Portuguese History

A Captivating Guide to the History of Portugal and the Portuguese Empire

Free Bonus from Captivating History (Available for a Limited time)

Hi History Lovers!

Now you have a chance to join our exclusive history list so you can get your first history ebook for free as well as discounts and a potential to get more history books for free! Simply visit the link below to join.

Captivatinghistory.com/ebook

Also, make sure to follow us on Facebook, Twitter and Youtube by searching for Captivating History.

Table of Contents

Part 1: History of Portugal

A Captivating Guide to Portuguese History from Ancient Times to the Present

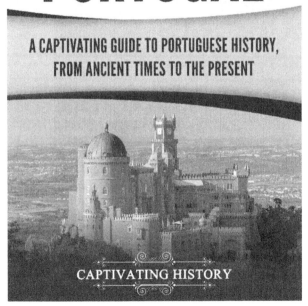

Introduction

Portugal has a very complex history that spreads all around the globe. The history of Portuguese discoveries, colonization, and trade guilds have been studied far and wide, but the history of mainland Portugal is often neglected. This book will concentrate on the events that took place in the Portuguese mainland, which is a small country locked between the Atlantic Ocean to the west and Spain to the east.

As the westernmost country in Europe, Portugal was regarded as a frontier nation, an outpost that was far from the European mainstream center of gravity. Although Portugal has only two neighbors—Spain to the east and the Atlantic Ocean to the west—Portugal can feel the closeness of Africa to the south, a country that was once a danger and, more recently, a temptation. Thus, it was Spain, Africa, and the opportunities presented with overseas voyages across the Atlantic that influenced and shaped the history of Portugal.

But Portugal has no geographical distinction in the Iberian Peninsula. It was never a geographically separate region, and Portugal is made of the western extensions of the geographic regions of Spain. It is interesting how Portugal developed a separate culture, language, and political worldview from the rest of the Iberian Peninsula when it was just a small part of a very large geographical entity. Nevertheless, Portugal was one of the first European kingdoms with stable borders.

As an independent kingdom, Portugal emerged only in the 12th century after the Iberian Reconquista. But its history starts much earlier. The first settlers of the early *Homo sapiens* and Neanderthals left behind extraordinary stone art in Côa Valley. The Romans would later make an appearance, as would the Germanic tribes. At this early stage, Portugal's history was indistinguishable from the history of Iberia since Portugal didn't yet exist as a political entity. But the waves of Roman, Germanic, and Islamic intruders, as well as the constant Hispanic influence, eventually shaped Portugal's society and culture. At the time, the people didn't have a unified idea of Portugal, and it was only when Christianity clashed with Islam during the Iberian Reconquista that the thought of an independent Portugal was shaped.

The early Portuguese kingdom had a tremendous task in front of itself. It needed to organize the popular medieval feudal system and, at the same time, defend its borders from attacks from the Arab and Hispanic kingdoms, as well as to fight the idea of pan-Hispanism. The Portuguese kings managed to defend their prized possession, and they slowly created the Portuguese nation. But the dynastical crisis of 1383 almost destroyed everything that had been achieved during the early kingdom. The rise of the Avis dynasty would finally strengthen the royal government.

The 16th century saw the rise of Portugal's golden age, which was when the kingdom prospered from its overseas discoveries. Nevertheless, this golden age was short, and due to the political and economic crises, the kingdom lost its independence. What followed was the unification of the Portuguese and Castilian crowns under the reign of the Spanish Habsburg dynasty. The Habsburgs first ruled Portugal in 1580 until the Braganza dynasty rose to power and assumed the throne in 1640. Under the Braganza rulers, Portugal prospered yet again. But the seeds of change had been sown across the whole of Europe during the 17th and early 18th centuries, and Portugal was no exception.

But while the Enlightenment and rational thinking sprouted in western Europe, Portugal struggled to follow. The old regime proved to be unfit to tackle the obstacles presented by the modern age, and new leadership needed to be implemented. These political developments within the country and its foreign policy led to the exceptional rise of Pombal, a political figure capable of modernizing Portugal and leading it into the future. However, the society of Portugal remained largely conservative and wished to go back to the old regime. Thus, Pombal had many enemies he had to remove to continue his work. His cruelty toward his political opponents would eventually be his demise. Nevertheless, Pombal proved his worth during the catastrophic earthquake of 1775, which leveled Lisbon. He personally assumed the command of the city's recovery and impressed observers with his capabilities.

The end of Pombalism brought back the old regime. This was also the period that saw the Napoleonic invasion, which caused the royal family to flee and seek refuge in Brazil. Portugal became a battleground for the British and French forces, and they fought for the control of Lisbon and its ports. The separation of Brazil and Portugal followed, which symbolized the end of the old regime. A series of weak rulers followed, and finally, the revolution came, after which the Portuguese Republic was proclaimed.

The political scene of the new republic was filled with power-hungry individuals like Salazar and his follower Caetano. The April Revolution of 1975 brought a new military government to Portugal but not the type of democracy that other European countries had. Portugal was left isolated and weakened. It took one more political coup, this time by liberal political parties, for Portugal to realize that the future was in decolonization and an acceptance of true democracy. From this point forward, Portugal's destiny was sealed as part of the European Community and the later European Union, which allowed the Portuguese to not only prosper economically but also come to terms with their imperialistic history.

Chapter 1 – The Prehistory

Prehistoric art in Côa Valley, Portugal.
Reino Baptista, CC BY-SA 4.0 <https://creativecommons.org/licenses/by-sa/4.0>, via Wikimedia Commons https://commons.wikimedia.org/wiki/File:Prehistoric_Rock-Art_Site_of_the_C%C3%B4a_Valley_-_Penascosa_-_Bull_@_2011-08-06.jpg

Modern scholars are not sure how long humans inhabited the territory that makes up modern-day Portugal. Their best estimation is that the first ones to settle the area were the hunter-gatherers that can be traced back to at least 500,000 years ago. Their simple tools were found in numerous sites, especially in the central and coastal areas of Portugal. They were not modern humans but rather *Homo erectus*, which was an ancestor of modern humans that was common in the areas of western Europe. Neanderthals showed up in these lands some 100,000 years ago, and they left behind the oldest human fossils in the territory of Portugal.

Modern humans—*Homo sapiens*—first arrived in Portugal some thirty-five thousand years ago. Their arrival was rapid, and they soon dominated the lands and pushed the Neanderthals to extinction. It remains unknown how and why this happened, but it is a common occurrence throughout Europe. There are many theories around the disappearance of the Neanderthals. Some believe they were absorbed into the large population of *Homo sapiens*, while others believe they were systematically slaughtered to extinction. There is also a possibility that the Neanderthals slowly died out over time and simply disappeared, likely because they were unable to adapt to the new climate and rivals. In 1998, at a site near Leiria in central Portugal, a body of a child was found whose morphological structure suggests he was a mix of Neanderthal and a modern human. The body is 24,500 years old, and this might suggest that, at one point, the Neanderthals lived alongside *Homo sapiens* and even interbred.

The most recent Ice Age reached its peak around eighteen thousand years ago. This was the end of the period of transition between the Neanderthals and modern humans, as well as the ice sheet that covered northern Europe. At this point, France and Spain were tundras, and the shores of Portugal were some forty kilometers into the sea compared to modern times. Only certain areas of the Portuguese coast, such as the Tagus Valley, had mixed forests and were suitable for hunter-gatherers to settle. The rest of the country consisted of icy tundras and plains with little shelter and food to offer. The first humans in northern Portugal hunted chamois (a type of antelope) and mountain goats that inhabited these cold places. In areas where the climate was more suitable for life, they hunted deer, rabbits, wild boars, aurochs (a type of wild ox that is now extinct), and horses. There is a possibility that fishing developed in the coastal regions, but the evidence for this remains elusive. At this point, humans developed small communities. It is estimated that the region of Estremadura in central Portugal had only around five hundred people, which was just enough for them to be a self-sustaining society.

The first inhabitants of Portugal left a legacy behind them: several thousands of rock carvings that stretch seventeen kilometers along the Côa River Valley. These carvings were discovered in 1992 during the construction of the dam. Many archaeologists raised their voices to preserve these valuable findings, and the dam construction was canceled in 1995. The carvings depict animals, especially aurochs and horses, but there are also depictions of humans and abstract figures. They were dated between twenty thousand and ten thousand years ago, and they represent one of the largest prehistoric rock art sites in the world.

After the peak of the last Ice Age, the climate started changing again, and the weather started getting warmer. The change was so rapid that eleven thousand years ago, the climate was pretty much what it is today. This was when the Mesolithic culture displaced its predecessor, the Paleolithic one. The people of the new Mesolithic period were still hunter-gatherers, but their conditions were improved by the milder climate. They had much more food resources than before. They were able to gather nuts, seeds, and fruit, and they even turned to fishing. Their tools included various traps, spears, fishing hooks, and barbs. The Mesolithic people were semi-sedentary, which means they would spend different seasons in different areas. They started building permanent huts near beaches and on river banks, and they no longer used animal-skin tents.

The Mesolithic way of life persisted in Portugal longer than elsewhere in Europe. This is because the climate in the area was good and predictable, which means there was no need for humans to adapt to new conditions. While the Neolithic period started early in Europe, the inhabitants of what is today Portugal were content, and they multiplied. But when the Neolithic period finally arrived in their territory, the changes it brought were revolutionary.

The Revolution of the Neolithic and Metallurgical Cultures

Western Europe already practiced agriculture and herding, and by 6000 BCE, this new way of life was widespread. The areas suitable for growing food and animals were quickly transformed into villages, and many tools, such as axes, knives, and pottery, entered everyday life. This might not seem like much, but this was the Neolithic Revolution. When it reached Portugal, it first appeared on its central and southern coasts and slowly spread to the interior. The northern territories were the last to adapt to the new lifestyle. But a long period of transition existed in which Mesolithic and Neolithic societies lived side by side. This period was over by 4000 BCE, and for the next two thousand years, the Neolithic culture dominated.

During the Neolithic period, the people of Portugal started cultivating legumes and cereals, and they started herding pigs, sheep, and cattle. These were the basics of their subsistence. The population started growing fast, and the need for permanent settlements rose. At first, the people built their villages in open, unprotected spaces, but they later chose naturally defensive sites, such as ridgetops and mountainsides. The society of the Neolithic period built megalithic monuments across Europe. In Portugal, the most significant one would be Almendres Cromlech near Évora. This is a complex of megaliths, and it is considered to be the biggest in Europe and is dated to the 6th millennium BCE. The function of these monoliths remains a mystery, but it is believed they were either used as primitive astronomical observatories or had religious connotations.

The transition between the Neolithic and Metallurgical culture was a slow, uneven process of adaptation without any sudden events that shaped history. Soft metals, such as silver, copper, and gold, were known since 2500 BCE. The southern Portuguese territory was one of the first European areas where copper was excavated and where copper tools were made. The abundance of copper pushed Portugal into developing this new technology very quickly. The first copper objects were ornaments, but early societies started producing copper axes, daggers, saws, and other tools soon after.

The first metalworkers used the process of cold hammering, with smelting coming much later. It is believed that they used the technology developed for ceramic making and invented smelting by accident. Casting was mastered last, but it was used the most. The specialists who produced the metal items often lived near the excavation areas, but their tools were taken far and wide. They soon became the norm throughout Portugal. The first bronze axes appeared around 2000 BCE, and it is believed they were introduced from northwestern Europe. By the end of the 2nd millennium, the bronze industry developed as the people discovered tin in the southern regions. But even before this, the people of Portugal developed what is called a secondary product revolution: the techniques of resource production and the utilization of agriculture and herding. This means that the people learned how to ride horses and use animals for transportation and plowing fields. They started drinking cow's milk, producing wool and textiles, and using plows and irrigation systems. But it seems that these technological and evolutionary advances were restricted to the southern areas of Portugal, as there is a huge lack of evidence for such developments in the north.

During this period of extensive copper production, Bell Beaker pottery appeared in Portugal. This is one of the most attractive and aesthetically pleasing forms of prehistoric pottery production. It is named "Bell Beaker" because the shape of the pottery resembled upturned bells. The major manufacturers of such pottery in Portugal were the areas of Lisbon and Setúbal. There were hundreds of production sites here, including the fortified settlements of Zambujal and Vila Nova de São Pedro. The increased demand for pottery and copper products led the early Portuguese societies to reach out and form relations with people elsewhere in Europe. They soon developed a vast network of trade across western Europe. Estremadura was particularly developed, probably because it was a central location with a developed river system that served as a trade route to many communities. Estremadura was also a very fertile region, and it soon began providing food to the rather dry areas of Portugal.

During the Copper Age, Portuguese societies formed small communities. The typical southern village housed no more than 350 people, but smaller settlements existed. These were likely seasonal, and they had only thirty to fifty people. The houses were very simple and built of local materials, such as wood and mud. The settlers mostly relied on natural defenses, but constructed ones were used. Some larger settlements had walls surrounding them as early as 2500 BCE. During the Bronze Age, Portuguese society expanded the system of villages to the fertile lowlands, where they built settlements without any natural defenses. In the Bronze Age, they started erecting hilltop fortresses, known as *castros*, but it remains unknown who exactly built them. Perhaps it was the nomadic cattle herders or settlers who had rival communities with whom they warred. At this time, Portugal had no invasions from the outside, so it is most likely that various communities fought for dominance in production and trade.

During the Copper and Bronze Ages, the societal elite started gathering power in their hands. But this increasing social differentiation continues to confuse scholars, as it is impossible to conclude who comprised the elites and on what they based their power. Evidence from burial sites shows that certain people were buried with ornamental weapons and jewelry, which is clearly a sign of prestige. The likely answer is that the early social elite in Portugal was composed of warrior leaders who were able to control the production and distribution of copper goods. There are various stelae found in Portugal dating from the Bronze Age, and they depict warriors and the various weapons they used, such as bows, daggers, and halberds. Even the funerary lids were engraved with similar images, and these are dated to 1200 BCE.

The burial sites also show a transition in the belief system of the early societies in Portugal. While the Neolithic people worshiped the bull's head and various phallic menhirs (tall, upright stones), the Copper and Bronze Age people prayed to mysterious eye-idols, which were often engraved on rocks, bones, or wood. They were also often painted on ceramic pottery. Scholars believe these idols were connected with solar or stellar symbols and represented the Mother Goddess. These idols were spread throughout the Iberian Peninsula, and it is believed they originally came from the Mediterranean. It is clear that, at this point, religious ideas from the outside started entering Portugal.

Iron arrived in Portugal through two routes: the Phoenician traders from the Mediterranean coast and the Celts from the northern parts of Europe. The earliest iron item discovered in Portugal was dated to 700 BCE, and it is a dagger with a bronze handle. Iron was stronger than bronze and could be easily shaped and sharpened. Thus, it is no wonder it rapidly entered regular use. Iron was also plentiful, and the people quickly learned how to smelt and forge it. Few items made of iron have been found in Portugal, which led early archaeologists to believe that the Iron Age may have started there later than in the rest of Europe. However, further research proved this to be wrong. Iron is a corrosive metal, and the Portuguese soil, especially in the north, is very acidic. It is more likely that all early Iron Age weapons and tools were destroyed by time. After all, Portugal was rich in iron mines, and the iron industry developed quickly.

The Iron Age brought another change within Portugal: the first inscriptions. They were found in funerary stelae dated to the late 7th and early 5th centuries BCE. The inscriptions were found only on the graves belonging to the elite, as well as on some coins and pottery. But the language and the script have yet to be deciphered. It is believed that the language belonged to the indigenous people that the Romans called Conii, and the script might have been derived from the Phoenician one. It is part syllabic and part alphabetic, which makes it very difficult to decipher. Although writing was used modestly in the Iberian Peninsula, the existence of these inscriptions shows cultural development.

Celticization

During the Iron Age, the territory of the Iberian Peninsula received waves of immigrants from the north. They were not all Celts, but most of them were. They brought with them a new culture, religion, social organization, and artistic expressions. They asserted their influence on the local people and changed their culture through a process known as Celticization. The ethnic composition of the country changed as well. The Celts were the people of north-central Europe, and they had Indo-European origins. They had a reputation of being fearsome warriors and excellent horsemen. During the 1st millennium BCE, they spread throughout Europe from Ireland and reached as far as the shores of the Black Sea. They came to Portugal in two waves; the first one occurred in the 6th and 5th centuries BCE, and the second one happened in the 2nd, 3rd, and 4th centuries CE. The Celts inhabited the northern and central regions of Portugal, while the south remained mainly populated by the locals. However, the Celts were always a minority in Portugal, and they were forced to share the land with the already existing society of non-Indo-European people.

The Romans and Greeks described the Celts who arrived in Portugal from both the first and second waves. The names of the

Celtic tribes were found in written evidence of Greek and Roman scholars, such as Avienius, who mentioned the Cempsi, and Strabo, who described the Turduli. The later ones founded many cities throughout Portugal, maybe even Ossonoba (today's Faro). Strabo thought that the Celts were wise and kind and that they had an important cultural influence on the region.

The Turduli were not the only Celtic tribe in Portugal at the time. They had to share the territory with the Celtici. Both of these tribes quickly adjusted to the southern regions, where their diet consisted of olive oil, wine, fruit, vegetables, and fish. In the north, the people had a much different diet. They lived in the infertile and mountainous regions. Herding goats and pigs were their main occupation, and they ate meat, butter, chestnuts, and bread made out of acorns. They drank beer rather than wine.

The society of Iron Age Portugal was based on kinship, and there were no kingdoms yet. Family alliances dominated, and they were reinforced by marriages. The groups of allied families formed clans. It seems that each clan occupied territory around a certain *castro,* and together, they supervised the distribution of their land. They also had their titular deities, which they worshiped as clan patrons. The leaders of clans were called chieftains, and it is believed that in some cases, but not all, this title was hereditary. A group of clans formed tribes or what the Romans called *gens* (nation or people with a common ancestor). They had their own tribal council, and they were the basis of the first loose ethnic confederations in the northwest, such as the Callaeci (also known as Gallaeci). But the Late Iron Age brought intense conflicts that undermined the existing tribal social structure. The military leaders started using their influence and power to consolidate their authority and gather personal prestige and wealth.

Orientalization

Southern Portugal and neighboring Andalusia underwent a series of cultural and economic changes during the period between 700 and 550 BCE, which transformed the society to resemble the ones established in the Near East. The society was no longer simple, and herding and agriculture were replaced with the growing industrialization that erupted with the opening of many iron mines. The use of iron became widespread, and pottery was no longer handmade but wheel-made. The settlements were no longer villages but *oppida*, large fortified towns. The artistic tradition evolved and developed into new forms, and writing was introduced. On top of this, new religious cults appeared. All of these developments are now referred to as Orientalization because they were all inspired by the ideas, technologies, and attitudes from the Mediterranean.

The western Mediterranean was regularly visited by the Phoenician traders from Tyre and Sidon. During the 8th century, these visits intensified because the Phoenicians were searching for new sources of raw materials and markets where they could spread their trade. They were a client state of the Assyrian Empire, and they founded several trading posts in Andalusia, which quickly developed into settlements. The Phoenician traders refused to mix with the local population, and they based their presence in the Iberian Peninsula solely on trade. Their main merchandise was perfumes, glass, ornaments, furniture, pottery, wine, and oil. They acquired raw materials from Portugal, such as iron and purple dye, which were highly valued. The Phoenician presence in Portugal was of a much lesser scale than in Andalusia, but apparently, they traveled the Algarve coast, where they bought silver, copper, bronze, gold, and tin. The Phoenician influences didn't only come from the merchants from Tyre but also through land routes from neighboring Spanish Extremadura. The Near Eastern practices of cremation and rites of worshiping the Phoenician fertility goddess Astarte entered Algarve through these trade routes.

The Phoenician presence in the Iberian Peninsula ended with the fall of the Assyrian Empire in 612 BCE. Around the same time, the Greeks became aware of Portugal, although the contact between them was very limited at the time. Greek objects reached Portugal indirectly through the Greek colonies in southern France and northeastern Spain. Nevertheless, the Greeks didn't assert much influence on the Iron Age Orientalization of Portugal. The main influence came from neighboring Andalusia, where the Tartessian Kingdom was founded by the Phoenicians and where the Oriental culture survived even after the Phoenician departure. The Tartessian objects were very popular in Portugal, and the locals even copied their production.

Another Oriental influence on Portugal came from the North African colony of Tyre, Carthage. The trade between this colony and south Iberia started during the mid-6th century BCE. The objects they traded were very similar to the Phoenician ones, and their influence was not as prevalent as during the early days of the trade. But over time, the Carthaginian influence became more political than cultural. During the 3rd century BCE, the Barcid family took control of Carthage and changed the character of the relationship with Iberia from trade to conquest. Southern Portugal became part of the newly established Iberian Empire, and Carthaginian-styled towns started popping up throughout Portugal, even as far as the mouth of the Tagus where Lisbon lies.

The famous Hannibal Barca (247–183/181 BCE) founded a Carthaginian settlement in the Algarve region, probably somewhere near today's Portimão. Its presence is known to us because it was described by the Romans, who called this settlement Portus Hannibalis. But the most spectacular Carthaginian site in Portugal has to be Garvão in Baixo Alentejo, which was a religious sanctuary dedicated to Tanit, a Carthaginian fertility goddess.

Chapter 2 – The Roman Empire

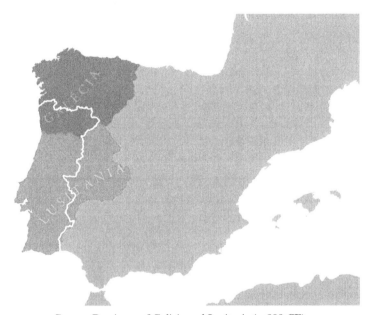

Roman Provinces of Galicia and Lusitania (c. 298 CE).

Carthage was the strongest Mediterranean empire of the 3rd century BCE, and it seemed that Portugal would be absorbed by it. The south already belonged to the Carthaginian leaders, and they had a very strong military presence in the Iberian Peninsula. The Roman Empire only observed the situation in Iberia but made no offers to deny Carthage's claim over it. It soon became obvious that it was unwise of Rome to assume such a passive role. In 218, Hannibal used his military base at Carthago Nova (modern-day Cartagena, Spain) to launch an attack on Rome. He crossed the Pyrenees and Alps and arrived in northern Italy. This is how the Second Punic War (218–201 BCE) started. The conquest of Hannibal in Italy is not important for the history of Portugal, but the Roman reaction is. They soon launched a counter-conquest campaign, and after many struggles, Carthago Nova fell in 209 BCE. It took the Romans the next three years to completely expel the Carthaginians from the Iberian Peninsula.

Before the Second Punic War, Rome never showed much interest in Iberia. But now, it was under their control, and they decided to stay since the peninsula offered cheap labor and rich deposits of minerals, as well as fertile land suitable for agriculture. In Spain, two Roman provinces were formed by 197 BCE: Hispania Citerior and Hispania Ulterior. The Roman control over these territories was predatory, as they exploited their riches and enslaved their people. This led to widespread discontent that very quickly escalated into open revolt. The people of the western shores of Iberia used the unrest in the Roman provinces to raid the Roman settlements. It soon became obvious that the empire would have to integrate the whole peninsula if they wanted to keep control over it.

The occupation of southern Portugal was quick and easy, and it was over by the second half of the 2nd century BCE. It seems that a military expedition was not needed, as the conquest was completed through persuasion and diplomatic efforts. The native Conii people became Roman allies, and they handed administrative control over the Algarve and Alentejo to the Romans. But the interior territories between the Targus and Mondego Rivers, as well as the mountainous regions in the north, were a different story. The

Lusitani, Callaeci, and other peoples lived there, and they mounted a heavy resistance against the Roman Empire. It would take Rome 175 years to subdue the whole of Portugal.

The Lusitani were hardy people living in the Beira region. Their settlements were fortified hilltop villages of the *castro* tradition, and their country was poor. The people were mainly shepherds, but they also practiced some small-scale agriculture. But to ensure their survival, the Lusitani started relying on raiding the neighboring fertile plains around Beira, mainly in Andalusia. The Romans came to respect the Lusitani as an effective and elusive fighting force, even though they were enemies. Their leaders were the first Portuguese names recorded in history, albeit in Romanized form. Among them were Punicus, who raided in 155 BCE, and Caesarus, who defeated Roman General Mummius in 153 BCE. Perhaps the greatest Lusitani war hero was Caucaenus, who embarked on raids in the Roman-controlled Algarve, captured the Conistorgis (the capital of the Conii), and continued to cross the strait and raid in North Africa in 151 BCE.

The Romans were very frustrated by the Lusitani raids. In 150 BCE, they organized a massacre in which the only survivor was Viriatus, a warrior who would later become the main leader of the Lusitanian resistance. Viriatus is traditionally portrayed as a simple shepherd who became a guerilla leader capable of charming his fellow countrymen and inspiring the Lusitanian population to revolt. He was active for seven years, between 146 and 139 BCE, during which he waged a bloody war against the Romans and inflicted several humiliating defeats on them. The Romans were forced to use bribery to organize his assassination. Viriatus became the first proto-Portuguese hero, but after his death, the Lusitani lost their will to fight. They turned their tactics into defensive ones since the raids no longer seemed worth their effort. In 138 and 137, the Romans penetrated the Tagus Valley and started their campaigns in the north, going as far as Galicia. But they never managed to subdue the Lusitani, although they did contain them.

The outbreak of the civil war among the Romans in Spain in 80 BCE allowed the Lusitani to reassert themselves. This time, they chose to fight alongside the renegade Roman governor of Hispania Citerior, Quintus Sertorius. For the next eight years, they fought the official Roman army that had been sent to Spain to get rid of Sertorius. But in 72 BCE, the governor was killed, and the rebellion ended. But the death of Sertorius proved to be only the beginning of the serious resistance to Roman rule. This resistance would last for several decades and would reach its peak during the governorship of Gaius Julius Caesar (100–44 BCE) and Gnaeus Pompeius or Pompey (106–48 BCE) in Hispania Ulterior.

During this resistance, the Romans managed to occupy much of the territory between the Tagus and Douro Rivers. The Lusitani submitted at this point and even started serving as mercenaries in the Roman army, especially during the following war between Caesar and Pompey. Therefore, the Lusitani were not subdued by the military efforts but by gradual acculturation. The only part of Portugal that remained outside of the Roman Empire was the north. Emperor Augustus (63 BCE–14 CE), Caesar's successor, was the one who dealt with this region. He campaigned in the area between 24 and 19 BCE and completed the conquest of not only Portugal but the whole Iberian Peninsula.

The Romanization of Portugal

The Romans remained in Portugal for almost 450 years, and they started the process of Romanization. However, there is no consensus between scholars to what extent the Romanization of Portugal occurred. The written and archaeological evidence differ greatly, and the classicists are prone to believing that the extent of Romanization was much greater than the archaeologists believe. Nevertheless, change did occur, and it was the most visible in the south of the country, where the Romans took control early on. But the south easily transitioned into Roman rule since it had been part of the Mediterranean world for so long. The south was more attractive to the Roman colonists than any other region of Portugal because it had a pleasant climate and an already developed economy. The central coast of Portugal was also Romanized easily, but the central and northern hinterlands were a different story. They were sparsely populated and were poor regions. Even the northern coast wasn't attractive to the Romans because it was remote, unfamiliar, and oriented toward the Atlantic Ocean, while the colonists preferred the Mediterranean Sea. Nevertheless, Romanization reached even these far-away regions, though very slowly and never completely.

The Romanization of Portugal meant the adoption of traditions and practices of Roman civic life. Urbanization was a consequence of Romanization. The 1st and 2nd centuries CE saw the quick development of towns. Even though they had existed beforehand, their names were heavily Romanized. Some of these names persist even today. But many of the settlements were newly founded by the Romans, such as Pax Julia (today's Beja). Most of the cities developed from already existing *oppida*, among them being Olisipo (Lisbon), Ossonoba (Faro), Salacia (Alcácer do Sal), and Ebora (Évora).

The Romanized towns were very different from what they were during their *oppida* stage of development. The design of the houses, public buildings, streets, and overall conception was completely Roman, and most of these cities survived through history and became modern-day metropolises. The concept of the cities and towns followed a familiar pattern, with features such as central forums, baths, markets, amphitheaters, and aqueducts. The imperial cult also appeared, and many Roman temples were built. The houses of the elite followed the peristyle concept (a row of columns surrounding the inner courtyard of the houses). These building projects demanded careful planning and considerable investment. The Roman civilization didn't lack any of that, but the local population had to learn and adapt to the Roman lifestyle.

The Romans didn't think that the Portuguese coast was particularly attractive, which caused the coastal towns and cities to be neglected. They considered the western coast to be a frontier to nowhere—it was the end of the world. But they valued the rivers of Portugal, which is why all the administrative centers were located on river crossings that headed east. The main administrative center of the Portuguese Roman territory was Emerita Augusta (Mérida), and it was so far to the east that it was actually in Spanish Extremadura. Lisbon, Porto, and Coimbra, the major cities of the later period, were not administrative centers during the early Roman period.

During the later days of the Roman Empire, villas and country estates grew in importance. They were profoundly Roman institutions, and they had an economic function attached to them. The majority of villas in Portugal were built between major mines, and they were surrounded by thick defensive walls, which offered protection to the mining convoys. However, they were not military in nature. Their main purpose was to exploit the agricultural and pastoral resources of the region. Since they were surrounded by fertile fields, orchards, and herds of sheep and cattle, they were the main producers of wine, oil, food, wool, and even garum (fermented fish sauce).

After the Flavian era (69-96 CE), the Romanization of Portugal slowed down. The building projects were finished, and there was no need for new ones. The construction of the new towns and cities would resume during the 4th century CE when the threat of barbarian invasions became real. At that time, new defensive points were built, and many towns that had already existed were given defensive walls. The cities started assuming their medieval appearance but not because of the extensive defensive building. Rather, it was because of the adoption of Christianity and the abandonment of old temples in favor of new churches.

The Romans built many roads, connecting the cities and towns of Portugal. Their purpose was military, administrative, and commercial. But the knowledge of the Roman roads in Portugal is very limited, although there is no doubt they were extensive. The main road stretched from the south to the north, connecting Lagos on the coast of Algarve and Odivelas. Here, it joined the road to Beja, from where it continued to the mouth of the Tagus. But the majority of the roads were constructed to connect the west to the east since that was the preferred communication route. The roads converged at Mérida and continued south to Andalusia.

The People of Roman Portugal

With the Roman rule of the peninsula and the construction of many roads and communication lines, the mobility of the people in Portugal increased. Professionals and merchants were now able to travel from one region to another without fear of entering enemy territory. But more importantly, they could travel from the peninsula to the other parts of the vast Roman Empire.

The laborers migrated more often and traversed greater distances because they needed to find better work opportunities. Eastern Portugal became their main goal due to its prosperous mining industry. Soldiers served in different parts of the empire, and after their service, they often settled far from their homes. Slaves were moved wherever they were needed. They could be bought in one part of the empire to be sold far away. All this movement helped break down ancient tribal differences, causing Romanization to accelerate.

The population of Portugal reached one million by the late 1st century CE. The society consisted of free people and slaves. The free people consisted of a small elite minority and the sub-elite majority who inhabited cities, towns, and villages. Little is known about this social layer, which represented the majority of the population, but the elite minority left a deep and visible imprint in the history of Portugal with their mansions, villas, burial sites, temples, orchards, and carefully maintained documentation. During the 1ˢᵗ century CE, the native leaders of Portugal were given Roman citizenship, and they were given principal municipal offices to hold. This was done because it was Roman policy to quickly win over the local leaders and integrate them into Roman society so they would keep the peace over the domestic population.

These local Romanized leaders were wealthy and powerful, mainly because they owned land. Once they received an administrative office, they would focus their wealth on their cities, financing public works such as the construction of forums, roads, baths, and theaters. These ambitious individuals would end up in the provincial capital, assuming higher administrative offices, or even move to Rome itself. It was rare for Portuguese natives to become Roman senators, but there are several names preserved in the Portuguese records.

As in the rest of the Roman Empire, the slave system was crucial for the development of Roman Portugal. Slavery had existed in the country since the Carthaginians conquered it. Many Lusitanians and other natives of the Iberian Peninsula were enslaved at that time. The Romans didn't spare the natives either. During their conquest, many local women and children were taken away to be sold in different parts of the empire. By the 1ˢᵗ century CE, a third of the Portuguese population were slaves. There were also slaves brought from different parts of the world, people who were enslaved because of a debt, children sold into slavery by their poor parents, and those whose ancestors were local slaves and were thus born into slavery. The law stated that all children of a slave woman were slaves by birth.

Slaves were needed for various purposes. They worked the fields, dug the mines, worked in the house, and performed various forms of service to the administration of the empire. The slaves who were exceptionally skilled or well-educated served as private tutors, doctors, scribes, accountants, business managers, and artists. They were usually from Greece, and they had professional backgrounds. Slaves had no right to own property or have legal families. Still, their owners often paid them some money, and slaves always had the option of buying their freedom. Freed slaves often remained close with their previous owners and continued to serve them, but they received legal rights they previously didn't have. In Portugal, some records show that some former slaves who were freed managed to rise to management positions and gain wealth through commerce, various professions, and the mining industry.

Roman Administration

After the initial fights during the conquest of the Iberian Peninsula, the Roman Empire had no major issues in the administration of the newly gained territory. The people of the western peninsula looked up to Rome as a symbol of civilization and prosperity, and they wanted to become just like Rome. Thus, they obeyed the Roman laws and administration. This attitude of the locals lasted up until the 5th century CE, though the focus shifted from the city of Rome to the imperial crown and the emperors.

The Roman administration of Portugal had three levels: provincial, district, and city. At the time, Portugal was inseparable from the Province of Hispania (the whole Iberian Peninsula). We already explained Hispania was divided into two large administrative units: Citerior and Ulterior. However, further divisions were needed once the population started growing and many new towns and cities were founded. Ulterior was split into the provinces of Lusitania (southern and central Portugal and parts of western Spain) and Baetica (Andalusia). The new capital of Lusitania was in the Roman-founded city of Mérida. Northern Portugal wasn't a part of Lusitania. Instead, it was assigned to Hispania Citerior, which was renamed to Tarraconensis. These administrative arrangements of the Iberian Peninsula remained in place until the reign of Emperor Diocletian (r. 284–305). He separated the northwest of Hispania and formed the province of Gallaecia, making Braga its capital. The emperor also created a new administrative office in Hispania, *vicarius*. Their task was to oversee the military and civilian administration of the peninsula. The headquarters of this office were in Mérida.

The provincial administration was further divided into various judicial districts called *conventus*. Lusitania had three such districts: Pacensis, Emeritensis, and Scallabitanus, with their capitals in Beja, Mérida, and Santarém, respectively. In comparison, Tarraconensis had seven *conventus*, and northern Portugal had one separate *conventus* named Bracarensis, with the capital in Braga. Each *conventus* had a separate assembly composed of the representatives of the cities that lay in its territory. The third administrative unit was the *civitas* (city), which simply consisted of the urban center and its immediate surroundings. In Lusitania, there were around twenty-four civitates, while in Portuguese Gallaecia, there was only one— Braga. This was probably because northern Portugal always had a fragmented society and the absence of major settlements that could grow into the cities.

The tribal political culture of Portugal was replaced with a unified Roman polity, even though, at the time, Portugal was never perceived as a separate entity. The Roman political map of the Iberian Peninsula was very different from what it is now or even what it was during the medieval period. This is why it is very difficult to think about ancient Portugal since it didn't differ at all from the rest of the peninsula. Most of modern-day Portugal was inside Lusitania, but the province extended to the east and included parts of what is today Spain. Even its capital, Mérida, was in Spanish Extremadura and not in what is now considered Portuguese territory. Modern-day Portugal is not even considered to be a direct successor of Lusitania.

Nevertheless, the Roman Empire greatly influenced the development of Portugal. By the end of Roman rule, the society, economy, and demographic patterns of the future nation were very visible. Despite the many changes that this country would go through during history, these patterns displayed a tendency of continuity. The literate Portuguese culture had already developed with their unique form of Vulgar Latin, which would later develop into the Portuguese language. The local variety of Roman architecture sprouted, and a unique material life developed. Although Portugal was a part of a much wider culture, by the end of the Roman Empire, it displayed separate characteristics.

Chapter 3 – The Germanic
Invasion and Kingdoms

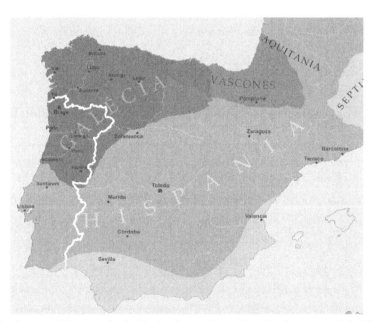

The Germanic kingdoms in the Iberian Peninsula, c. 560. The Suevi control the blue territory and the Visigoths the green.

The Roman rule in Lusitania and Portuguese Gallaecia was undisturbed for centuries. During the 3rd century CE, the Frankish intruders plundered the Iberian Peninsula. They came as close as Tarraconensis, but they never managed to penetrate what is today Portuguese territory. The news traveled fast due to the Roman system of communication, and even the towns in Lusitania and Gallaecia reinforced their walls and prepared defenses. However, by the 5th century, neither of these two provinces was directly attacked by the outside barbarian tribes. The big change came in the autumn of 409 CE when bands of Vandals, Alans, and Suevi crossed the Pyrenees passes and entered Hispania with no one to stop them.

Three years earlier, these barbarian tribes had breached the Rhine frontier and settled in Gaul but not before they brought havoc to it. They were constantly searching for new territories to pillage, and Hispania proved to be the perfect target. Hydatius and Orosius, the Gallaecian chroniclers of the 5th century, describe in general terms what happened in the period between 409 and 411. The intruders crossed great distances very quickly, and they entered Gallaecia and Lusitania while pillaging, looting, and killing the residents. The villagers had no option but to seek safety behind the walls of major cities or even ancient *castros*. The increased population in the cities brought famine and plague, adding to their misery. Rome was already weak, and the emperor couldn't spare his legions for such a remote province. The imperial authority in Lusitania and Gallaecia simply disappeared, never to return.

Throughout Hispania, the Roman Empire's power collapsed with incredible speed. Only Tarraconensis managed to resist for some time. Of course, there were pockets and defensive spots that the barbarians failed to take. The invaders chose to ignore these places because the rest of the peninsula brought enough riches. In 411, the barbarians decided to divide Hispania among themselves and permanently settle there. It is unknown what procedure they used and how they decided which tribe would settle where, but Orosius and Hydatius claimed it was by lot. This suggests that the invading tribes made no notice of Roman rule in the area and that they were strong enough to ignore it if it even existed then. Nevertheless, there is some evidence that suggests an alliance existed between the barbarians and the imperial cities of Tarraconensis. In any case, Lusitania and Carthaginensis (a region in Hispania) were settled by the Alans; Gallaecia by the Suevi and Hasdingi Vandals; and Baetica by the Silingi Vandals. Only Tarraconensis remained Roman.

The lawlessness and terror due to the barbarian invasions ended with their settlement in 411. The tribes gave up pillaging and started taking up agriculture, which proved to be more efficient in feeding their vast families than the constant danger of war. But the period of peace was very short. In 416, the Visigoths entered Hispania and rekindled the violence. The Visigoths were Roman *foederati* (foreign tribes, states, and peoples that had a treaty with Rome), and they inhabited southern Gaul. But they were pressed from the north by the Franks and were running out of resources and food. They had to search for new territory, and the Romans directed them toward the south, where they would make deals with the Alans and the Vandals. But the Visigoths decided to attack, and under the leadership of their king Wallia (r. 415–418), they invaded Hispania and defeated the Alans in Carthaginensis and the Vandals in Baetica. These tribes ceased being political factors in the region. Instead of settling here, the Visigoths returned to Gaul in 418 after the death of their king.

The Hasdingi Vandals of Gallaecia decided they were not satisfied with the mountainous terrain allotted to them in 411, and they entered Lusitania and Baetica, sparking another conflict. But although they brought destruction and violence to the region, they didn't linger there. By 430, they were on their way to conquer North Africa. They continued to raid in Lusitania, but even that was rare, and they never again bothered the whole Iberian Peninsula. Of the four tribes that crossed the Pyrenees only twenty years prior, only the Suevi remained.

It is important to understand that the Germanic tribes that invaded Hispania at the beginning of the 5th century were migratory. Their main goal wasn't only to loot and pillage but also to settle. This is why they brought their women and children with them. These migratory but non-nomadic tribes were pushed out of their homelands by famine and the Huns. They entered Hispania with the intent to abandon raiding and start an agricultural and pastoral society. Although they came in great numbers, they weren't overwhelming. All four tribes amounted to 200,000 people, which wasn't enough to replace the already existing population of Hispano-Romans. They wouldn't have even been able to penetrate the peninsula if they had faced the full Roman army. But at the time of their migration, the Roman Empire was at its decline, and there were no effective legions or authority that would organize the defense of Hispania. The Roman Empire never even bothered to restore the authority in Portuguese territories after the barbarians left.

The Kingdom of Suevi

The Suevi established their kingdom in Hispania with their capital at Braga in southwestern Gallaecia. Their kings, Hermeric (r. 406/19-438) and Rechila (r. 438-448), gradually took over the whole peninsula except for Roman Tarraconensis and eastern Carthaginensis. The expansion started with Hermeric, who launched attacks on the territory that previously belonged to Hasdingi Vandals in Gallaecia. The terrain here was rugged and unapproachable, and the local population stoutly resisted the conquest. The Suevi had no other choice but to conclude a peace, but they soon broke it. They launched another sudden attack, hoping that it would catch the locals by surprise and that no defense would be mounted. The tactic worked, and the Suevi continued using the attack-peace-attack pattern for the decades to come, during which time they took control over the whole peninsula. Rechila started an attack on Lusitania and Baetica, and he imposed his rule over these territories. In 439, he conquered Mérida, and he took Hispalis (today's Seville) in 441. By the middle of the 5th century, the Suevi had both Lusitania and Baetica under their control and probably western Carthaginensis.

Rechila also started raiding Tarraconensis, but his son who succeeded him, Rechiarius (or Rechiar; r. 448–456), concluded peace with the Romans. After only three years, the Suevi king broke the peace and invaded Roman territory. Although they didn't manage to establish themselves in Tarraconensis, they took many of its inhabitants. The Suevi were at the peak of their power in the mid-5th century, and it seemed as if they would subjugate the whole Iberian Peninsula. In 446, the attack on the Romans was renewed. Although Roman General Vitus took the lead and tried his best to defend Tarraconensis, he was defeated, and no more attempts were made to expel the Suevi. Rome simply didn't have enough troops to spare due to Italy and Byzantine suffering from barbarian attacks. The locals proved unwilling to defend the Roman rule, and they even helped the Suevi by joining the enemy forces. By the 460s, the imperial commander of Tarraconensis was appointed by the king of the Visigoths and not the Roman emperor. Rome completely lost control over the territories in Iberia.

The Suevi occupation of Tarraconensis didn't provoke the Romans, but it did stir up the attention of Rome's ally in southern Gaul: the Visigothic King Theodoric II (r. 453–466). He entered Hispania leading an enormous army, and in 456, he defeated the Suevi in the name of the Roman emperor. The decisive battle took place near Asturica (Astorga) at a place called Campus Paramus. After this victory, the Visigoths continued to Braga, which they sacked. They then desecrated the Roman churches since they were Arians. Nevertheless, the Visigoths decided against killing and raping the residents. King Rechiarius was captured and executed, and the major regions of Lusitania, Carthaginensis, and Baetica were occupied by King Theodoric II's army.

The invasion of the Visigoths ended the short-lived Suevic control but not the core of the kingdom. It remained autonomous, nestled in the rugged terrain of Gallaecia. The leadership of this surviving kingdom passed to a certain Maldras, who may have been a local Hispano-Roman or renegade Visigoth. But the Suevic Kingdom's recovery was slow, and the local leaders fought for power. They resumed the raids in Lusitania but never managed to expand their kingdom. Nevertheless, they persisted until the late 6th century. In 585, the succession of the kingdom was disputed, and the king of the Visigoths, Leovigild, took the opportunity to intervene. He deposed the last Suevic king, Audeca, and annexed the kingdom after 150 years of its existence.

The Visigoths

The origins of the Visigoths are obscure, but they were a Germanic people. It is believed their homeland was somewhere near Scandinavia, but there is no conclusive evidence to confirm this. They first came into contact with the Romans on the Danube frontier after they migrated southeast. They settled in Dacia, and there they were converted to Arian Christianity in the late 4th century. But they were poorly treated by the Romans, and they revolted. They defeated and killed Roman Emperor Valens and migrated to northern Italy. In 410, they even sacked the city of Rome. In the late 4th century, the Roman emperor had no other choice but to grant them territory in southern Gaul where they could settle as *foederati*. After this, they became active in Hispania too. The successor of Theodoric II, who took over Lusitania and Baetica, King Euric (r. 466–484), occupied most of Iberia. Roman Hispania officially ended. In 476, around the same time, the last western Roman emperor, Romulus Augustus, was deposed.

The Visigoths remained in power in most of southern and central Portugal until the Muslim conquest some 250 years later. During their reign, much of Andalusia was reclaimed by the Eastern Roman Empire, and it possibly included small parts of southern Portugal. Perhaps this is why Algarve was influenced by Byzantine culture. They also kept a close connection with Constantinople and North Africa. Northern Gallaecia remained part of the Suevic Kingdom until the Visigoths finally absorbed it in 858. Therefore, Visigothic control over the Portuguese territory came in stages, and it took them a whole century to finish the process of creating their pan-Hispanic realm.

The Visigothic kings never took up residency in the territory that is today Portugal. Their capitals were in Toledo, Barcelona, Toulouse, and Tortosa. The closest they came to the Portuguese border was in 549 when they moved the capital to Mérida. For the population of the western Iberian Peninsula, the Visigothic court was a distant concept, and royal visits were very rare. Nevertheless, the Visigoths had a well-organized administration of the territories they possessed, with each province governed by a duke (*dux*). The administration of major cities was in the hands of counts (*comes*). The Visigoths were meticulous lawmakers, and they often had help from the Hispano-Roman officials who issued the legal codes. The earliest known code belonged to King Euric, but successive kings often revised the code.

King Leovigild (r. 568–586) is considered the most successful warrior king of the Visigoths who tried to exercise central control over his realm. But this was difficult due to the poor communication and reliance on the already existing local administration. Moreover, the local magnates often fought for power. Between 579 and 583, Leovigild faced a revolt launched by his son, who tried (and failed) to make a separate kingdom in Baetica and southern Lusitania. Leovigild and his successor adopted quasi-Byzantine traditions, such as the use of the throne, the royal purple cloak, and an elaborate crown. They enforced royal authority through civil and military judges who were authorized to punish offenders with mutilations and executions.

The successor of Leovigild, Reccared I (r. 586–601), converted from Arianism to Roman Christianity in 587. The connection with the Byzantine court diminished, and the Catholic bishop of Toledo offered his strong support to the king in establishing central authority. The Roman Church soon became a staunch upholder of the centralized government, and they even allowed the Visigothic kings of the 7th century to proclaim themselves *rex et sacerdos* (the priest-king). The adoption of Catholicism accelerated the blurring of the ethnic borders between the Visigoths and the Hispano-Romans. But that didn't mean that the kingdom of the Visigoths secured stability. It was often involved in political crises, particularly concerning succession.

Society and Economy of the German Kingdoms

From the late 5th century, the relations between the Visigoths and the Suevi were mainly peaceful, though tensions remained. The Suevic Kingdom sought to institutionalize itself, and a *modus vivendi* ("way of living") was established with its neighbors. As time passed, the Visigoths and Suevi mixed, with mixed marriages becoming the norm. However, there were never large numbers of Suevi. The majority of the population in their kingdom was Hispano-Roman, and it is believed that the Suevi never had complete control over Gallaecia and their parts of Lusitania. The Visigoths had a presence in these regions since their victory at Campus Paramus, but their numbers were very small. It is unknown how many of them permanently settled in Gallaecia and Lusitania, but the rough estimate suggests that there were no more than 150,000 in the whole Hispania in the early 6th century. In Portugal, their numbers were even lower.

The structure of the society in Portugal wasn't any different under Germanic rule than it was under the Romans. The elites and nobles still owned the majority of land and other properties, and the majority of the population consisted of dependent tenants (*coloni*), freedmen (*liberti*), and slaves. Other groups of society existed in the form of small landowners and free professionals and artisans. The invading Germanic peoples never sought to destroy the native nobles or the existing social system, and it continued to exist undisturbed. But the Hispano-Roman leaders clung to their Roman identity and considered their barbarian conquerors to be uncivilized. They were slow to realize that the Roman Empire had abandoned Hispania forever. Once they did realize this, some of them decided to follow.

Although some of them abandoned their home country, the majority remained and tried to arrange treaties with the Suevi and later the Visigoths. In the end, the old elite decided it was best to collaborate with the invaders to secure their survival. The Suevi and Visigoths slowly added their own families to the elite social layer while avoiding disturbing the balance. They implemented a system based on *hospitalitas*, where the Germanic families took control over two-thirds of an estate while the rest remained in the hands of the previous owner. But since the Visigoths preferred to settle in what is today Spain, this system didn't have any impact on the Portuguese territory.

Tenant farmers were legally free, and some legal protection was offered to them. However, they were bound to the land on which they worked. They had to pay the tithe, perform forced labor if unable to pay the taxes (corvée system), and were obliged to serve in the military. The former slaves had a distinct social status up until the middle of the 7th century, and they were obliged to continue working for their former owners, who were now called patrons. Slave labor was fundamental to the economy of both the Suevic and Visigothic kingdoms, especially in Portugal, where it had been in place since the times of the Carthaginian conquest. The slave population was always very large and very diverse. The majority of slaves continued to perform the hard labor no one else wanted, such as digging the mines, working the fields, and serving the professionals. The minority of them held administrative positions for merchants or professionals or served as concubines of the elite.

Women had equal social status as men, and they could be nobles, free, or slaves. But in general, women were valued less than men because the Visigoths had a warrior society. There were laws set in place to protect women, but the punishment was milder than for the same crimes committed against men. For example, the punishment for killing a woman was much less than for killing a man of the same social status. However, the laws of the Visigoths favored women compared to the Roman laws. Women had equal rights as men in regards to inheritance and property rights, while under Roman laws, the property of women, for the most part, had to be controlled by male relatives.

The economy of the Germanic kingdom period was unchanged. Wars and constant invasions brought some economic insecurity, but once the kingdoms were set up, business continued as usual. The Suevic and Visigothic kings issued coins, the mining industry continued to work undisturbed, and the merchants came and went using port cities, such as Porto and Santarém. Merchants regularly came from Greece and Syria, and they traded spices, silk, slaves, and religious relics. Construction sites were everywhere, although the buildings the Germanic people built didn't always survive history. The most prominent examples of the Germanic style of building are the basilicas in Évora and Egitania. The Germanic rule didn't provide many monuments and mosaic art pieces, but friezes were popular at the time.

Rural life seems to have suffered the most during the invasion of the Germanic barbarians. Recent excavations in Baetica show that several hundreds of villages stopped functioning during the violent period of the conquest, possibly because the people abandoned their homes and searched for safety behind the city walls. It is believed that the scale of the destruction in Lusitania and Gallaecia was lesser because these regions had natural defenses, which means the people probably didn't have to abandon their villages. In many parts of the Portuguese countryside, the Roman lifestyle continued. There is evidence that supports the idea of continuous villa life in Gallaecia even during the turbulent 5th century.

Religion and the Church

The main institution that came with the rule of the Germanic kings was the Roman Catholic Church. It spread fast, and by the late 6th century, the church became the most powerful organization in western Iberia. But that doesn't mean the church had an easy time gaining this power. The Suevi were still pagans when they arrived, and they didn't receive Christianity until their king, Rechiarius, was baptized in 450. After his death, one of his successors fell under the influence of the Arian preachers. There is no evidence to claim who the first Arian king of the Suevic Kingdom was, but Arianism first appeared around 470 and would remain active until 550. But although the royal family adopted Christianity in one form or another, the kings never pushed the religion on their subjects. Their efforts to convert the whole kingdom were, at best, short-lived.

Catholicism returned around 550, but by that time, the Visigoths had already diminished their influence. The Visigoths were Arians even before they came to Hispania, and they brought their faith with them. They, too, would finally convert in 586 when King Reccared finally adopted Catholicism. But while the Visigothic royal family was still Arian, the majority of their subjects adopted Catholicism thanks to the works of various missionaries. Western civilization was firmly settled in Catholicism by the end of the 6th century, and it seems that the Visigothic kings had no other choice but to adapt to the situation. Arianism was anathematized during the Council of Toledo in 589.

During the reign of the Germanic kings, the church was mainly an urban institution. Every major city had a complex of church buildings and properties clustered into precincts that included a central church, cemetery, chapels, a bishop's palace, and other ecclesiastical buildings and land. Two metropolitan sees controlled the territory of what is today Portugal: Mérida and Braga. The Mérida see controlled Lusitania and cities including Lisbon, Beja, Faro, and Évora. The Braga see controlled the whole of Gallaecia and its thirteen dioceses. In 681, the preeminence of Toledo was established with the power to oversee the religious institutions of Visigothic Iberia.

In the countryside, the Christianization of the population was slow. Eventually, a system of parishes developed, and the first priests came to settle in the villages, replacing the missionary preachers. In Iberia, there was a strong sense of asceticism, and the first monasteries were modeled on those in the Middle East and North Africa. However, the specific origins of the monasteries in Portugal remain unknown. There are mentions of communities of nuns as early as the 5th century, especially in Braga, but the first monastic rule dates from a century later. Its founder was St. Martin of Braga, who converted the Suevic king to Catholicism.

After the Visigothic Kingdom converted to Catholicism, the bishops supported the crown, and the church and the state started working together. The bishops were often chosen to assume the royal offices, and the king was the leader of the ecclesiastical councils in Toledo. These councils often ruled on both secular and religious matters. The Catholic Church in Hispania also had to face some challenges to establish its authority. The Hispano-Romans largely remained pagan in Gallaecia, except for the stubborn Arianism that remained active in the Visigothic communities. They continued to practice some of the Roman pagan customs, such as marriages on certain dates and the lighting of lamps and candles at major landmarks. They sometimes even continued worshiping ancient monolithic constructions.

But the most problematic challenge the Catholic Church experienced in Gallaecia was Priscillianism, named after a noble Priscillian who demanded radical reforms of the church during the last days of Roman rule in Hispania. He stressed the importance of studying the sacred texts, and he advocated the rigorous forms of asceticism, vegetarianism, and celibacy. He also insisted on the equality of men and women. The existing Christian Church saw this as an effort to undermine its authority. Priscillian was eventually charged for sorcery, and the emperor found him guilty and ordered his execution in 386. Priscillianism persisted for the next two centuries. The Suevic conquest of Gallaecia didn't help in suppressing this sect, and even once it was eradicated, it continued to echo throughout Gallaecian society. It is believed that Priscillian's remains were brought back to Gallaecia and that he was buried under the cathedral at Compostela.

The main enemy of the church and Visigothic Catholic society during the 7th century were the Jews. They were seen as stubborn unbelievers. Their presence had been established among the Christian society of Hispania since Roman times. They were tolerated, for the most part, by the early Suevic and Visigothic kings, even though both royal and ecclesiastical councils approved some laws against them. For example, the Jews were forbidden from assuming royal and administrative offices, owning slaves, and building synagogues. But the real persecution of the Jews began with King Sisebut (r. 612-621), who issued a policy of forced baptism. King Chintila (r. 636-639) expanded this policy. With the church's approval, he brought about a decree by which all the Jews who would not accept baptism had to be expelled from his kingdom. The effective implementation of this new law never came, and the Jews continued to live within the realm.

The later kings brought new decrees that discriminated against the Jews, ranging from the prohibition of circumcision and Jewish ceremonies to reducing the whole Jewish community to slavery. Their property was confiscated, and all Jewish children under six years old were taken away and given to Christian families. There is no consensus among modern scholars for the reasons behind such anti-Semitism in the late Visigothic Kingdom. It is possible that as non-Christians, the Jews were scapegoats. They were likely blamed for the famine and plague that ensued at the end of the Visigothic rule of Hispania. The Jews persisted and survived Germanic rule, and they even found some relief in the more tolerant atmosphere of the early Islamic rule of the 8th century.

Chapter 4 – Gharb al-Andalus

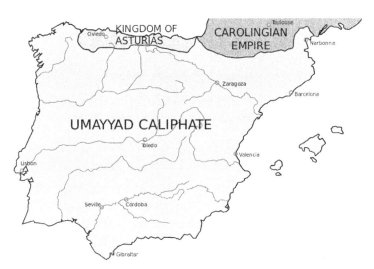

The Iberian Peninsula under Umayyad control, c. 750.

The Islamic Conquest

The Visigothic Kingdom was conquered exceptionally fast. In 711, Tariq ibn Ziyad crossed the Strait of Gibraltar with his army and defeated the Visigoth king Rodrigo in southern Baetica. Tariq was a commander of the Umayyad forces of North Africa, and after defeating Rodrigo, he led his army straight to the heart of the Iberian Peninsula. There is very little known about why the Umayyads conquered Iberia in the first place. Some people cite Caliph Uthman, the son-in-law of the Prophet Muhammad, who said that the road to Constantinople was through Hispania. But this seems less likely because conquering Constantinople through the western reaches of Europe seems implausible. Modern scholars believe that the Muslims had military and religious motives that drove them to cross the strait; however, pinpointing them has proved to be impossible.

One Muslim source from the 9th century claims that when the Umayyads conquered North Africa and took over Tangier, one Visigoth outpost remained undefeated. This outpost was under the control of the count of Ceuta, Julian, who sent one of his daughters to the Visigothic court at Toledo for education. This daughter was allegedly raped by King Rodrigo. When Julian heard of this, he used his connections to the Umayyads and helped them cross the strait on his merchant ships. This episode may well be a legend, but both Muslims and Christians sang ballads about it. While the Muslims praise the daughter of Julian and claim she was a sanctified virgin, the Christians sing about her as an evil seductress. The real evidence shows that there was a civil war or at least a power struggle between the king and the nobles in the late Visigothic Kingdom. Julian possibly took in the relatives of the late King Wittiza when the bishops crowned the usurper Rodrigo. It is also possible that Julian approached the Muslims and asked them for help to restore the old dynasty in Hispania.

Tariq and his army were given not only merchant ships from Julian's outpost but also his forts on the mainland. This helped them to launch a full-scale invasion. The initial success of Tariq prompted the governor of North Africa, Musa ibn Nusayr, to cross the strait with a much larger army and continue the conquest of the peninsula. He occupied Toledo in 712 without much effort, as most of its inhabitants fled the city. By 716, the Muslims took control of all the important strategic points and main cities of the Iberian Peninsula. They divided them between Musa ibn Nusayr, his son Abd al-Aziz, and Tariq—the three leaders who soon conquered the whole of Hispania. Wherever they turned, they encountered little to no resistance.

For a long time, it was simply accepted that the Visigothic Kingdom fell due to the sudden and unexpected attack by the Umayyad Caliphate. This opinion was formed because there was no contemporary evidence that would provide information on what had happened. The earliest existing source is from the late 10th century, and it only touches on the events from the Muslim point of view. But recent studies of the Chronicle of 754 (written by a Christian in Andalusia) suggest that there were Umayyad raids on Hispanic territory predating the conquest. That means that Tariq's invasion wasn't the first time the Christians and Muslims met on the battlefield and that perhaps the Visigoths even anticipated the Arab conquest.

The conquest may have started as nothing more than a raid, and the Muslim goal was to loot the Iberian cities and return to Africa with their prize. They decided to mount a full-scale conquest only when they realized there was no organized defense. The Umayyads switched their tactics and started offering the cities the opportunity to surrender before they would attack them. This allowed them to take control over many cities without any destruction, which, in turn, ensured the compliance of the population. The cities that accepted the surrender would have to pay tribute to the Muslims, but the people were offered protection. They were also allowed to keep their property, faith, and even local autonomy. The cities that refused to capitulate were conquered through battle. All male citizens were executed, and women and children were enslaved. Most places chose to capitulate, though, so the conquest was achieved relatively peacefully. However, the Christians wouldn't believe in the tolerance of the Muslims, and many people fled the cities and hid in the mountains, expecting violence to erupt. Although these fearful people saved their lives by fleeing, they abandoned their land, homes, and properties, leaving space for many Berber immigrants (indigenous people of North Africa) to come and settle.

The Islamic Rule of Iberia

The toponym "al-Andalus" is used by modern-day scholars to designate the Muslim rule of the Iberian Peninsula. However, the term itself is dated to the 8th century, as it was inscribed on coins minted in 716. It is the name the Muslims gave to their newly conquered territory. For a long time, scholars believed it meant "the land of the Vandals," though some people are recently challenging this translation. "Gharb al-Andalus" designated the western part of the conquered peninsula, which mostly consisted of today's territory of Portugal. During the early stage of the Islamic rule, Gallaecia wasn't part of Gharb al-Andalusia, as the area wasn't attractive to the Umayyad settlers. They preferred the southern and central regions of Roman Lusitania since the climate there was warmer and drier, already well-developed, and close to Córdoba, a major Islamic center. Gharb al-Andalus was never a distinct province or administrative unit during Islamic rule like Lusitania was during Roman rule. At the time, Portugal was part of a large unified administrative unit of al-Andalus, so scholars have trouble separating it culturally or historically from the rest of the peninsula.

A generation after the complete conquest, al-Andalus was still dependent on the administrative unit of Umayyad North Africa, and it was treated as part of it. A military governor was appointed from Kairouan in Tunisia, but it was ultimately ruled by the caliph in Damascus. The links in this chain of command were soon weakened by the revolt of the Berbers in Tangiers (740) and by the conflict between the Muslims in al-Andalus itself. The Umayyad caliphs were overthrown in 740 and replaced by the Persian

Abbasids, who had their capital in Baghdad. They proved to be more distant from Iberia, which made al-Andalus a perfect place for a surviving Umayyad prince to escape to. He was known as Abd al-Rahman I (731–788), and he proclaimed the peninsula to be an independent Umayyad state and himself as its emir. Everyone accepted his authority, and he ruled from Córdoba from 756 until his death.

The emirs of Córdoba proved to be able rulers, with a few exceptions, until the 10th century. However, they had to deal with many internal problems, such as tribal and ethnic interests of different groups of society and their religious preferences. They also had external enemies against which they had to defend their realm. At first, they faced the dangers of the Abbasid Caliphate of Baghdad. Once this passed, the Christian rulers from the north pressed on al-Andalus. To raise the prestige of the Umayyad realm and counter the dangers of outside threats, Abd al-Rahman III (r. 912–961) assumed the title of caliph. He made Córdoba a magnificent city, with its imposing but stylish palaces and mosques. As he was a great patron of the arts and education, Rahman III was praised throughout Europe, and his court was proclaimed to be the most sophisticated on the continent. His reign and the reign of his successor, al-Hakam II (r. 961–976), were proclaimed to be a period of peace and prosperity in al-Andalus.

During the Umayyad emirate and later caliphate, al-Andalus was divided into several administrative districts called *kuwar* (sin. *kura*). They were overseen by a governor (*wali*), and they roughly correspond to the Roman *jurisdictio* (a district under singular administration of justice). The governors were responsible for the military affairs and the upholding of law and order in their *kuwar*. The Muslim judges were called *qadis*, and they had jurisdiction over all communities. Christian and Jewish communities were allowed to retain their judges, though only in the matters that concerned their internal affairs. The *kuwar* were further divided into *Madina*, administrative units of several towns and their surroundings. The villages were called *dayas,* and their inhabitants were the workers dedicated to certain large landholdings. The villages of autonomous peasants existed too, and they were called *qarya.* All villages were soon named *aldeia,* and the word entered the modern Portuguese language.

Al-Andalus was subjected to raids by the northern Christians and seafaring Vikings, and the government had to install defensive marches in their frontier regions. In Gharb al-Andalus, the march was administered first from Medinaceli, but later, it was moved to Badajoz. Cities had to be fortified, and a network of watchtowers and castles was raised all over the country. Each city had an inner fortification or a citadel (alcáçova), which contained a water cistern, food storage, and administrative buildings, as well as the houses of the military leaders and city officials. The frontier cities that were under constant threat of attack had much bigger alcáçovas than the cities in inner al-Andalus, which were considered to be safe.

Al-Hakam II was the last prominent ruler of the Umayyad al-Andalus, and his successors rapidly lost their fortunes. Al-Hakam was succeeded by his son, who was only twelve years old. Thus, his chief-minister al-Mansur took the opportunity to manipulate the young caliph. Al-Mansur became a ruthless tyrant who remained in power from 980 until 1002. Nevertheless, he was an exceptional military commander who managed to defend al-Andalus from invaders from the Christian north. However, to dominate the affairs of al-Andalus, he had to dismantle the Umayyad bureaucracy and replace all the state officials with his supporters. He also distrusted the local army and often relied on the Berber mercenaries from North Africa. These mercenaries later attacked the local Andalusian population, which led to revolts and the further disintegration of the caliphate.

After al-Mansur died, political chaos ensued in al-Andalus. This period is remembered as the *fitna* (anarchy) in history, during which the caliphate was fractured by a violent power struggle. The result was the division of al-Andalus into many small kingdoms; at one point, there were up to sixty of these small kingdoms, which were known as *taifas*. Gharb al-Andalus was split into two large *taifas*—Badajoz and Seville—and four smaller ones—Huelva, Mértola, Silva, and Faro. In time, these smaller kingdoms were absorbed by Badajoz and Seville. Southern and central Portugal was part of Badajoz, which was ruled by the Berber family of Banu al-Aftas. Although the capital of this *taifa* was outside of modern-day Portugal, it encompassed most of it at the peak of its power. Some scholars even believe that Badajoz was a precursor of modern-day Portugal, as it was near to achieving complete autonomy of the region.

However, the fragmentation of al-Andalus inspired the Christian rulers of the north to react, and they resumed their attacks on the Iberian Peninsula. This caused the death of the *taifas* since they had no power to resist such attacks individually and displayed no intentions to unify against their common Christian enemy. Instead, the local rulers started bribing the Christians and paying them tribute in exchange for safety. This tribute was named *parias*, and the Umayyad princes institutionalized it. They spent enormous amounts of riches, so much so that the whole period of the 11th century in al-Andalus became known as the "Age of Parias." When Toledo fell to the Castilians in 1085, the system of paying tribute collapsed, and the danger of the Christian occupation became very real. The remaining Umayyad princes called on the Almoravids for help, which was an Islamic military group that had recently come to power in Morocco. The Almoravids crossed the Strait of Gibraltar and helped al-Andalus to defeat the kings of León-Castile. But the leader of this Islamic military group, Yusuf ibn Tashfin, decided to incorporate al-Andalus in his emirate. The Almoravid rule of Iberia was short-lived, as they soon abandoned al-Andalus and retreated to defend Morocco, which they started losing in the 1120s.

The Society and Economy of al-Andalus

Many Hispano-Romans converted to Islam after the establishment of al-Andalus. Other Muslims who settled in the peninsula were the Arabs, mostly Yemenis, and the Berbers. The Arabs comprised a small elite minority, while the Berbers represented the majority of the Muslim population of Iberia. They came from the Maghreb region in Africa. The migratory Muslims came to the peninsula in several waves over two centuries and settled mainly in Algarve and other southern regions. Their numbers were never large, and they never surpassed more than several thousand. Only a minority of the Muslim immigrants brought their families to the newly conquered territory. Most of the immigrants were young bachelors who intended to marry local women.

The Arabs and Berbers who came to the peninsula remained loyal to their origins and tribal way of life. They even attempted to settle the members of the same or similar tribes in distinct areas, but this proved impossible long-term. The Arabs and Berbers never mixed, and they often clashed. But over time, the ethnic lines blurred, and the conflicts eventually disappeared. With such sparse numbers of immigrants, the majority of the Muslims in al-Andalus consisted of converts and their descendants. The neo-Muslims came from all levels of society, and they were called *muwallads*.

The Muslim society of al-Andalus was socially divided into the aristocracy (*hassa*) and the common people (*amma*), but this division was never as rigorous as in the Christian north. The aristocracy was concentrated in the cities and towns, and they held the administrative offices. In some cases, these offices were hereditary. They also owned a lot of lands, and they supported themselves by renting it out. The commoners were tied to the land they worked on, and it seems that little had changed for them since Roman times. They often revolted against their position in society but ultimately failed to get rid of their dependence on the land. The slave system was entrenched in al-Andalus as much as it had been in the Roman and Visigothic times. The Muslims often raided the Christian north of the peninsula and took slaves from there. They also traveled through Europe and crossed Gibraltar. They brought slaves from Christian kingdoms and sub-Saharan Africa, adding to the enormous diversity of Iberia.

The Muslim rule of al-Andalus was heavily focused on the development of the cities, as they were an urban-oriented society. It is no wonder that during the Umayyad period, great cities, such as Córdoba, Seville, Lisbon, Coimbra, and Beja, developed into grand urban centers. They housed several thousands of inhabitants, mostly the professional middle class. They were artisans, merchants, and artists, as well as scholars, lesser officials, and small landholders. The middle class was not a distinct social group, although they were different from both the *hassa* and *amma*. The society of al-Andalus was patriarchal, and although women held social positions equal to men, they had strictly family roles. This doesn't mean they couldn't become cultured. Women from the royal and aristocratic families were given an education, and they studied law and religion and wrote exquisite poetry. The majority of court women were slaves who either served as pleasure providers or who served the royal family. But Andalus rulers were known for often marrying their slave concubines, thus raising their social status.

The Christians remained in Iberia even after the Muslim conquest, though their numbers were significantly reduced. Many decided to convert to the faith of their conquerors, but many also decided to emigrate to other Christian countries in Europe. Those who stayed and remained faithful to Christianity but accepted the rule of the Muslims were called Mozarabs. Their social structure was the same as before the conquest, with a hereditary nobility and an intermediate class of merchants and professionals. There was also a dependent class of tenants bound to the land, as well as slaves. The Mozarabs became a minority in al-Andalus by the 11th century. Jews were also present, though in very small numbers. It is estimated that there were only around one thousand Jews in Gharb al-Andalus. They were given the same tolerance and treatment as the Christians, which was an improvement for the Jewish community that suffered under the Visigoth rule.

Christianity and Judaism under the Muslim Rule

Early Islam was very tolerant of other religions. Although they institutionalized their religion and made it official, they allowed Christians to practice their rites, keep their churches, and even build new ones on several occasions. The episcopal and parish organization of Christian al-Andalus remained intact, and their monasteries continued to operate undisturbed. In the initial period after the conquest, the Christians were even allowed to keep their internal administration, though when this was canceled is unknown. The caliphate wanted some control over the appointment of the bishops, but this wasn't anything new since the previous Visigothic government had the same power.

Although the Muslims proved more tolerant toward other religions, some changes did happen. In major cities, the mosques replaced many churches. In several cities and towns, the Christians were confined in ghettos. Although they had the freedom of movement, they were forbidden from settling anywhere else. The priests no longer held official positions in the government, and the churches were often forbidden from ringing the bells within the cities. Christians were allowed to convert to Islam if they wished, but Muslims were not allowed to take up Christianity. Muslims were allowed to marry Christian women or take them as concubines, but Christian men could not do the same with Muslim women. The Christians also had to pay higher taxes than the Muslim residents.

All of these prohibitions and limitations on Christians were less worrisome for those who lived in the rural parts of al-Andalus, although the constant pressure could always be felt. However, this pressure was more political than religious, as the government wouldn't allow the church to pursue any long-term Christian interests. There was never open persecution of Christians in Muslim-ruled Iberia, at least not until the late 11th century. Still, the Latin language was completely displaced, with Arabic replacing it. The Arabic language, culture, and education became the norm, and all ambitious Christians had to conform to it. There was an ever-present incentive to abandon Christianity and convert to Islam, which the majority of the population eventually did.

The Islamization of the peninsula led to the weakening of the Christian Church, and soon enough, it struggled to survive. The episcopal organization was intact, and it continued functioning as late as the 12th century. However, almost nothing is known about the Christian leaders of al-Andalus. The bishops were appointed in major cities such as Lisbon, Faro, Beja, and Évora, but their names have been forgotten. Only several names of the bishops of Coimbra were preserved, and they all belonged to the 9th and 10th centuries. The monasteries continued operating, especially in the territories north of Mondego, but nothing is known about the monasteries in the south. The south of what is today Portugal had two major Christian pilgrimage spots: the tomb of St. Vincent at Cape and the sanctuary of the Virgin Mary in Faro. The Muslim authorities respected these pilgrimage sites immensely and never disturbed them. Several Christians resisted the Muslim rule, and they were executed and became martyrs. One such was St. Sisnando, who was executed at Évora in 851.

The Muslim officials were suspicious of the ecclesiastical contact that the Christian Church of al-Andalus had with the outside Christian world, and they acted on it. The church became inward-looking and very isolated. Such isolation led to the development of different dogmas, which only further strengthened the loneliness of the al-Andalus Christians. One of these dogmas was the belief that Jesus Christ was the son of God only by adoption. In Gharb al-Andalus, the doctrine of Adoptionism was accepted, even though it was condemned by Rome. But in truth, the development of such different doctrines only served to display the need that the church felt to bridge the religious differences between the Christians and their Muslim rulers.

A small community of Jews existed in Gharb al-Andalus, and they were treated better by their Muslim masters than by the Christian Visigoths. Nevertheless, during the late 11th century, both Jews and Christians suffered under the rule of the Almoravids and Almohads. The number of Jews significantly declined in al-Andalus, and the synagogues that existed in Lisbon, Beja, Silves, and Évora were nearly empty.

The Christian North

When Musa ibn Nusayr finished the conquest of Iberia, he was recalled back to Syria. He left the whole peninsula under Islamic rule, except for several remote areas in the north that remained Christian. In 722, these Christians, led by a certain Pelayo, defeated the Muslim forces. Pelayo (Pelagius) was a leader of the mountain people who had a long tradition of resisting any invaders. After his victory, the Muslims considered the territory not worth the trouble, and they never attempted to take it again. But the rest of Portugal was firmly under Muslim rule, and the Christian Reconquest (also known as the Reconquista) would last for the next five centuries until the last Muslim enclave surrendered in 1249. The slow pace of the Reconquest could be explained by the people's unwillingness to fight for their religious freedom, which was because they were not oppressed or persecuted. They would rather make deals with the Muslims and live in peace than suffer the consequences of war.

However, the situation in the north changed during the late 11th century as religious fanaticism started blooming. Religious motivations became enough for the Reconquest, though it was never the only motive behind it. The territorial ambitions of the Christian leaders led to the development of an intense conflict, and they used religion to inspire the people to fight for them. After Pelayo's success against the Muslims, he was proclaimed king of Asturias (a region in northwestern Spain).

Pelayo's successor, Afonso I (693–757), laid claim on the inheritance of the Visigoths and confirmed the border of his kingdom, which lay in the western and central territories of the Cantabrian Mountains and in the central region of what is today the Province of Asturias. Later, the kingdom would absorb Galicia and the Basque Country. The Kingdom of Asturias sent regular raids southward into the Muslim territory. However, Afonso I was aware he could not hold onto these territories, so he uprooted the Christians living in the cities of Portucale, Braga, and Viseu and moved them to the north. By doing this, he left an empty, uninhabited zone between Asturias and al-Andalus. However, not all modern historians believed that such a buffer zone existed. And when they do, they cannot agree on its size. Nevertheless, in the 9th century, the Asturias king moved into this zone and established his presence there.

From the mid-9th century, the parts of northern Portugal, Minho, and Trás-os-Montes were incorporated in the Kingdom of Asturias. Alfonso III (c. 848–911) expanded his territory to incorporate everything north of the Douro River. By the late 9th century, this area already had Christian settlers and a working Asturias administration. The town of Portucale was captured in 868, and control over it was given to Vímara Peres, who became its count. Under his family, the town prospered and became a bishopric by the end of the century. Braga had to be rebuilt since the city was left destroyed after the conflict with the Muslims. However, the bishop wouldn't return to this old capital of Gallaecia for another century. Count Peres worked hard to attract the Christians from the north and those who remained in the Muslim south to come and repopulate the area of Entre Douro e Minho.

Another count, Hermenegildo Guterres, was established in Coimbra, a territory that was heavily Islamized and whose inhabitants predominantly consisted of the Mozarabs. This area was also opened to Muslim attacks, and its count quickly realized that if he wanted to keep the peace, he would have to implement cultural tolerance in Coimbra and maintain good relations with the Muslims in Córdoba. Coimbra and Portucale are often regarded as the predecessors of the Kingdom of Portugal, especially Portucale, which gave the country its name. Portucale is a derivation of the Latin *Portus Cale* (Port Cale). In Roman times, Cale was a town at the mouth of the Douro River, and it had a small harbor on its banks, where the Suevi later built a fortress. This town was a major communication junction, and in time, its significance grew immensely. It was later named Porto, and it became Portugal's second-largest city.

After the death of Alfonso III, the king of Asturias moved his capital to Spanish León, and the kingdom became known as León. This move occurred because the Christians felt confident in their ability to face the Muslim threat. But the Muslims were the ones who restarted the conflict. Under the reign of al-Mansur, they started raiding the territories of León and caused widespread destruction. Many Christian inhabitants of the Kingdom of León were captured and taken to al-Andalus as slaves. Coimbra was retaken by the Muslims in 987, and after it, the city of León fell. King Vermudo II (Bermudo; r. 984–999) had no other choice but to submit to Muslim dominance. To seal the peace, he married his daughter to al-Mansur.

The caliph wasn't satisfied. In 997, he launched an attack on the territory of today's Galicia and northern Portugal, where the city of Compostela was burned to the ground. He spared the shrine of St. James, but he robbed the cathedral of its bells and doors. He later melted these to make grand chandeliers for the Córdoba mosque. This confirms the predatory nature of al-Mansur's raids, and he never really intended to assert control over the northern Christian territories.

Chapter 5 – Independent Medieval Kingdom

King Afonso II as depicted in the Castilian Compendium of Chronicles of Kings, 14th century.

After reading of the events that took place in the Iberian Peninsula during the Muslim rule, the emergence of the Kingdom of Portugal during the 12th century and its later expansion and consolidation of the border in the 13th century seem surprising. Portugal as a political idea had never existed before, and the people who lived within the territory had no common language or a distinctive tradition and culture that would set them apart. The appearance of Portugal was sudden, but it can be explained by a short-term political development, which was especially influenced by the Christian Reconquista.

As the Christian Kingdom of Asturias and later León expanded, its kings faced the problem of keeping the fringe territories under their firm control. The areas of Portucale and Coimbra were especially troublesome. These two regions bordered Muslim al-Andalus, and their counts had to employ an army and were given important military functions within the kingdom. They used these to consolidate their power, expand their estates, and ensure the succession of their family lines. They created dynasty continuity and local autonomy to a certain degree.

The kings of León-Castile became aware of the ever-growing autonomy of Portucale and Coimbra. In the mid-11th century, they started reasserting their authority in these regions. The counts were formally dismissed and replaced by the king's loyal supporters. The count of Portucale wouldn't accept the loss of prestige, though. In 1071, he organized a revolt. King García of León-Castile managed to defeat him and even kill him. The family of Vímara Peres lost its political significance after two centuries of having Portucale under their control. A similar thing happened to the count of Galicia, who revolted in 1088.

The new governors of the outlying territories of León-Castile were discouraged from acting independently. Alfonso VI appointed Raymond of Burgundy as the governor of Galicia. He was a foreigner and had no familial ties to the region. This made him a perfect candidate, as he would be more likely to remain loyal to the king. Alfonso himself was tied to Burgundy through a marriage with the sister of the duke of Burgundy. Raymond came to León-Castile to take part in the Reconquista, and the king noticed his efforts and gave him the hand of his only legitimate daughter, Urraca.

Another Burgundian noble appeared at the court of Alfonso VI: Henry of Burgundy, who would prove crucial for the foundation of the Kingdom of Portugal. He was not related to Raymond, but Henry's brother later married Raymond's sister, binding the two noble families together. To reward Henry, Alfonso decided to split the territory he had given to Raymond. What was once ancient Gallaecia was now split along the flow of the Minho River. Raymond took control over Galicia, while Henry received the Portucale-Coimbra territory, also known as Condado Portucalense.

The combination of Portucale and Coimbra into a single administrative unit was a crucial step for the later formation of Portugal. Earl Henry proved to be a loyal servant of León-Castile, and he married Alfonso's bastard daughter Teresa. But after the death of Alfonso VI in 1109, Henry took the opportunity of the ensuing civil war to quietly retreat to his earldom and govern it as a true autonomous ruler in his own right. He simply abandoned his feudal obligations to the crown, and there was no one powerful enough to force him to come back. Henry himself died in 1112, and he left his earldom to his wife Teresa since their son, Afonso Henriques (r. 1139–1185), was still a minor.

But because Teresa was a woman, the clergy and other nobles pressured her to remarry. The Trava family of Galicia insisted that Henry's widow should marry one of them. This family already enjoyed great prestige and influenced Alfonso Raimúndez, the son of Raymond of Galicia, since Pedro Fróilaz de Trava was his tutor. The Trava family's main goal was the reunification of the Galicia and Portugal-Coimbra regions into an independent kingdom.

Teresa eventually succumbed to the wishes of the Trava family. She married her daughter to a Trava, and she even later became involved in a love affair with Fernando Pérez de Trava, the son of Pedro Fróilaz. Even though they were never married, Fernando started governing Portucale. The nobles and bishops of Portucale-Coimbra left Teresa's court. In 1127, a rebellion started against the rule of Fernando Pérez de Trava and Teresa. The leader of the rebellion was Teresa's son, Afonso Henriques. It is not clear why Afonso decided to move against his mother, but it is possible he took the side of the discontented nobility with whom he had personal ties.

The most notable relationship Afonso had was with the Mendes family, whose members were responsible for his education and upbringing. He lived with the Mendes family, and they were the ones who took him to the Zamora Cathedral where he was knighted. Under such circumstances, it is no wonder he took their side in the contest between Galicia and Condado Portucalense. The decisive battle between the forces of Afonso and his mother Teresa took place on June 24th, 1128, at São Mamede. Afonso defeated and expelled the Travas, and Teresa withdrew to Galicia with them.

The Emergence of Portugal as a Kingdom

After his victory at São Mamede, Afonso emerged as the sole ruler of a large part of the Iberian Peninsula between the Mingo River in the north and al-Andalus in the south. He did not call himself a count; instead, he assumed the titles of *infante* and *príncipe*, both of which implied his royal descent. For the time being, he continued to acknowledge the kings of León-Castile as his superiors to whom he claimed loyalty. But in 1131, Afonso moved his court from Guimarães to Coimbra to distance himself from the northern nobility. This allowed him to focus his attention on the southern parts of his domain and beyond. The nobles who helped him seize power were left to enjoy their spoils in the north. The region of Coimbra and the southern areas beyond it lacked the established nobility, which meant that Afonso could impose his will there undisturbed. Moreover, Coimbra was the perfect spot to set up a military base from which Afonso could continue the Reconquista.

In 1139, Afonso defeated the Muslims in his most celebrated battle, that of the Battle of Ourique. The place of the battle remains a mystery, but its magnitude and the influence it had on Afonso were great. After this battle, he started styling himself as *rex* (king), although he was never officially crowned. Instead, his followers raised him on a shield, celebrating his victory as if he was one of the Germanic warrior-leaders of old. The shield, therefore, became a symbol of his reign and a symbol of the foundation of Portugal. The shield was hung above Afonso's tomb after his death in 1185, and the medieval Portuguese believed that it fell from its stand whenever a king died in their country.

The fact that Afonso Henriques assumed the royal title didn't break the bond and obligations he had with the Kingdom of León-Castile. The attitude of King Alfonso VII was crucial in Afonso's recognition as a sovereign ruler of Portugal. Navarre and Aragon were already separate kingdoms that remained in a feudal relationship with León-Castile. Alfonso VII thought the more kings he had under his vassalage, the bigger his personal prestige would be. Thus, he wanted to reach an agreement with Afonso. At Zamora, the papal legate Cardinal Vico mediated the negotiations between Alfonso and Afonso, and in 1143, the agreement was reached. Afonso I of Portugal was crowned king. Unfortunately, no document of these events survived, so we do not know what their agreement involved. Scholars speculate that Afonso probably promised he would never aspire to gain the territories that belonged to León-Castile and would focus on reconquering Gharb al-Andalus.

In 1157, Alfonso VII died, and the Kingdom of León-Castile was divided between two sons of Alfonso VII. Ferdinand II of León tried to assert his dominance over Portugal. But these tensions were quickly quashed when Afonso offered his daughter's hand in marriage to Ferdinand. This marriage signified the definitive status of Portugal as an independent kingdom. Afonso now only needed to persuade the pope to recognize him as king. He promised to pay an annual fee to the papacy and to become the vassal of the Holy See, all in an attempt to lobby for papal approval of his royal titles. Initially, the pope accepted the tribute, but he wouldn't recognize Afonso as a king, only as a duke. Finally, in 1179, Pope Alexander III issued a bull in which he addressed Afonso Henriques as king. Portugal was finally recognized as a kingdom under the apostolic protection of St. Peter. By that time, Afonso had managed to expand his kingdom to the Tagus River, a territory that previously belonged to Gharb al-Andalus.

The Expansion

The 12th-century Christian leaders of Iberia regarded al-Andalus as occupied territory, and it was their moral and legal obligation to free it. It was only natural for Afonso Henriques to expand his newly founded kingdom southward to the territory of Gharb al-Andalus. As the successor of the Visigoths, it was Afonso's sacred duty to recover the lost territories. This view also had strong papal support, and Afonso's efforts to expand his kingdom merged with the efforts of all Christian leaders to reconquer the Iberian Peninsula. It is important to remember that Portugal didn't exist before and that the "Reconquest" didn't mean returning the previous Portuguese territories. It simply meant returning the Iberian territories under Christian rule. But Afonso's reasons were also personal; he knew the more territory he controlled, the more prestige he would have. He didn't plan to conquer the territories and make Portugal as we know it today. He only wanted to enlarge the territory he controlled, and he would take any opportunity that presented itself.

The Reconquest of Portugal was over only 110 years after the reign of Afonso Henriques. The first expansion in the 1140s pushed the southern border to the Tagus River. Most of the conflicts during the early stage of the Reconquista occurred in Ribatejo and Estremadura. Although the Portuguese Army tried to push farther south, they were not successful in asserting their control over those territories. In 1147, Afonso managed to take Santarém, a strategically important city in the Lower Tagus Valley, and later that year, he conquered Lisbon. But when he tried to push south into the open plains of central Alentejo, he met stronger resistance. It took him three attempts before he could finally take Alcácer do Sal in 1158. But in the next two years, the Portuguese Army and the foreign crusaders the king employed took many towns, such as Cáceres, Beja, Évora, Moura, Serpa, Juromenha, and Monsaraz. The Crusade against Islam was called on by Pope Urban II in 1095, but at the same time, the pope exempted the Christians of the Iberian Peninsula from joining the Crusade in Palestine. Instead, he expected them to get rid of Islam in their own peninsula. When the European Crusaders came back from Palestine, they continued their fight by joining the Iberian Reconquista, swelling the armies of the Iberian Christian kings with their numbers. Nevertheless, the first phase of the Portuguese conquest ended with Afonso's failure to take Badajoz in 1169.

If he had taken Badajoz, Afonso would have possessed an important strategic city that would have allowed him to eventually seize control over the whole of Lusitania. This was unacceptable to Ferdinand II of León, and he sent his army to help the Muslims defend the city. Afonso was even captured and spent some time as Ferdinand's prisoner. His leg was also injured, and his general health suffered, so he started delegating more responsibilities to his son and successor, Sancho. The young prince didn't manage to do much, for, at the time, the Muslim cause experienced a revival. The Muslim princes called for help from North Africa, and the

Almohad army responded. The Reconquest efforts of Portugal were not only halted but also reversed to some degree. Through the 1180s and 1190s, the Almohads took over some of the lost territories of Gharb al-Andalus, and they took back almost all of the towns that had been previously conquered by the Christians. The Portuguese were pushed back to their old border at the Tagus River.

It was obvious the Muslims couldn't keep their momentum since they were not unified, and their realm was divided among various princes. The Christian army, led by the kings of Castile, Aragon, and Navarre, defeated the al-Andalus Muslims at a battle that took place in 1212 at Las Navas de Tolosa. This was the most decisive battle of the later Reconquista, and it marked the beginning of the end of al-Andalus. The Christian rulers of the Iberian Peninsula finally started advancing against their enemies. For a time, Gharb al-Andalus became the only Muslim enclave, but even it would eventually fall. The Portuguese Army rushed to take Alentejo in 1230, which was followed by the conquest of Algarve in 1249. This was the end of the Portuguese Reconquest, but they were denied the right to take Algarve by the king of Castile. However, with papal support, Portugal gained this territory in 1297. Regardless, the notion that Algarve was a separate entity persisted throughout history, and the Portuguese rulers styled themselves as kings of Portugal and Algarve.

It is impossible to conclude how many Muslims lost their lives during the Reconquista. The new Christian rulers of the territories that once belonged to al-Andalus were less tolerant than the Islamic ones. They welcomed the Mozarabs and allowed them to reconvert to Christianity, but they saw the Muslims as less desirable. They were pushed southward until they finally crossed the Strait of Gibraltar and sailed to Morocco. Those who decided to remain behind were systematically slaughtered. At this point, the whole of Europe had a very strong anti-Muslim sentiment, and these massacres were considered a sacred duty to cleanse the land of the infidels. But despite the bloodshed, the Muslims remained a constant presence in Christian Portugal, and they became known as Mudéjars (the subjugated). They were either forcefully Christianized or allowed to practice their religion but lost some of their civic rights. In Portugal, they remained a minority for around 250 years. Islam was finally outlawed in Portugal in 1497, and the majority of Mudéjars left the kingdom for good. Those who remained were baptized, but they usually continued to practice Islam in secret.

The Development of Portugal

During the 12th century, the central government and the institutions of Portugal remained underdeveloped. The king traveled around the country, and he was accompanied by his royal council, or *curia*. This council was composed of the king's royal advisors, who were also the leading vassals. They owed him their loyalty, counsel, and military support. The *curia* also represented the central judicial tribunal, and they administered justice in their extensive travels while following the king. There were different officials on the council, of which three of them stand as the most prominent: *mordomo*, *alferes*, and the chancellor. They were the king's executives, and although the first two titles eventually transformed into honorary ones, the chancellor became the most prominent figure of the kingdom. The *mordomo* (majordomo) supervised the king's estates. The *alferes* was the banner carrier and main military general of the kingdom. The chancellor had the most responsibilities; he carried the royal seal, drafted all the laws of the kingdom, and supervised its fiscal administration. However, at the start of the 13th century, the chancellors lost some of their significance when King Denis (r. 1279–1325) formed a new office, the confidential secretary, which would take over some of the functions that were previously in the hands of the chancellors.

Much of the king's revenue and his capacity to govern Portugal were compromised by the grants that were issued to vassals in return for their military service. To strengthen their position and centralize the government more firmly, Sancho I and his successor, Afonso II, did whatever was in their power to draw back some of the concessions. The idea to do this came from Chancellor Julião Pais, a Bologna-educated lawyer. He used the law as his primary instrument to strengthen the central government. In 1211, Afonso II declared the king's law to be supreme, even above the church's right to deal with temporal matters. Later, Chancellor Mestre Vicente promulgated the law that granted the king of Portugal the same rights the Roman rulers had under Roman law. By doing this, he proclaimed that God directly gave Portuguese kings the right to rule, not the popes. All the kings of medieval Portugal adopted this doctrine.

In 1220, the crown initiated an inquiry that would determine the right of the vassals to own their lands or if the interests of the crown had been usurped. Monasteries, which were widespread across medieval Portugal, felt threatened by this. They owned vast amounts of land, and they were previously given many privileges and immunities as vassals of the kingdom. However, their wealth deprived the king of much of the revenue. The church also aggravated the crown by claiming the right to tax exemptions, spiritual authority, and judicial independence for the clergy. The Reconquista had been an expensive endeavor, though, and the crown needed to recoup its financial losses.

Much of Sancho I's reign was marked by increasing post-war famine and the plague. Social unrest followed, and the king had to fight the nobles and clergy for both lay and ecclesiastical interests, which would bring new revenue to the royal treasury. He even entered into an open conflict with the bishops of Coimbra and Porto, who denied him meddling in ecclesiastical affairs. His successor, Afonso II, strove to strengthen the king's authority. Although his health was constantly compromised (it is believed he suffered from leprosy), he proved to be an exceptional ruler. Unlike his grandfather (Afonso I) and father (Sancho I), Afonso II didn't seek to expand his kingdom. He took a different approach to governance, but once he tried to take away the rights and immunities of the aristocracy, he had to deal with a revolt. The northern nobles united under the leadership of Mendes de Sousa, who had the support of Alfonso IX, King of León. Luckily, the Kingdom of Castile supported Afonso II. The Portuguese prelates also rushed to support their king because even though he attacked their revenues, they still preferred a stable government over the fragmentation of the kingdom.

Afonso II quelled the rebellion successfully and immediately returned to his centralizing policies. The relations between the crown and the church deteriorated once again. Afonso wanted the church to accept his court and to start paying taxes. The clergy threatened to revolt. His main opponents were the bishop of Coimbra and the archbishop of Braga. Dom Estevão Soares da Silva, Archbishop of Braga, had once been a close friend of the king. But his insistence on ecclesiastical freedoms eventually resulted in the defeat of Afonso II, who sought peace in 1223. By then, the king was already on his deathbed and couldn't do much when the papacy got involved and demanded the resignation of ministers who advised the king against the church. Afonso was dead by the time peace was reached, and the church took the opportunity to influence his fourteen-year-old son and successor and impose humiliating terms on him. Sancho II (r. 1223–1248) was a minor, and as such, he was put under the tutelage of the archbishop of Braga, Dom Estevão. He was also forced to pay a large indemnity to the archbishop for the losses caused by his father's reckless behavior. The centralizing policies his predecessors had pursued were now completely halted.

Afonso III and King Denis

When Sancho II reached adulthood and started ruling in his own name, he rekindled the old conflict between the crown and the church by demanding royal rights. The ecclesiastical leaders filed complaints to the pope, who once again had to intervene. Sancho was never a strong monarch, and not only did the clergy denounce him, but he was also deserted by many nobles. In 1245, he was deposed by Pope Innocent IV, and his younger brother, Afonso III, replaced him, though not without a brief civil war.

Afonso III (r. 1248-1279) proved to be a much more capable king than his older brother. He made Estêvão Anes his able chancellor, and together, they restored order to Portugal. Afonso also had better opportunities than his brother to start his endeavors. By that time, the Reconquista was over, and the kingdom's economy had started recovering. The colonization of the newly acquired territories began, and additional charters were issued to include these territories in the Kingdom of Portugal. By the mid-13th century, the relations with the church were improved, though not at a satisfying level. The king had to accept that the royal and ecclesiastical laws were supreme in their respective spheres, though some cases still sparked arguments.

The number of royal officials increased during the 13th century, and the administration of the kingdom became more efficient. Afonso summoned a *cortes* (council) in 1254 at Leiria. This was not the same council of nobles and clergy, as it also included higher clergy and representatives from all the major towns of Portugal. In 1258, Afonso resumed the centralization policy of his predecessors and started a commission that would inquire into the alleged usurpation of the royal lands and rights. The church revolted against such inquiries, and Afonso had to pull back. Just like his father before him, he was made to submit to the ecclesiastical wishes on his deathbed by none other than the pope.

The son of Afonso III had the longest reign of all the Burgundian kings of Portugal. King Denis (Dinis; r. 1279-1325) came to the throne as a teenager and ruled for forty-six years. It became obvious during his rule that the king had increased authority and an obligation to assume some of the key functions. He ruled for a long period of time despite the constant threat of rebellion. His son and brothers launched several rebellions against the crown, but they didn't achieve much. His assumption of authority is best seen in the growth of the centralized court that had been founded by Afonso II. In the beginning, there was only one judge who dealt with the judicial issues of the whole kingdom. Denis raised the number of the principal judges to four. He also created a network of judicial districts in all the provinces (*julgados*) and employed a royal judge in each of them.

Denis was also known for his extensive travels around his kingdom, during which he issued laws, dispensed justice, and promoted agriculture, trade, and the development of towns. This is why he was also called the "Farmer King." Denis also acquired papal support for his concordat that investigated some titles and land ownership of the Portuguese nobles. In exchange, he had to promise he would leave the clergy out of this investigation. The pope also banned the church in Portugal from acquiring more land for the time being. The investigation revealed some claims over the land to be invalid, and the nobles lost control over them. Denis did the same thing with the military orders, which had gained vast lands during the Reconquista. But unlike other European kings, Denis never sought to disband them. Instead, he took them under his royal protection, as he did want to nationalize them and subject them to the crown so he could use their resources. In 1288, he again approached the pope and secured his support for the royal appointment of the master of the Portuguese Order of Santiago. When the Templars were disbanded by the pope in 1312, Denis took them in and used them to create a nationalized military order, the Military Order of Christ (founded in 1319).

Denis was the sixth king of an unbroken line of Burgundian kings of Portugal. The kingdom had existed for almost two hundred years and covered a territory of approximately ninety-two thousand square kilometers (eighteen thousand miles). But even though his reign was long and he proved to be one of the ablest Portuguese rulers, the conflict between the crown on one side and the church and nobility on the other was far from over. Nevertheless, the monarchic institutions appropriate for a medieval kingdom took shape in Portugal, and the political climate in Europe favored the crown. Its society was still feudal, and the monarchy was as successful as any other in western Europe at the time.

Chapter 6 – Portugal during the 14th Century

Afonso IV
https://commons.wikimedia.org/wiki/File:AfonsoIV-P.jpg

By the early 14th century, a key ingredient for the establishment of the Portuguese nation was established: the Portuguese language. It was used in both written and spoken form throughout the kingdom.

Portuguese is a composite language that took the structure and vocabulary of the early Galician used in the northwestern Iberian Peninsula. It also borrowed heavily from other dialects, especially those used by the Mozarabs (e.g., Lusitano). Therefore, the Portuguese language absorbed many Arabic words and integrated them. During the early kingdom, Latin was still the official language, though Portuguese started entering official documents. King Denis made the Portuguese language exclusive for the secular government, which left Latin for the church.

The Portuguese language started entering literary works in the 14th century. Writers used it to compose *cantigas*, which is poetry heavily influenced by traditional Muslim poetry, as well as the ballads of Provence. Other literary works were written in Portuguese, such as astrology, science books, and genealogies of noble houses. Due to this, a common Portuguese culture took shape in the region. In 1290, King Denis issued a charter through which the University of Coimbra was founded. This meant that the Portuguese inhabitants no longer had to leave their kingdom to acquire education.

The Economy of the 14th Century

Portugal reached its peak of prosperity and stability during the early 14th century. It had the largest population in its history at that time, but the population was not evenly distributed. The northwestern region was the most heavily populated, followed by Estremadura. The mountainous northeast and central regions were sparsely populated, with only two people per square kilometer. The majority of the people lived off of agriculture and herding animals, but they didn't own the land or cattle they worked with. The ownership was in the hands of the royal or ecclesiastical institutions and a small number of elite individuals. The crown had most of its possessions in Alentejo and Trás-os-Montes, where it accumulated well over half of the land. These royal possessions would later be broken up and divided between ecclesiastical offices and lay beneficiaries. The Order of Santiago gained the most, as it acquired around 25 percent of Alentejo. The land owned by the nobles was also large, but it was more fragmented since it was controlled by individual lords.

The large landowners had to administer and maintain one or more domains, although they were rarely a continuous tract of land. These domains were called *granjas* or *quintas*, and they had a large residence under the administration of a steward. These domains had a diverse landscape, as they usually consisted of woods, cultivated fields, wastelands, and pastures. Although some nobles had the *quintas* in their possession, most of them were in the hands of the military orders, bishoprics, and monasteries. The *quintas* were never exploited directly by their owners. They were fragmented into smaller units and rented to tenants. The owners got their income from the rent and dues, which were paid in both money and kind.

The basic unit of the tenant system was the *casal*, a farm large enough to support one family of peasants. It was a mixture of arable land, woods, and pastures. In the northwest of Portugal, the *casals* were very small, often amounting to only one hectare. Later, the powerful magnates tended to divide the *casals* into even smaller units and rented as separate farms. However, most of the peasant families held several of these small units and sometimes even several *casals*. Large estates were present only in Alentejo and Ribatejo. The rest of Portugal was made out of a complex patchwork of small farms.

The form of tenure established in the early 14th century in Portugal was *emphyteusis*. This tenure had been around since ancient Greece, and it represents a perpetual contract between the owner and the tenant. It gave the tenant the right to exploit the land as long as he paid the taxes and rent and properly cared for the estate, which involved making constant improvements. This meant that the peasant families had security, and the rates he had to pay were fixed.

Portugal's rural economy hadn't changed much since Roman times. The staples of life were still bread and wine, and the *casals* were self-sustaining types of farms where the peasants produced everything they needed. They grew grains, fruit trees, vegetables, and wine. The principal crop was wheat, although the Portuguese soil is not best suited for it. Wine production was so widespread that tenant contracts often specified that the rent needed to be paid in a certain amount of wine. Chestnut trees were popular for the production of flour and timber. The Portuguese villagers also grew a wide range of European vegetables, such as cabbage, carrots, beans, and spinach. The southern areas grew figs and oaks, which were used to produce corks. Medieval Portugal already exported significant amounts of cork to other European and Mediterranean countries.

The farmers also possessed pigs, goats, sheep, and poultry. The cattle were the most precious animal, and they were sparse. They were mainly used to produce milk, milk products, and fertilizer, but they were also as draft animals. Commercial herding was present only in southern and central Portugal where there were conditions for large herds. Here, the cattle were kept mainly to produce meat and hides. The wool in Portugal was produced mainly by the Cistercian monks of Alcobaça, and they also possessed the largest flocks of sheep. Shepherds would take their flocks north during the summer, and in winter, they would head south to Alentejo.

Besides agriculture and cattle-raising, the Portuguese economy also relied on the aquatic industry. River mouths were abundant with shellfish, and there is evidence that shellfish had been exploited since prehistoric times. Other than ocean fishing, the Portuguese developed freshwater fishing since the country is full of streams where trout is plentiful. From maritime fishing, the Portuguese would acquire tuna, sharks, sardines, and hake. Whaling was also starting to develop, and the Portuguese seafarers were skillful hunters.

Commercial Capitalism in Portugal

Portugal remained mostly rural during the 14th century, but a prosperous network of towns and cities was already developed. Much of this network was acquired during the Reconquista, and its main hub was in the Muslim south. The Portuguese towns of the north were very different from those in the south. After all, they had origins in different cultures, as well as in very different geographical regions. The southern towns were larger, with houses built of plaster and mud. The smaller northern towns were usually built of granite and had heavier walls. The southern towns reflected the tradition and culture of their Muslim inhabitants, while the northern towns kept their Romanesque style. The towns raised after the Reconquista were typically Christian. They were laid in parallel streets with a cathedral in the main square. The contrast between the traditional northern and southern cities and towns can be seen even today.

In the 14th century, the towns became economic centers. Portugal's urban growth was remarkable in the early 1300s, with Lisbon growing up to four times its size from 1147. This city became the most important one in the kingdom, though other towns and cities also grew. New ones popped up all over the Portuguese landscape. Coimbra in central Portugal doubled its size since the Reconquista. The crown was always involved in the development of the urban centers, especially in the south, where Torres Vedras and Óbidos lay. Templars were also investing in the development of the cities, especially Castelo Branco and Tomar. Some ex-Muslim cities, such as Faro and Évora, prospered under Christian rule, but many more declined and were forgotten.

The cities and towns were the meeting points where the trade between Portugal and Spain developed. Roads that were abandoned during the Christian-Muslim struggle were once again filled with merchants and their caravans. But the seaports were where Portugal outshone everyone else in Europe. Portuguese ports started developing during the Reconquista, as the sea trade routes between northern Europe and the Mediterranean world reopened. International shipping brought traffic to the Portuguese ports, and the kingdom used the arrival of many foreign ships to impose taxes on them. The seaborne trade that Portugal developed would be of great significance for its future exploration endeavors. Portugal's main export products were wine, cork, salt, fruit, and hides. However, the kingdom had to import great amounts of grain since its persistent but insufficient production couldn't feed all the people. Other imports were usually luxury items, such as spices, textiles, and artifacts. The result of the Portuguese trade development was a balanced import and export flow, as well as a constant outflow of gold and silver.

The Black Death in Portugal

The beginning of the 14th century was a period of extreme change in Europe that would eventually come to affect all of its inhabitants. The climate started cooling off, which made northern Europe unsuitable for agriculture. There was no more yearly surplus in the granaries of the European kingdoms north of the Alps, which caused famine. The population had to move to the warmer southern regions to survive. Constant hunger made people weak, and those who were born between 1315 and 1322 were usually much weaker and more susceptible to diseases. The cooler climate lasted until the start of the 16th century and is what marks the transition period from medieval Europe to the modern age.

At first, Portugal wasn't affected by the cooling, and its climate continued to be benign. Wheat was never an abundant crop in the region, and occasional famine would occur. Portugal started feeling the effects of global cooling around the 1320s. Agriculture declined, but it still didn't influence the majority of the population.

It is unknown if Portugal lost its citizens due to great famine as the northern kingdoms had. Another catastrophe hit Europe at the same time: the Black Death. And it took many lives. Climate change didn't affect only Europe. In Asia, the droughts caused many rodents to seek food in the cities, where the concentration of people is always high. These rodents brought about the disease. Well, more accurately, the rodents brought about the fleas that fed on the blood of diseased animals and then transmitted the bacteria *Yersinia pestis*, which causes the bubonic plague, to humans. The plague arrived in Portugal in 1348, probably through the busy port cities such as Lisbon. It spread quickly, and the disease was soon present in all corners of the kingdom. The massive migration of the people to more fertile lands helped spread the Black Death, not only in Portugal but also throughout the whole of Europe, Asia, and North Africa.

At first, the rural parts of the kingdom were not severely affected by the pandemic, as the population there wasn't as dense as in the urban centers. But in just one year, the plague killed one-third of Portugal. Monasteries and nunneries, where people lived in very tight-knit communities, suffered the most, and they became the nuclei from which the disease spread. Although the initial outbreak was fairly quickly contained, as the number of the diseased started dropping already in 1349, in the next 150 years, there were seventeen more plague outbreaks. They were never as massive as the one in 1348, but they contributed to the decline of the population.

The Black Death wasn't the only catastrophe that hit Portugal in this period. There are contemporary sources with references to at least eleven earthquakes that hit Portugal during the 14th century. Several civil wars started, adding to the toll on the population. The disruption to everyday life caused by all these misfortunes was enormous. The people didn't have time to recover from the Black Death before another catastrophe hit. Overall, Portugal's population declined from 1.5 million at the beginning of the 14th century to under 900,000 at the beginning of the 15th century.

The Black Death and the other misfortunes that occurred in Portugal caused an increased feeling of insecurity and the need for the people to search for salvation. The people turned to God for the answers to their adversity. The cult of the Virgin Mary grew, as well as saints who were revered as healers and physicians. But aside from salvation, the society of Portugal also searched for a scapegoat. The Jews were the primary target. Their numbers in Portugal started increasing during the 13th and 14th centuries, and as non-believers, they were the cause of many deaths in the eyes of Portuguese Christians.

For the government, the most problematic effect of the Black Death was a shortage in the labor force. This affected all sectors of the Portuguese economy. This also meant that the market conditions turned in favor of the poor and working classes of society. The laborers had to become more geographically mobile, which weakened the feudal ties they had to the land. The cities started offering higher wages to the workers, along with better conditions, which resulted in a huge shift of the population from the countryside to urban areas. The cities that lost a significant amount of their population quickly repopulated. They became overpopulated, and many of them (especially Lisbon) doubled their size and were forced to build new city walls to accommodate the new population. However, this increase in urban society led to the increase of urban poverty, and the workers quickly became aware of their marginalized status. They turned to begging, thieving, and even murdering to survive.

The economic crisis that ensued was more devastating in the rural areas of Portugal. Because of the labor shortage, production fell, and many small farms were abandoned. In the areas of Trás-os-Montes and the Mondego Valley, some estates remained abandoned until the late 15th century. The landowners were unable to find new tenants who would take on the farms and resume the production. The harvest of grains decreased significantly, and even some vineyards were neglected. The nobility now had to concentrate on grazing land for their cattle, while others expanded their hunting grounds. The land that was used to grow vegetables and fruits was converted into vineyards and olive tree orchards. This meant that the country was no longer able to meet its basic needs for grain, and the dependence on foreign wheat grew.

The government had to react by enforcing new laws that would prevent the people from abandoning the farms. In 1349, the first set of laws was issued that prohibited new people from settling within the city walls. It also tried to legislate the production of cereals. The workers resisted, especially in Lisbon and Porto, as well as in the countryside. The measures that the crown undertook weren't enough to curb the economic crisis that followed the Black Death. By 1367, the state revenue had fallen by 50 percent. Because of this, the king and the nobles started taking an interest in trade. It would prove to be an exceptional alternative to their dependence on agriculture. Afonso IV (r. 1325-1357) and Peter I (r. 1357-1367) quickly realized that revenue growth could be restarted by taxing the trade and even directly participating in it. By the reign of King Ferdinand I (1367-1383), the crown owned merchant ships and started the lucrative business of trade.

During the late 14th century, Portugal recorded promising international trade growth, and those who were involved in trade started prospering. Its exceptional commercial ties were created with Italy and northern Europe. The safe harbor of Lisbon attracted merchants from England, Genoa, Venice, and Catalonia. Portugal offered them wine, olives, salt, hide, and fish. The local merchants also started their overseas routes, mainly because they were supported by the crown and because of the new market opportunities. Non-Portuguese merchants had limited rights to export, which encouraged domestic merchants to take on the journeys. Peter I and his son Ferdinand I encouraged shipbuilding, and they even granted concessions to the nobles who would cut the timber in royal forests.

At this point, most of the Portuguese merchants traded individually, and they didn't yet start companies. Even when they banded together, it was to safely travel, not for a share of profits. However, Portuguese commerce was developing, and marine insurance was introduced to offer the merchants a feeling of safety. The bookkeeping became systematic, and the Roman numerals were still in use in Portugal. Arabic numerals would become popular only in the 15th century.

Afonso IV and Peter I

King Afonso IV came to the throne of Portugal in 1325. He was a brave man, and he was more of a warrior-king than his predecessors. He had no interests in courtly intrigues, art, and literature. His reign started after a civil war he waged against his father, King Denis. But the causes for this war weren't political disagreements between father and son but personal reasons. Afonso suspected that his father planned to proclaim his illegitimate son, Afonso Sanches, as his successor. King Denis did exclude Afonso from the political life of the kingdom, which looked like a move to challenge his succession. After Denis died, Afonso quickly made a deal with Sanches and assumed firm control over the kingdom.

The kingdom was peaceful, and the new king's main preoccupation was the relations between Portugal and Castile. Although these relations started peacefully, with the two kings signing a friendship treaty in 1327, the tensions continued to grow. By 1336, Afonso IV had occupied some of the Castilian territories, and Alfonso XI of Castile occupied a portion of the Portuguese territory. The hostilities continued until 1340 when the Marinid Sultanate sent soldiers across the strait and attacked Andalusia. Afonso hurried to help Castile in its defense, and the two kings enjoyed a victory over the Muslim invaders at Río Salado. After this joint effort, the relations between Portugal and Castile remained friendly.

However, the situation within the kingdom wasn't peaceful anymore. The nobles revolted, as they felt they needed to protect their seigneurial rights and privileges. At first, the majority of nobles supported Afonso IV in his fight against Denis, but the hardships of the 14th century continued pressing on the landowners. They demanded royal patronage because their rural enterprises were failing. However, the crown was in the same situation and had no spare resources to give away. The resentment of the nobles grew over the years, and it finally culminated in 1355 in an open revolt against Afonso. They were under the leadership of none other than Prince Peter, Afonso's successor. The revolt ended quickly, but the personal drama that ensued would have long-term political effects on Portugal.

Prince Peter was infatuated with a Galician noblewoman, Inês de Castro. But Inês was a lady-in-waiting of Peter's wife Constanza, who happened to also be his cousin. Nevertheless, the prince decided to live openly with Inês after his wife died. Afonso disapproved of this because he didn't like the influence her Galician family had on his son, as they tried to persuade him to claim the Castilian crown. Afonso realized that this would be a threat to his foreign policy, and he became directly involved in the assassination of Inês de Castro. She was murdered in 1355, the same year Prince Peter revolted against his father. Historians believe that her assassination was only a pretext for his rebellion, with the real reason being his lust for power. However, his actions after he claimed the Portuguese crown two years later speak differently. As soon as he came to the throne, he persecuted everyone involved in the murder of his lover. They were all eventually caught and executed.

As a king, Peter faced similar social and economic troubles as his father. But unlike Afonso, he decided to avoid any conflict with the nobles of Portugal. He shared the values of the nobility, and he was not as stubborn in pursuing centralizing policies that would deprive the aristocracy of their seigneurial rights and privileges. Nevertheless, Peter's attitude toward the nobility was extremely selfish. He only rewarded his relatives, especially the people of the Castro family. He legitimized two of his bastard sons he had with Inês, though the church never approved of it. He also gave generous patrimonies to Inês's brother, Dom Álvaro Pires de Castro. As for his relations with Castile, it seems that Afonso was wrong, as Peter continued the friendship policy with the neighboring kingdom. He never meddled in the internal affairs of Castile, and he maintained the peace.

Ferdinand I and the Wars with Castile

In 1367, Peter's only legitimate son, Ferdinand, succeeded the throne of Portugal. History remembers him as an incompetent ruler. He was short-tempered and impulsive, and he continuously made bad political decisions. His reign was marked by many disasters and is remembered as a time of trouble. One of the first bad political decisions he made regarded neighboring Castile. King Peter of Castile was killed in a battle in 1369. His bastard half-brother, Henry (Enrique) of Trastámara, declared himself king. However, Ferdinand I of Portugal was the closest male relative, and he took in many fleeing supporters of King Peter of Castile into his court. They used their influence on the Portuguese king to sway him and make him demand the Castilian crown. Ferdinand thought of this as a good opportunity to unite the crowns of Portugal and Castile, and he proclaimed himself the king of Castile. He then proceeded to occupy Galicia, where he met no resistance.

But Henry of Castile had French support, and he quickly moved to occupy the parts of Portugal closest to his kingdom. His invasion was so aggressive that he pushed the Portuguese into retreat, and Ferdinand was forced to sue for peace in 1371. The treaty was signed in Alcoutim. Ferdinand had to renounce his claims on the throne of Castile, but he did gain several towns that previously belonged to Castile. He also agreed to marry Henry's daughter. But

Ferdinand never got to marry her. Instead, he chose the niece of João Afonso Telo, Leonor, who was his court favorite. The hostilities with Henry of Castile resumed.

Meanwhile, English interests in Portugal increased, which was sparked by the Anglo-French Hundred Years' War (1337–1453). The French supported the crown of Castile, so it was only natural for the English to persuade Portugal to enter their sphere of influence. This position was also supported by the increase in trade between England and Portugal immediately after the Black Death. The relationship with the English was one of the factors that influenced Ferdinand I not to marry the daughter of Henry.

An English noble, John of Gaunt, was married to Constance, one of the daughters of Peter of Castile. Through this marriage, he laid claim to the Castilian crown. Ferdinand agreed to support John's claim in exchange for a military alliance between Portugal and England. In response, King Henry (Enrique) of Castile sent his fleet to block the Tagus River. He also led his army across the border and captured some of the cities. In 1373, he reached Lisbon and besieged it. Ferdinand wasn't ready for a major conflict since the English were not able to dispatch their army that fast. He had no other choice but to sue for peace again. The treaty was signed at Santarém, and Ferdinand had to renounce John of Gaunt and enter an alliance with Castile.

The Castilian wars were very destructive for Portugal, as Henry's forces continued to devastate not only the cities but also the countryside. Braga, Lisbon, and Coimbra were hit hard. Even after the treaty was signed, the Castilian military presence in them continued and led to many internal conflicts that brought misfortune to the local population. The wars also brought back the plague and famine, and prices skyrocketed, making it impossible for the commoners to sustain themselves. The crime rate increased, and popular unrest was often seen. In Lisbon, one major unrest was led by a tailor named Fernão Vasques.

Ferdinand proved able to deal with these local events more than he was foreign policy. He didn't only strive to pacify the people with the use of the military, but he also endlessly worked on revitalizing the local economy. In 1375, he issued *Lei das Sesmarias*, a land management plan to restart agricultural production and regulate exports. Workers who had property below a specified value were forced to remain on their land and work it for the next two generations. They were given the means to work the land, such as animals and tools, but they received fixed wages.

A new foreign relations crisis emerged at the end of the 1370s. The English military was unable to stop the French and their Castilian allies from raiding their coast, as they lacked the power to face the Castilian fleet. Portugal owned many galleys, and England once again approached Ferdinand, offering a closer alliance. This was also the period in which the Western Schism occurred. Portugal and England supported Pope Urban VI of Rome, while France and Castile stood behind Clement VII of Avignon. The rivalry between the Anglo-Portuguese alliance and the Franco-Castilian one reached religious and sentimental levels.

When Henry of Castile died in 1380, he was succeeded by his very young son, John (Juan) I. John of Gaunt saw this as the opportunity to renew his claim on the Castilian throne. Ferdinand concluded that he could use this chance to retrieve some of the Portuguese cities captured by Castile in the previous war. Ferdinand and John of Gaunt reached a deal and worked together on their plan to attack Castile. However, the Anglo-Portuguese Army didn't have competent leadership, and their effort ended with young John I raiding Portugal and taking over some of the border cities and castles. However, neither Castile nor Portugal had the means to support a prolonged conflict. The two rulers made peace by the summer of 1382, but this time, the terms were exceptionally favorable for Portugal. Ferdinand had to recognize John as the king of Castile, but in turn, he would marry off his only child, Beatrice, to John's young son. However, John's wife died soon after, and the king of Castile agreed to take Beatrice himself. This marriage alliance meant that, in the near future, the crowns of Portugal and Castile would be united. However, the only result of such a marriage was a dynastic crisis in Portugal. It left the people wondering if their next king would be a Castilian usurper or a Portuguese bastard.

The Dynastic Crisis

At the time of Ferdinand's death in 1383, his daughter Beatrice was only eleven years old. She had been married to John I just months before. The contract through which she was married stated that Portugal would be under her and John's control until their marriage produced a son and that son reached fourteen years of age. Should Beatrice fail to give John a son, the Portuguese throne would pass directly to the crown of Castile. In the meantime, Leonor Teles, Ferdinand's wife, was to rule Portugal only as a regent. Though Castile and Portugal were now united by this marriage, and there was a prospect of a joint crown in the future, the marriage contract also demanded that Portugal and Castile would never become one political entity. Instead, they were to be governed separately.

The nobles of Portugal never disapproved of the legal rights of Beatrice, the king's daughter. But they couldn't accept the regency of Leonor Teles. They thought that this was the working of Leonor's *éminence grise*, her confidential agent João Fernandes Andeiro. By the time of Ferdinand's death, Andeiro became the dominant figure in the Portuguese court and perhaps even Leonor's secret lover. There is no evidence to support this claim, but it was a rumor at the time that the nobles of Portugal believed. They also believed he was the true father of her infant son, who had died in 1382. The Portuguese nobles who were not a part of the inner circle of the regent resented Andeiro, and Leonor herself was despised. After she assumed her role of regent, Portugal displayed all the signs of an upcoming civil war.

The main opponent of Leonor's regency was John of Avis, the bastard half-brother of Ferdinand I. He was an intelligent man in his twenties who enjoyed the respect of many nobles. To move him as far from Lisbon as possible, Leonor decided to make John a military commander of Alentejo. But he wasn't ready to give up his efforts to remove Leonor, and he organized a small band of nobles with whom he broke into the royal palace on December 6th, 1383. They murdered Andeiro. The city burned, and violence broke out. Leonor realized she had lost control of Lisbon. She was forced to flee for her life and settle in Santarém.

John of Avis assumed de facto control over the royal city, but he was in a very vulnerable position. His coup was illegal, and it caused widespread upheaval. John of Castile decided to react. He crossed the border and slowly advanced toward Lisbon, giving John of Avis time to give up his claims. Though he had the option to flee to England, John of Avis decided to stay and fight. He even entertained the idea of marrying Leonor Teles to make his claim over Portugal a legitimate one, but she declined his proposal. Leonor approached John of Castile in the hopes he would help her regain her regency, but he locked her away in a Castilian castle. The clash between John of Castile and John of Avis was unavoidable, and although the king of Castile had his army with him, the people of Portugal felt that their interests lay with John of Avis. The noble houses were split, and some offered support to the Castilian crown while others remained loyal to the Portuguese John.

The supporters of John of Avis needed to work quickly on legitimizing his regency. They met in Lisbon in December 1383 to proclaim him regent and the protector of the realm. But John of Castile was near Lisbon, and many Portuguese towns and castles had already submitted to him. By February 1384, he had arrived in the capital. He expected the surrender of John of Avis's supporters. But he was wrong; the opposition they formed against him was very strong. John of Avis had a very talented military mind among his supporters: a young nobleman named Nuno Álvares Pereira. He led the armies against John of Castile in Alentejo, and in April 1384, he won an extraordinary victory. After that, he became bold and led his forces to take over the towns and strongholds that supported the Castilian crown. By September, the Castilian army was exhausted and decimated by the plague. John of Castile was forced to raise the siege of Lisbon.

These events led to the increase of John of Avis's prestige, and many nobles who previously supported John of Castile turned to him. In Coimbra, in April of 1385, John summoned a *cortes*, which had the task of determining the fate of the Portuguese throne. Beatrice had few supporters at this point, but Dom João de Castro, the older son of Peter and Inês, had much more support. However, his claim to the Portuguese throne was overridden by the fact that he fled to the Castilian court and that the church refused to legitimize him as Peter's son. The only real choice was John of Avis, and on April 6th, 1385, he became John I, King of Portugal.

Although he was proclaimed a king, John of Avis had yet to secure his throne. John of Castile was preparing another invasion, and John of Avis knew he had to fight for his right to rule. But he needed allies, and he turned to England. He approached John of Gaunt, promising him help if he resumed his claim on the Castilian throne. John of Avis also approached English King Richard II and signed the Treaty of Windsor in May 1386, in which both kings promised military help to each other, as well as trading rights for their citizens in each other's kingdom. Richard promised he would support John of Avis as the legitimate ruler of Portugal and help him against anyone who tried to overthrow him. This Anglo-Portuguese alliance would prove to be long-lasting.

John of Castile crossed the border in July 1385 with a large army, numbering approximately twenty thousand soldiers, among whom were some Portuguese and many Frenchmen. They marched straight to Lisbon, and John of Avis decided not to hide behind the city wall. Instead, he met them in open battle. He positioned his army of seven thousand men on defensive spots around the ridge called Aljubarrota. When John of Castile arrived, he quickly assessed the situation and ordered his army to be patient and not rush into the dangerous trap set by the Portuguese. He and his military advisors saw that the full-frontal attack would be a disaster, even though their army was larger. But the hotheads and the inexperienced soldiers in his army disobeyed and engaged the Portuguese defenders. By noon, the whole Castilian army was drawn into the fight.

The battle lasted barely an hour before John of Castile's forces were defeated. The Portuguese defenders held the higher ground, and they used a 14th-century military innovation, the crossbow, to shower the advancing Castilian army with deadly arrows. John of Castile was forced to flee, and his campaign in Portugal ended with an inglorious defeat. The Battle of Aljubarrota confirmed the legitimacy of John I and the House of Avis. The Portuguese refused to conform to the idea of a united Iberian Peninsula since they now had a well-defined national identity. After the battle, John of Avis raised an abbey at Aljubarrota as a sign of his gratitude to the higher forces for his victory. This abbey was never completed, even though its construction lasted for 150 years. Nevertheless, it still stands as an unfinished monument and a symbol of the new dynasty and the kingdom's independence. Known as the Batalha Monastery, this place would serve as the tomb for the royal members of the Avis dynasty.

Chapter 7 – The House of Avis and the Golden Age of Portugal

The wedding John I and Philippa of Lancaster (15th-century art)
https://commons.wikimedia.org/wiki/File:Casamento_Jo%C3%A3o_I_e_Filipa_Lencastre.JPG

After the Battle of Aljubarrota, Portugal remained an independent kingdom in the Iberian Peninsula. John of Avis became the new king. But his enemy, John of Castile, continued to style himself as the king of Portugal, which was a clear sign that he intended to return and assume the throne. Once again, John of Avis approached John of Gaunt to make an alliance. To secure it, he agreed to marry Philippa, the daughter of John of Gaunt. The wedding was performed on February 10th, 1387, with much celebration. The marriage proved fruitful, as Phillipa gave John five sons and one daughter that survived into adulthood. All of these children would later leave a mark on the history of Portugal. But Philippa didn't serve only to give birth to the successors of the Portuguese throne. She asserted her influence on the court and introduced several English royal customs that would remain part of the Portuguese royal tradition. However, John I's military alliance with Gaunt wasn't very fruitful. Together, they attacked Castile and even reached León, but the resistance to their efforts was so great that Gaunt finally decided to make peace and give up his claim on the Castilian throne. When John of Castile died in 1390, all prospects of the invasion of Portugal ended.

Regardless, the royal families of Portugal and Castile would not make peace for years to come. John I was ever wary, and he didn't want to tie his family even more to the Castilians for fear that future generations would lay claim to the Portuguese crown. This was one of the reasons he married Phillipa, who was wholly English, unlike Gaunt's second daughter Catherine, who was half-Castilian and had ties to the Castilian crown. In 1405, John I married his daughter Brites to an English earl, tying Portugal and England in an even tighter alliance. He had similar plans for his legitimate children and married them to princesses from Burgundy, Aragon, Hungary, the Holy Roman Empire, and Urgel rather than to the Castilian princesses. This way, the Castilian royal family would have no more claims on the Portuguese crown.

John I of Portugal was also the first emperor of the Portuguese Empire. His most significant military victory was the conquest of Ceuta, a city in Africa. With this victory, the empire began the establishment of the first Portuguese colony in Africa. The

Portuguese Empire, or Portuguese Colonial Empire, was the longest-lasting modern European colonial empire. It ended only in 1999 when Portugal decided to end its sovereignty over Macau. It was also one of the rare empires that had territories across the globe, with colonies in North and South America, Asia, Oceania, and Africa.

John I's Successors

John I continued the centralizing policies of his predecessors, and he banned the nobles from acquiring vassals. Instead, he proclaimed that only a king could have vassals. Moreover, he started neutralizing powerful nobles with royal marriages. He would then transfer the titles and lands of a certain noble to the members of the royal family who stepped into the marriage. For example, he married Afonso, his son, to the daughter of his main military commander and count of Barcelos, Nuno Álvares Pereira. Afonso automatically became the count of Barcelos and gained all of the possessions that came with the title, leaving Pereira completely neutralized. John I did this to protect the royal patrimony, and his successor, King Edward (Duarte), continued this policy and even gave it its definitive form in 1434 by issuing the law known as *Lei Mental*. This law defined royal patrimony as inseparable and inalienable. The patrimony was always inherited by the oldest surviving son or grandson and never by female family members or distant male relatives. This law would remain in Portugal for the next four hundred years.

However, the king could always make an exemption, and Edward did so for the first time in the year the law was issued. The first exemption was granted to Afonso, Count of Barcelos, the king's half-brother. Other important nobles were granted similar concessions. King Edward died of the plague in 1438. He was succeeded by his six-year-old son, Afonso V. Edward's widow, Eleanor of Aragon, became her son's regent. This arrangement was suitable for many nobles, as they saw the opportunity to influence

Edward's widow into reversing the *Lei Mental* policy. But another group of nobles was against the female regent, and they claimed that it wasn't the wish of the late king that mattered but the decision of the *cortes*. They claimed that only the council was able to name the regent.

In 1438, Eleanor agreed to share the regency with her son's oldest uncle, Prince Pedro. The nobles demanded that Pedro rule alone, but Leonor wouldn't accept this. She had very little support, though, and once Pedro moved his army against her, Eleanor fled Lisbon and sought refuge in Castile. She continued to plan her return to Portugal, as well as the removal of Pedro, but in 1445, she suddenly died. Pedro was now secure as the sole regent of the empire, and he started removing Eleanor's allies and supporters from the high offices. Prince Pedro's regency lasted from 1439 until 1446, and he did an exemplary job in administering the kingdom. Nevertheless, he started losing the support of the nobles. The most difficult personal blow was the loss of his younger brother's support, Prince John. Pedro's opposition started gathering around his half-brother, Afonso of Barcelos.

In 1446, young Afonso V finally reached majority and became eligible to rule alone. But Pedro managed to retain the title of regent, and he secured his position in court by engaging his daughter Isabel to the young king. Afonso was weak and unable to resist his uncle's schemes, but Pedro's enemies started putting pressure on the king. Afonso V finally dismissed Pedro as a regent in 1448. Having nothing else to do at the royal court, Pedro returned to his stronghold in Coimbra. His opposition, which was led by Afonso of Barcelos (now also Duke of Braganza) and his son, Count of Ourém, continued to pressure Afonso V. In September 1448, they persuaded him to annul all the grants and appointments done by Pedro during his regency. Pedro wouldn't go down so easily. Instead of accepting his defeat, he dispatched his army to Lisbon. But by that time, he had lost most of his support, and at the Battle of Alfarrobeira, which took place on May 20th, 1449, he was defeated and killed.

Afonso V ruled Portugal for almost forty-three years, the longest of any Avis monarch after John I. During his rule, Portugal went through the transition from medieval to modern times. Afonso V was one of the early monarchs who received a humanist education under Italian tutors. He was the first king in Portugal to found a royal library. Nevertheless, his policies and his behavior remained very much medieval. He was very liberal in granting lands and titles to the nobility, and the result was the increase of the nobility's power, though this power was in the hands of very few nobles. The leading Portuguese magnates were Prince Henrique (also known as Henry the Navigator) and the dukes of Braganza, the successors of Afonso of Barcelos. When Henrique died childless in 1460, the House of Braganza became the most powerful Portuguese noble house. The king's younger brother, Ferdinand, was named the duke of Beja in 1453, and the House of Braganza received the Duchy of Guimarães. Its members assumed the newly introduced titles of marquis and viscount. Other noble houses also received new titles, and by the end of Afonso's reign, there were three marquises, twenty-five counts, one baron, and one viscount. The nobility during the reign of King Edward consisted only of several counts. However, this increase in the number of nobles heavily depleted the royal estate since the king had to grant lands to go with the titles.

Unlike his predecessors, King Afonso was eager to tie his royal line with Castile. Perhaps this was due to his dream of becoming the first Iberian emperor, and he thought he could achieve this through marriage ties. This dream of his came close to coming true when weak King Henry IV of Castile invited Afonso V to assume the governorship of his kingdom since he was dying. Afonso's younger sister was married to Henry and had a daughter, Joanna, with him. Henry invited Afonso of Portugal to marry Joanna. This might have come to pass, but the Castilian nobility proclaimed Isabella, Henry's half-sister, the rightful queen of Castile.

Afonso V was aging at the time of these events, and it is unknown why he reacted by proclaiming himself to be Joanna's champion. Maybe he was persuaded by the exiled Castilian nobility who supported his niece, or maybe he wanted to return the family's honor since Joanna was proclaimed not to be Henry's daughter but a product of an affair between a Castilian nobleman and Henry's wife. Whatever the reason may be, Afonso decided to invade Castile in 1475. He advanced with a small army to Palencia, where he married his niece, Joanna. To gain the right to rule Castile, he had to defeat Isabella and her husband Ferdinand II of Aragon, who proved to be a very able military and administrative leader. The decisive battle took place not far from Toro in 1476, during which Afonso was forced to retreat.

Afonso V lost not only the battle but also his prestige. He was forced to recognize the legitimacy of Isabella and her husband and renounce all claims on the throne of Castile. He sent Joanna to a nunnery since he had no more use of her. In 1477, Afonso abdicated the throne in favor of his son John II and dreamed of spending the rest of his life as a hermit in the Holy Land. However, he ended his days in a monastery in Sintra.

John II

Although Afonso V abdicated and retired in 1477, John II was not crowned as king until his father died in 1481. Afonso included John in the affairs of states and prepared him for kingship from a young age. He ruled shortly, from 1481 until 1495, but he left a deep impact on the history of Portugal. During his reign, the kingdom expanded overseas, and John II significantly increased the prestige of the Portuguese crown. He summoned his first *cortes* immediately after becoming the king, displaying his determination to assert his authority over the nobility. John II was much tougher than his father, and the noble magnates feared him. Indeed, he recalled all of the privileges, titles, and land grants of the nobles. To get their titles and grants back, the nobles had to swear loyalty to John and recognize him as their ultimate superior. In 1481, at Évora, a great oath-taking ceremony took place.

The only man powerful enough to oppose the king was Fernando, the third duke of Braganza, who was able to raise a private army of his own, numbering over thirteen thousand soldiers. The clash between the duke of Braganza and John II was inevitable. In 1482, the duke and his supporters planned to dispose of the new king. However, they never managed to act on their plans because one of the duke's men betrayed them. The duke of Braganza was arrested on counts of treason, and he was promptly executed. All of his properties, castles, and lands were confiscated and remained in the hands of John II until the end of his reign. The failure of Braganza's conspiracy was a heavy blow for all the nobles who opposed the heavy centralization of the kingdom.

A new leader of the opposition presented himself only a few months later: Dom Garcia de Meneses, Bishop of Évora. He gathered the resentful noble families around a common cause—the deposition of the king. However, the leadership of this second plot was soon taken over by Dom Diogo, Duke of Viseu, brother of Eleanor of Viseu, John II's queen. He planned to become the next king and return the pro-seigneurial policies of Afonso V. John learned about the conspiracy in 1484, and he summoned the duke of Viseu to his chambers, where he executed him. The king then proceeded to arrest and execute other ringleaders, but he spared those family members of the nobles who were not directly connected with the plot. Therefore, the younger brother of Dom Diogo, Manuel of Viseu, was allowed to live and even assumed his brother's titles. He was also given the title Duke of Beja, becoming one of only two people who received new titles during the reign of John II (the first being John's bastard son Jorge).

In 1491, Prince Afonso, the only son of John II and Eleanor of Viseu, died in a riding accident. Portugal entered another succession crisis since Afonso was the last legitimate male successor of the House of Avis. The next in line for the Portuguese crown was Manuel, Duke of Beja, who was also a member of the Avis family since he was a grandson of King Edward. The king put his efforts into legitimizing his bastard son Dom Jorge, but the papacy refused to grant him recognition, mainly because of the resistance Queen Eleanor displayed. Eleanor had the support of the Castilian royal family—Ferdinand and Isabella—a couple endorsed by Spanish Pope Alexander VI, who even named them the "Catholic King and Queen" for defending the faith in Castile against the Jews. With such opposition, John could do very little, and he was forced to accept the succession of Manuel. John II died in 1495 when he was only forty. The cause of his death is unknown, but many believed (and some still do) that Queen Eleanor poisoned him.

The Golden Age

The period between the 1490s and 1540s is considered to be the golden age of the Kingdom of Portugal, an era during which this country gained significance in world affairs. It was the Age of Discovery. Portuguese explorer Bartolomeu Dias sailed around the Cape of Good Hope, and the Portuguese pioneers founded their first settlements in overseas territories, such as Morocco, Brazil, and Southeast Asia. These explorations brought new revenues for the kingdom and were highly endorsed by its rulers. The internal affairs of Portugal settled as the kingdom avoided yet another succession crisis. The economy was prospering, and with it came the general good mood of the citizens and the development of arts and science.

King Manuel I (r. 1495–1521) came to rule against all odds after the death of Prince Afonso and the death of his five older brothers. He was not prepared to rule, but he was endorsed by the nobility who thought he came to rule by divine right, just as the biblical King David, who was the last-born but came to rule a kingdom. Manuel accepted this justification of his succession, and he came to believe that he was the instrument of God and that he had a sacred task on

Earth. He decided that the sacred task for which he was put on Earth was the crusade against Islam. His ultimate goal was to free Jerusalem and destroy all Islamic power bases in the Christian East. He hoped he would become the emperor in the East and that he would bring peace to the Holy Land under the name of Christianity. But his dreams of a crusade never came to pass. Nevertheless, Manuel is remembered as the most successful king of Portugal.

The population of Portugal rose during the reign of Manuel I, and due to the overseas explorations, the economy was growing. Portugal became the main commercial intermediary between Europe and Asia, a position previously held by Venice. As for the affairs within the kingdom, Manuel reformed the bureaucratic system and made it more centralized. The judicial courts were reformed, and taxation was modernized. He published the Manueline Ordinations, a set of codified laws. During his reign, the Catholic Church went through reforms, as the king financed many foreign missions. When Manuel I died of the plague in 1521, he was succeeded by his son John III, during whose reign the golden age continued, though it already displayed signs of decline.

John III was only nineteen when he came to the throne of Portugal, and he proved to be a very cautious monarch. Because of this, Portugal's era of explorations and economic ascendance came to an end. John III's reign and that of his immediate successor is considered to be the era of imperial consolidation and rationalization. Expansion continued, but John was much more pragmatic about it. He reduced the crown's involvement in overseas expansion and trade, as well as in imperial administration. This is why his government always struggled to find manpower and finances for royal commitments. Some territorial acquisitions had to be abandoned, especially in Morocco. The second half of John's reign was when Portugal started withdrawing from some of its colonies in Africa and Asia, although it continued pursuing expansion elsewhere in the world.

Chapter 8 – The End of the
Golden Age

Eighteenth-century depiction of all Portuguese throne pretenders during the succession crisis of 1580
https://commons.wikimedia.org/wiki/File:Frontispiece_-
The_History_of_the_Revolutions_of_Portugal_(Vertot,_1735).png

The Portuguese golden age started declining sometime during the 1540s. This decline was apparent in many spheres of life, such as the economy, arts, education, imperial expansion, and individual rights of the citizens. Even the royal family experienced several tragedies that posed a threat to the integrity of the nation. The second half of John III's rule was marked by a sudden change in the king's behavior. He went from an intelligent and humanist ruler to a bitter man. However, this change in his personality can be explained by the tragedies that struck the imperial family. All nine of John III's children died before him. The king was crushed by the death of his children, and he abandoned the public responsibilities he had toward his kingdom. His wife Catherine ruled in his name, but she was not prepared for such a task. The end of the royal dynasty seemed near.

But not all was lost to this family tragedy. The youngest son of John III, Prince João Manuel, died and left his wife, Joanna, pregnant and alone. There was one more grandchild of the Portuguese king: Don Carlos, the son of Philip of Spain and Maria, João's daughter, who died in childbirth. Carlos was the heir to the Spanish throne, and if he succeeded John III, the Iberian Peninsula would be finally united under a single ruler. Portugal would not have it, as the independence of the kingdom was sacred. They anxiously awaited the birth of Joanna's child. She birthed a son, who was born on January 20th, 1554, only eighteen days after his father's death. The fate of the whole kingdom depended on this child, Sebastian, who became the king in 1557 at the age of three.

Sebastian and Henry

Since his birth, Sebastian was seen as a hero, as he defended the independence of the Kingdom of Portugal. He was to save the nation from being absorbed into the Iberian Spanish Empire, and he proved to be a good ruler. But in his efforts to preserve Portugal, he needlessly died in a battle in North Africa, leaving no heir behind.

Before Sebastian reached adulthood, Portugal was governed by regents. The first among them was his grandmother, Catherine, the widow of John III. She continued the governance started by her husband, and she didn't replace the old ministers and officials. Nevertheless, under her leadership, Spanish influence started seeping into Portugal. After all, she was a sister of Charles V, Habsburg king of Spain (in 1519, he became the Holy Roman emperor). Catherine remained loyal to the Spanish Habsburg line even after the death of Charles V and the succession of his son, Philip II. But her allegiance to her family made her unpopular among the Portuguese nobles who wished to preserve the independence of their kingdom. In 1562, Catherine was forced to resign as the regent, and the *cortes* chose Cardinal Henry (Henrique) in her place. This cardinal was the great-uncle of young Sebastian and the younger son of King Manuel I. His regency was neutral, and he tried to make Portugal a friend of the Holy Roman Empire, Spain, England, and France.

The regents of Portugal during Sebastian's minority were mainly preoccupied with the question of his marriage and the continuation of the Avis dynasty. There were many princesses to choose from, and the state officials started searching for a bride as soon as the prince turned five. The favorite candidate was Elisabeth (Isabel) of Bohemia, as her father was about to be elected as the Holy Roman emperor. Another candidate was Margaret of Valois, a French princess. However, Philip II of Spain lobbied against this marriage, as he didn't want Portugal to tie itself to France. In 1568, Philip's wife died, and he changed his mind about Sebastian and Margaret. He would prefer to see Elisabeth married to French King Charles IX, while he himself would marry Anna of Austria, the daughter of the Holy Roman Emperor Maximilian II, who was also his own niece. Although the *cortes* agreed to this marriage scheme, Sebastian, who was now fifteen years old and the sole ruler of Portugal, refused the marriage proposal.

Sebastian assumed power a year earlier at the age of fourteen, and it immediately became evident he had no interest in women. There are speculations among scholars that he was homosexual, but there is no evidence to confirm this claim. Perhaps he was simply too occupied with the warrior lifestyle that he led and had little interest in marriage and the continuation of his line. Sebastian was also obsessed with the idea that he was chosen by God to rule and to fulfill a sacred mission. This led him to believe he had to fight for Christianity, and he believed the Muslims were his natural enemy. He led a great expedition to North Africa and even agreed to marry the daughter of Philip II if he could secure Spanish military help against Morocco. But Philip refused to answer, as he was concerned with gaining Portugal for himself. Sebastian embarked on his expedition to Morocco alone in 1578, still unmarried and without a son to succeed him. As stated above, it is believed he died in North Africa, though Portuguese myth tells a story about a promised king who sleeps and will awaken when the need is greatest. Some believe that Sebastian is this king who sleeps under the mountain.

Sebastian was the only living descendant of John III, but he wasn't the last Avis. His successor was found in Cardinal Henry, the previous regent of Portugal. As a son of King Manuel I, he was the only male belonging to the Avis royal family. However, he was already old, and as a servant of the Catholic Church, he was unable to marry and produce a legitimate heir. Henry asked the papacy in Rome to permit him to marry so that the Portuguese royal line could be prolonged, but the pope declined this request. Henry was king of Portugal for only two years, from 1578 until 1580, and he spent these years searching for the perfect candidate to inherit the throne. The dynastic crisis that occurred in Portugal would lead the country into a new era of Habsburg rule.

The Crisis of 1580

At this time, Portugal had four possible candidates who could succeed the throne. One of them was António, the bastard son of

Louis, who was the third son of King Manuel I. António was popular in Portugal, but he was a bastard, which made him ineligible to rule unless he could prove his parents were secretly married. The second candidate was none other than Philip II, King of Spain. He was also related to King Manuel I, as he was the son of Isabella, Manuel's oldest daughter. He was an extremely powerful Habsburg ruler, but he didn't have the support of the Portuguese, who detested the possible unification of the Iberian Peninsula. The third candidate was Catherine, the daughter of Manuel's youngest son, Duarte. She was a direct descendant of the Avis family through the male line, which gave her a stronger claim than that of Philip II. However, she was a woman, and because of this, she was an extremely unpopular candidate and dismissed early on. The fourth candidate was Ranuccio Farnese, the son of Duarte's older daughter Maria. But Farnese was even more unpopular because he had been brought up in Italy. He was not Portuguese enough to satisfy the xenophobic tendencies of the 16th-century *cortes*.

Although Henry wanted to preserve Portugal's independence, he was aware that if he refused King Philip II's claims, he would put his kingdom in danger of future invasion. António was unable to prove his legitimacy and was dismissed as a possible heir, which left Philip as the only viable option. The negotiations for the succession of the Portuguese throne started between Henry and Philip, but they never really ended. When Henry died in 1580, Philip laid his claim on the throne, although the dying king never really confirmed him as the chosen heir. Henry left the final decision to the *cortes*, but this council was divided. Most of the noble houses supported Philip II, but the representatives of the towns preferred any other option but the Spanish king. However, there were no more options left. To persuade the Portuguese nobles that he was their only choice, Philip employed Cristóvão de Moura, a Portuguese nobleman who was heavily influenced by his Castilian mother, to be his main negotiator. Moura lobbied consistently for Philip, and he even resorted to bribery to win some of the nobles and clergy over.

Upon the death of Henry, António tried to resume his claim to the Portuguese throne by relying on his popularity. He entered Lisbon, but he was denied the crown by the five governors who ruled temporarily until a proper heir was found. Philip didn't want to enter Portugal as a conqueror, so he decided to wait patiently, as he was sure that he had the birthright to the Portuguese crown. Nevertheless, as time passed, he grew impatient and started preparing his army. He finally sent an ultimatum to the Portuguese governors, giving them one month to proclaim him the king before he moved his forces. His deadline expired in June of 1580, and the governors still refused to recognize him. Philip had no other choice but to move his army across the Portuguese border. Upon hearing this, António rushed to proclaim himself king, and this time, he entered Lisbon without any resistance. Three of the five governors supported Philip, and they abandoned the city and rushed to meet the Spanish king and his military force, which was made up of twenty thousand Spanish, Italian, and German soldiers.

By late June, the Spanish military had closed in on Lisbon by both land and sea. António was surrounded. He had no money and very few supporters, but he was determined to defend the city. To make matters even worse, the inhabitants of Lisbon were suffering an epidemic of influenza, which rendered them unable to mount a proper defense. António was able to gather a small militia force numbering only eight thousand souls. The defensive line was set up along the Alcantara creek, and the fighting began on August 25th, 1580. The resistance was quickly broken by the Spanish troops, who killed more than two thousand of António's makeshift army before the rest of them surrendered. The short Battle of Alcantara sealed the fate of Portugal. António was wounded during the battle, and he fled to Coimbra to gather more followers. His rebels were vigorously hunted by Philip II, and António was forced to flee, first to England and finally to France, where he died in 1595.

The epidemic was still raging in Lisbon, and Philip II refused to enter the city. Instead, he summoned the *cortes* to Tomar, where he was finally proclaimed the king of Portugal. He surprised everyone by respecting the Portuguese terms of succession that the *cortes* imposed on him. Although Spain and Portugal were united under one crown, they were to remain separate political entities—a dual monarchy. Thus, Portugal retained all of its liberties and customs. All offices of the Portuguese crown, including trade, were to remain in the hands of Portuguese officials. The kingdom was to keep its currency, and Portuguese would continue being the official language. Moreover, the Portuguese officials created a council that would reside in the king's court in Spain and advise him on the matters of Portugal. The dual monarchy provided many benefits for Portugal, such as the abolition of custom taxes on trade goods between Castile and Portugal, increased military safety, and provisions of grain that were grown in Spain.

The Institutional Changes in Portugal and the Question of Autonomy

Philip II of Spain ruled Portugal as Philip I. He remained in Lisbon until 1583 to secure his throne and oversee the unification of the two monarchies. He proved to be a generous ruler who rewarded his supporters, and many Portuguese noble families found a trustworthy ally in their new Castilian king. Philip also made sure that the succession promises he made in Tomar were respected, and he interfered in local affairs only when necessary. The majority of the work and even decision-making was left in the hands of Portuguese officials. In 1582, Philip's heir, Diego, Prince of Asturias, died, and the king felt the urge to return to Madrid. But Philip wouldn't depart before summoning a *cortes* and begging them to accept his next heir, Prince Philip.

With Philip's departure from Portugal, many institutional changes occurred. One of the conditions of Philip's succession was for him to install a Portuguese viceroy who would govern the country in the king's absence. In 1583, Philip chose his nephew, Cardinal Archduke Albert of Austria, the great-grandson of King Manuel I. He proved to be very adept as a viceroy, and he governed Portugal for the next ten years (1583–1593). He brought forth a period of great stability. Before assuming his position as a viceroy, Albert was appointed as the papal legate, and he successfully combined the authority of the church and the state. Although his period was very stable, and he brought forth many institutional changes that eased the administration of the kingdom, he wasn't popular with the people.

Once Albert was recalled to Madrid in 1593, the government of Portugal was handed to a board of governors, which consisted of the archbishop of Lisbon and four nobles. But they didn't last long, as the new king in Portugal, Philip II (Philip III of Spain), who succeeded the throne in 1598, appointed another viceroy. He chose the marquis of Castelo Rodrigo, Cristóvão de Moura, who was one of the greatest supporters of the Habsburg line in Portugal. Philip II was the second and last Habsburg king who would stay in Portugal, although his visit lasted for only three months in 1619. After him, none of the Spanish Habsburg rulers bothered to come to Lisbon. During his rule, there were eight viceroys, and his successor, Philip III (Philip IV of Spain), returned Portugal to the board of governors on this one occasion and continued the practice of appointing viceroys.

The Portuguese came to realize that there was a significant difference in the governance of their country between the appointed viceroys and the board. The viceroys lived in the palace and enjoyed the full powers and prestige of a king. The governors weren't allowed to reside in the royal palace, and although they had similar powers as the viceroy, they didn't enjoy royal dignity. However, the viceroys and the board of governors had no power to summon a *cortes*; only a king could do that. Since the Habsburg rulers were usually absent from Portugal, the meeting of the *cortes* became a rarity. For the fifty-eight years of Habsburg rule, the *cortes* met only three times: in 1581 to swear allegiance to Philip I in Tomar; in 1583 to do the same for his successor, Philip II; and in 1619 when Philip II stayed in Lisbon for three months.

Another institutional change that occurred in Portugal during the Habsburg rule was the creation of a council in 1582. This council had six members, all Portuguese nobles, and their task was to remain in the Portuguese royal palace and advise the king on the country's affairs. Another council was created in 1591 with the task of controlling the royal treasury and the finances of the Portuguese Empire. The third council was founded in 1604 to supervise the administration of the empire; this was the India Council. This was when Portugal started mirroring the system of the council that was already in place in Spain. But the complexity of this system and the absence of the king meant that administrative decisions took a much longer time to be realized.

Although Portugal retained autonomy and all of its freedoms, this was mainly formal. In practice, this autonomy was restricted and susceptible to corruption. Whenever the interests of Spain conflicted with those of Portugal, its autonomy was pushed aside. Even the exclusively Portuguese councils were simply bypassed with the creation of special committees, whose members were both Spanish and Portuguese. These committees were then given powers greater than the Portuguese councils, and they were capable of making decisions that would ignore Portugal's interests and work for either Spanish ones or those of the united crown. Philip II of Portugal was the first to ignore the condition that the appointed viceroy needed to be Portuguese, as he appointed a Castilian noble. A similar thing happened in 1634 when Princess Margaret of Savoy became a Portuguese viceroy. These Castilian viceroys served the purpose of curbing Portugal's autonomy and working in their own interests. By 1635, it had become obvious that the autonomy of Portugal had eroded to such an extent that the locals started demanding the end of the union.

Chapter 9 – The United Crown

Count of Olivares painted in 1643

When Philip I succeeded the throne of Portugal in 1581, he united the Iberian Peninsula under one crown. To celebrate the occasion and to connect the two parts of his kingdom, he ordered the construction of a bridge over the Tagus River at Toledo, which would link Lisbon to Madrid. This project wasn't only a transportation and communication network in the making but also a symbol of the nations' joint economy and prosperity. Initially, many benefits came with the union. After the 1620s, the economy of the dual monarchy started suffering; the costs began to mount, and they started outweighing the gains. There were different reasons for this failure of the united economy, and it had little to do with the Portuguese ability to respond to the economic trends of the period.

With the ascension of the Habsburg rule, Portugal's population started declining. There are many theories as to why this happened, and while some suggest pandemics and natural disasters, it is more plausible that the main reason was migration. People started leaving Portugal for other Portuguese colonies, Spanish America, and most commonly Spain. It is estimated that around six thousand people left Portugal annually in the late 16th to the early 17th century. With the demographic decline came the slowdown of consumption and the stagnation of wages. There were very few people left who were willing to work the land, and agriculture halted its development. Portugal's chronic shortage of grain became even more obvious, and the need to import much larger quantities rose. Maize was introduced as a crop from America, but its popularity never grew enough to make it a product worth exporting. The country had to import one-third of its grain needs, and it spent enormous amounts of gold to keep famine at bay.

In the early 17th century, Portugal experienced agricultural reform, with its main focus on increasing grain production. Leaders and officials believed there was too much uncultivated land, and their idea was to use all of it to plant cereal crops. In practice, though, this land was used for grazing cattle and for collecting raw materials, such as wood, clay, and stone. Another reason cereal production in Portugal often failed was the climate and the condition of the soil, which were unsuitable for the production of grains. The local producers, therefore, preferred to invest in olive trees, vineyards, and fruit than in wheat. The Habsburgs showed an interest in reforming Portuguese agriculture, but they approached it with the wrong idea. Instead of investing in the crops that the soil could produce in abundance, they insisted on cereals and ultimately failed with their reforms.

The Habsburgs had a much bigger influence on Portuguese finances and international trade. The kingdom became part of a much bigger trade bloc after the unification, and its place in the Iberian Peninsula allowed it to expand its trade to all the known continents at the time. Spanish-controlled America was finally opened to Portuguese traders, but Brazil remained exclusively a Portuguese market. This meant that Portuguese traders gained access to American silver and gold while keeping their monopoly on seaborne trade between Europe and Asia.

As for domestic trade, Philip I (Philip II of Spain) immediately abolished the custom taxes after the unification, which meant the whole Iberian Peninsula was now one commercial entity. Cross-border opportunities for small local Portuguese traders suddenly opened, but this only added to the population decline, as many artisans, traders, businessmen, and sailors decided to move to Castile. Seville, the largest city of Spain at the time, suddenly grew, with more than 25 percent of its citizens being Portuguese. Many of them were Jews who were forcefully converted to Christianity ("New Christians"). Although they were now Christian, they were still regarded as less valuable, and a series of restrictions were imposed on them. They were allowed to start and develop their own businesses, but they had to pay higher taxes. These restrictions started easing up with the Habsburg rule. The New Christians started growing their wealth, and they took control over the trade with the New World and even lent money to the crown.

The economy of Habsburg Portugal started faltering when the economy of the whole Iberian Peninsula and the Habsburgs were endangered. Although the union brought Portugal new opportunities in a wider world market, it also brought the loss of control. In the American market, the Spanish traders who had already established their business there would not calmly accept the Portuguese takeover. They forced the Habsburg king to impose a series of embargoes on Portuguese traders. But the crown didn't stop in America. In 1585, the embargo was extended to include the Netherlands and England, which were important clients for Portugal. The promise made in Tomar that the Portuguese trade would be untouched and in Portuguese hands was thus broken.

The Habsburg rulers didn't predict the outcome of the embargo. The crown's seaborne trade interests started dropping, as many traders chose to become private businessmen and replace the European market with the Asian one. The crown started losing its trade income rapidly, and the only place it could continue investing was Portuguese-controlled Brazil and Spanish America. Brazil became the main source of sugar and tobacco, and the Portuguese ports started prospering again since they were in the perfect position to accept the ships coming from the west. Another major immigration wave occurred in which the Portuguese left their country to seek opportunities in Peru, Mexico, and Brazil.

Foreign Relations

The Portuguese people hoped that the unification would bring them protection from outside enemies. The Habsburg monarchy in Europe was at its peak during the 16th century, and it brought confidence in Spain's power. This power could also be seen in the Spanish and Portuguese joint plans of the conquest of China, Japan, and various territories of Southeast Asia. But by the 1580s, the Habsburg prestige was in decline, and the Portuguese realized that Spain would not bring them security.

Portuguese relations with the Dutch and English before the union were always friendly. But these were Protestant countries, so they were in conflict with Catholic Spain. Even in the colonies, English ships attacked Spanish ones and confiscated the goods brought from the Americas. The English also often helped the Dutch during their open conflict with Spain. The Portuguese throne pretender António sought refuge in England, and the English crown backed his efforts against the union and Philip II of Spain. This was the main reason Philip imposed an embargo on England and the Netherlands in 1585. These embargoes were lifted on a few occasions and reimposed in 1621 and again in 1647. They were very effective at stopping trade between the Iberian Peninsula and the Protestant countries of England and the Netherlands, but several private enterprises continued operating. The Dutch herring industry heavily depended on salt imported from Portugal, and the embargo seriously threatened its existence. However, Portugal felt the consequences of the trade ban too.

After the union of the crowns and the imposition of the embargo, England started treating Portugal as an enemy. The Portuguese settlements on the Cape Verde Islands were under constant attack, and the Portuguese ships carrying products from Spanish America were never safe. King Philip II of Spain responded by launching an invasion of England in 1588, sending the Spanish Armada off the coast of Portugal. This armada included twelve Portuguese ships and five thousand men. In the ensuing war, all of these ships and men were lost, leaving the Portuguese shore open to attack.

In 1589, António and his English friends Francis Drake and John Norris landed near Lisbon and tried to take the Portuguese throne by force. However, the locals offered them no support, and they were forced to retreat. If they had succeeded, Portugal would have, without a doubt, become an English dependency. António promised his English friends not only substantial payment but also yearly payments in perpetuity, control over the forts on the Tagus, the sacking of Lisbon, and freedom to trade in all Portuguese colonies.

The English attacks on Portuguese ships continued, and one such incident would spark the interest of the British traders in India. When the Portuguese ship *Madre de Deus* was captured in 1592, it was sailing back from India loaded with spice, precious stones, silk, indigo, and other overseas products. It also contained its logbook, which explained, in detail, a safe route to India. This incident inspired the creation of the British East India Company and the eventual demise of Portuguese trade in Asia.

The Dutch East India Company was founded in 1602, and it entered the Asian market very aggressively. The Dutch expelled the Portuguese traders from Tidore and Ambon and, by 1606, from Melaka. The next year, they attacked and conquered Mozambique. The Portuguese East India Company, which was created in 1628, was powerless against such aggression. By 1640, the Dutch had taken over all the enterprises east of the Cape of Good Hope, becoming the most powerful European force in the region. The Dutch also raided the Portuguese possessions in the Atlantic and laid waste to the islands of São Tomé and Príncipe as early as 1598. In 1621, the Dutch founded their very own West India Company and started making their first settlements in the Americas. In 1624, they captured Brazil. Although the Portuguese managed to regain it the next year, the ability of the newly founded Dutch company to achieve such a feat in the first place serves to display their aggression and power.

The Reform of Olivares

When Philip III of Spain (Philip II of Portugal) died in March of 1621, his successor, Philip IV of Spain, was sixteen years old. Although he was of legal age, he was very inexperienced and under the heavy influence of his court favorite, Count of Olivares. This count was loyal to Spain, and he devoted his life to working in the interest of his kingdom. For the next two decades, he ruled Habsburg's Iberian monarchy from the shadows. He proved to be a much more versatile and able ruler than Philip IV and perhaps even a stronger one than Philip II. Olivares rose to power when the monarchy was already faltering. To save it, he had to implement a series of reforms. The dual monarchy's main problem was the financial burden it had to carry. American silver was no longer as abundant as in the 16th century, and Olivares needed to find new sources of revenue. The only possible way to do so was to breach the constitutional rights of the neighboring ex-kingdoms (Aragon, Navarre, and Granada that merged with Castile in the 15th century) and override the autonomy and liberties of its people.

In 1624, Olivares drew up his reforms and presented them to the king. To save the declining economy, he planned to centralize the government through a process of gradual integration. To achieve this, Castile had to carefully navigate the laws and constitutions of its neighboring regions and adjust them to its own. By doing this, the transition to a centralized government would be smooth, and it wouldn't aggravate the people. Olivares considered this integration beneficial for outlying regions too, as they would receive more attention from the centralized government than from a king who was always absent. The people would gain access to increased opportunities for their businesses, admission to government offices, and royal patronage. This would secure the people's support for the reforms. However, the monarchy would have to sacrifice its exclusively Castilian character and become a true Iberian empire.

For Portugal, the centralization of the government meant military and fiscal reform. The centralized monarchy would need to have a single army, and the kingdoms would have to contribute to it with provisions and men. This plan was publicized in 1626, and almost immediately, it faced strong resistance in Portugal. Portuguese interests were put aside, and although some nobles accepted the new duties and started personal military service, no one else was enthusiastic about the reforms. A similar thing happened with Olivares's fiscal reforms in Portugal. He wanted to impose new taxes, but he couldn't do it without the approval of the *cortes*. However, Olivares was resourceful, and he turned to collect "voluntary" subsidies that financed projects that were beneficial for Portugal. He persuaded the Inquisition to pay a significant amount of money for the Portuguese war efforts in India. He turned to regular clergy as well and collected even more subsidies for the same cause.

In 1626, a combined Castilian-Portuguese Army managed to recapture Bahia (in northeastern Brazil) from the Dutch. The Portuguese realized that their interests often coincided with the Spanish. However, the military efforts put significant pressure on the finances of both Portugal and Castile, and the people wondered if the success in Bahia could be repeated. Spain was at war with England from 1625 until 1630. In 1635, it started yet another war, this time with France. Portugal experienced a significant loss in 1627 when its whole fleet was destroyed by a storm in the Atlantic Ocean. Thousands of men perished, both Spanish and Portuguese. After such losses, it was hard to persuade the people of the benefits of a military union when all they wanted was peace. The population started resisting the efforts Olivares made to raise money for future campaigns.

Olivares had no other choice but to order 25 percent of the salaries paid by the crown to be suspended until enough funds were raised for the forthcoming military expedition, which would recover Pernambuco (Brazil) from the Dutch. This put pressure on most of the elite, as they received pensions, grants, and incomes from the state. The governors of Lisbon couldn't allow the elite to bear the cost by themselves, so they suggested a collection of subsidies that would be split between all the municipalities in Portugal. This meant that all citizens would have to pay. The city representatives opposed this idea. Having no other solution, Olivares imposed his idea in 1635, which included the introduction of a new tax on wine and meat, as well as increasing the tax on the sale of land and other properties by 25 percent. The Portuguese had nothing against paying the taxes, but they expected them to be just. These new impositions were beyond the people's ability to pay, and everyone wondered why the crown didn't collect the money for military expeditions from its resources. The obvious consequence of imposed taxation was the elevation of social tensions.

The Revolt of 1640

In 1637, social unrest in Évora, Portugal, exploded. Olivares wasn't concerned with these sparks of rebellion because he relied on the local nobility to suppress them. But several weeks into the unrest, it became obvious that the Portuguese nobles had no intention of using force to quell the revolt. Instead, they preferred peaceful negotiations. The results weren't satisfying, and the nobles didn't even manage to calm the situation. Several preachers and nobles encouraged the people to protest. The church officially supported the king, but even the clergy wanted a peaceful solution to be found instead of raising an army against the Portuguese people. However, Olivares needed the unrests to disappear quickly, and he gathered Castilian troops and intervened in Algarve and Alentejo. Order was restored in Portugal by the next year. Nevertheless, the Portuguese nobles started distrusting the government, and their anger would erupt three years later in a renewed revolt.

The discontent of the Portuguese continued to simmer throughout the period of 1637 to 1640. But no charismatic leader showed up to direct the angry masses and lead them against the government. Although the common people resented the nobility for avoiding the taxes, they were even angrier with the government and Olivares's reforms. The Habsburgs never had strong support among the Portuguese people, but whatever support they had was gone. The lower clergy also had very strong anti-Habsburg sentiment, but it was unlikely they could provide the people with a much-needed leader. The bourgeoisie remained neutral and observant. They consisted of wealthy merchants who understood that as much the Portuguese hated Spanish rule, the Spanish had developed an anti-Portuguese stance.

In 1638, Olivares summoned a gathering of Portuguese nobles in Madrid, intending to persuade them of agreeing to constitutional changes that would ease up the money-gathering for the war efforts. But nothing significant came out of this meeting, except for the agreement to abolish the Portuguese council. Some of the nobles invited to the gathering didn't bother showing up. Most notable was the absence of John, the eighth duke of Braganza and the grandson of Catherine, who was one of the people to claim a right to the throne back in 1580. Olivares always considered the duke of Braganza a serious threat to the Habsburgs rule, especially since the myth of King Sebastian became related to the House of Braganza. Many new prophecies identified John as the sleeping king who would come to aid the Portuguese in their time of need. The French were also aware of the popularity the duke of Braganza enjoyed, and they contacted him in 1634, intending to use him against their common Spanish enemy.

In the autumn of 1638, Olivares managed to collect enough resources to send the Luso-Spanish fleet to recover Pernambuco from the Dutch, but they achieved nothing significant. The failure of the united fleet only served to prove that Spain and the Habsburgs were no longer able to protect Portuguese overseas possessions. Other military failures in Europe occurred as well. From 1638 to 1640, Spain lost twenty thousand sailors and one hundred warships in total. The French used the opportunity to attack Catalonia, and the Portuguese were afraid that they would be next. Olivares desperately sought to negotiate peace with both the Dutch and the French.

This was the background that set the stage for the events of 1640. Olivares's final demand from Portugal was to provide eight thousand men for the war effort in Italy, but the Portuguese objected. They didn't see a reason why they should fight outside the borders of their kingdom, and they ignored this final demand.

Two years earlier, Olivares had appointed the duke of Braganza as the chief of the Portuguese Army in an effort to sway the noble to the Habsburg cause. Now, he regretted this decision, as Braganza put the Portuguese Army outside of Spanish control. When Catalonia exploded in revolt in May of 1640, Braganza had to make a quick decision about the possibility of leading the Portuguese revolt.

Braganza was sure he had the support of the people, and he knew he could easily claim the Portuguese crown. But he was too cautious and did not act until October of 1640. But even before Braganza's decision, the nobles had plotted against the regime. Around forty young nobles planned the assassination of the crown's viceroy, Margaret of Savoy. They openly offered the crown to John, Duke of Braganza, who finally accepted it. The coup was scheduled for December 1ˢᵗ. The duke needed to remain uninvolved until the coup was successful. One false step could bring disaster to not only John personally but also all the involved noble families and Portugal as a whole.

Olivares ordered the Portuguese Army to take up arms and help repress the protests. He also ordered the nobles to do the same, and he threatened them with property confiscations. The Castilian nobles responded to the call, but the Portuguese, including the duke of Braganza, declined. A week later, they put their plot into motion. The viceroy's palace in Lisbon was their primary target, and they easily overwhelmed the guards and reached Miguel de Vasconcelos, Portugal's Secretary of State. They shot him and threw him out the window. They arrested Viceroy Margaret of Savoy but didn't hurt her as initially planned. Instead, they dispatched her to

Spain unharmed. The rebel nobles didn't encounter any serious resistance in the palace, and the bloodshed was very minimal, as the few Castilian guards who remained quickly surrendered. Within hours, Lisbon was in the hands of the rebels.

Chapter 10 – The Restoration

The Acclamation of King John IV by Salgado.
https://commons.wikimedia.org/wiki/File:Joao_IV_proclaimed_king.jpg

John, Duke of Braganza, officially became king of Portugal on December 15th, 1640, and he immediately summoned the *cortes*. By doing so, he displayed his power, and by accepting the summons, the *cortes* officially recognized his authority. The *cortes* session began on January 28ᵗʰ, 1641, during which John was sworn in as the king of Portugal and started his rule as John IV (r. 1640–1656). John and his supporters started spreading propaganda through the country's press, stating that Philip II of Spain usurped the throne back in 1580 and that John IV was only reclaiming what was rightfully his. The propaganda went further, claiming that the Habsburgs ruled unjustly and that they exploited Portugal and squeezed it for money and resources. Philip IV, the current king of Spain (he had been Philip III of Portugal), was specially painted in a bad light, with the press claiming he was a tyrant and that the *cortes* had rightfully deposed him. The union with Spain was officially done, and the traditional Portuguese king was once again on the throne.

The purpose of this propaganda was to attract all of the Portuguese nobles who had moved to Spain earlier and those who were loyal to the Habsburg rule. These nobles posed a danger to John's rule, and Olivares knew this. After Olivares learned of the coup, he summoned all of the Portuguese nobles residing in Madrid (around eighty of them) and swore them to the Habsburg cause. As for the clergy in Portugal, their devotion to the restoration of the Portuguese king was divided. While the archbishop of Lisbon wholeheartedly supported John, the archbishop of Braga remained loyal to Philip IV of Spain (Philip III of Portugal). The rest of the higher clergy either supported the new regime or remained neutral.

The new regime was also very popular with the commoners, businessmen, and religious orders, especially the Jesuits, who would soon become very influential in John's court. But despite this popularity, John had to remain cautious since danger still existed. The nobles who supported the Habsburg rule even attempted to kill John in August 1641, but their plans were discovered in time. The main culprit of this conspiracy was the archbishop of Braga, but other Portuguese nobles were also involved, which posed a new concern for the king. All of the participants were ordered to be public beheaded to set an example.

Among those who refused to support the new king, the most difficult to deal with was the Inquisition. This was established in 1563, and its main task was to eradicate Judaism. Their target was the New Christians, the converts who claimed to practice Christianity but were often found to secretly practice Judaism. The Portuguese Inquisition was able to support itself because it often confiscated the properties and earnings of the New Christians. These converts were exceptional businessmen, and the previous Habsburg regime had relied on their loans to keep the royal treasury full. John needed the New Christians for the same reason, and he was prepared to give them protection against the Inquisition. But the Inquisition opposed him. The king had no legal power to remove the Inquisition officials, and the hatred for the New Christians was widespread. The populace, especially the nobles, ended up supporting the Inquisition's stance, and the persecution against the Jews continued.

Another problem John had was that the Spanish-oriented pope refused to recognize him as the legitimate ruler of Portugal. This caused enormous problems within the kingdom because, without a legitimate ruler, the new bishops couldn't be appointed. By 1649, Portugal had only one bishop left, with all the other sees falling vacant. The pope would not acknowledge the legitimacy of the new Portuguese dynasty until 1668 when peace with Spain was finally concluded. Until then, Portugal had to endure religious condemnation.

John IV is remembered as an extremely cautious ruler. He never left Portugal and rarely traveled outside of his Duchy of Braganza. Perhaps it was his wariness that made the Portuguese Restoration a bloodless and peaceful event. Although he had enemies and people who openly opposed him, they only acted against him on one occasion in 1641. But John was put in a role he was not prepared for, and he always relied on the advice of his secretary, António Pais

Viegas, and court favorite António Vieira the Jesuit. The king was always wary, even in his final years as a ruler, and because of it, historians often portrayed him as a weak king.

The Diplomacy of John IV

One of the most urgent tasks John had to deal with after the coup of 1640 was to secure the support of overseas Portuguese colonies. He dispatched special couriers to all corners of the empire to announce the restoration of the Portuguese king. The news was celebrated everywhere—in Bahia and Goa in 1641 and in distant Macau in 1642. The Jesuits strongly supported Portugal's new king, and their presence in the distant lands of the empire made the transition of loyalties smooth. The only Portuguese settlement that refused to acknowledge John and remained loyal to the Habsburgs was Ceuta in North Africa. But this was expected, as Ceuta was geographically closer to Spain, and it heavily depended on Spanish supplies. After securing the support of the colonies, John founded a new council in 1643, the *Conselho Ultramarino*, whose task was to administer all the overseas possessions.

Although the Braganza regime was widely accepted, that didn't mean Portugal would avoid a war for its independence. Spain would not simply abandon the dual monarchy, and the Habsburgs already regarded Portugal as their possession. Unfortunately for Portugal, the Portuguese military wasn't equipped or in shape for war. They didn't have enough weapons, horses, or supplies, and the fortresses on the country's border were all neglected. The most experienced Portuguese military leaders were away, either fighting for the Habsburgs or in far-away colonies. Spain, on the other hand, was already involved in wars with France and the Netherlands, and it also had to deal with local rebellions in Catalonia and Andalusia. Although its army was stretched on many fronts, Spain attacked in 1641.

The first clash between Spain and Portugal was small, consisting of several quick battles and the raiding of villages and border towns.

Portugal used this time to rebuild its force and repair the neglected fortresses. It also spared its main army by focusing on defense rather than engaging in offensive operations across the border. The first offensive came in 1644 when a small Portuguese force successfully won a battle at Montijo, Spain. However, this victory wasn't enough, and the war continued, with neither side gaining any advantage. Portugal could not afford a prolonged war, and in the late 1640s, Spain started concluding its war with the Netherlands and the revolt in Catalonia. Since Spain could now reroute its army and concentrate on Portugal, the sense of urgency was overwhelming. John IV died in 1656 before the independence of Portugal was concluded.

But aside from the military conflict, John had to concentrate his efforts on a diplomatic war too. Spain worked hard to persuade other European countries to refuse to recognize Portugal's independence. During the dual monarchy, Portugal had no foreign offices of its own. Instead, Spain dealt with all the foreign relations. This is why now, after the Restoration, Portugal had no people trained in diplomacy, except for one: Francisco de Sousa Coutinho. He dispatched envoys to various European courts, not only to ask for Portugal's recognition but also to secure foreign help for their cause. Coutinho especially focused on securing recognition from France, a longtime enemy of Spain. But at that time, France was reluctant to make any more moves against Spain, and it refused the diplomatic efforts of Portugal, which included the offer of a marriage between John's daughter Catherine and Louis XIV, as well as Tangier or Mazagão.

The only other country that was likely to recognize and support Portugal at the time was England. In January 1642, the Portuguese representatives managed to successfully acquire recognition from King Charles I. However, Portugal was left disappointed, as England soon entered a civil war and was unable to offer any diplomatic or military help. The disaster only deepened in 1649 when Charles I was executed, and Portugal found itself in a short war against the Commonwealth of England. Because John gave shelter to the British fleet commander Prince Rupert, the government of Oliver Cromwell decided to block the Tagus River, forcing Portugal into negotiations. The result was a new Anglo-Portuguese treaty that gave generous commercial rights to the English. In return, Portugal gained the protection of Cromwell's England. This alliance was a major step forward for Portugal since England's maritime power was continuing to grow. England also stepped into a war with Spain in 1650, which took the military pressure off of Portugal.

Afonso VI (r. 1656–1683) and Peter II (r. 1683–1706)

The Braganza dynasty wasn't secure on the throne of Portugal when John IV died. His eldest son had died in 1653, and he was the one who received the necessary training and education to rule. John's less adequate second son, Afonso VI, inherited the throne. It wasn't a lack of training that hindered Afonso but rather his physical and mental weakness. When he was still an infant, he contracted meningitis, which rendered him handicapped. He was only thirteen years old when he came to the throne, and his mother, Queen Luisa de Guzmán, acted as regent. Although she was Spanish, she continued the struggle to acquire the recognition of Portugal's independence.

The first major Portuguese victory came in January 1659 when around five thousand Spanish soldiers were taken prisoner at Elvas, a city on the border with Spain. But that same year, Spain finally made a lasting peace with France and was able to focus its attention on the Portuguese problem. Luisa had no other choice but to completely rely on help from England. Cromwell's government allowed her to purchase arms and recruit twelve thousand Englishmen, which would greatly help Portugal against Spain. Shortly after these events, Charles II of England was restored to the throne, and luckily, he continued the friendly relations with

Portugal. In 1662, a new Anglo-Portuguese treaty was signed and sealed by a marriage between King Charles II and Princess Catherine, sister of King Afonso VI. England also promised protection against Portuguese enemies and officially recognized the Braganza dynasty as legitimate. However, this English support didn't come without a price. Portugal had to confirm the concessions given to England in 1654 and give away control of Bombay and Tangier.

After Afonso reached the age of eighteen, he finally terminated Luisa's regency and allowed himself to be influenced by his private secretary, Luís de Vasconcelos e Sousa, Count of Castelo Melhor. For the next five years, Melhor greatly influenced the king. He proved to be loyal to his country as an effective leader. He was equally determined to acquire Portugal's recognition of independence. But unlike the Braganzas, Melhor was aware that further war with Spain would strain Portugal and that the country would not be able to recover financially. He focused on settling the matter through diplomacy rather than conflict. But he never effectively ended the war, as he knew the continuous struggle put pressure on Spain too, which would make the Habsburg rulers more likely to accept terms that would be more favorable for Portugal.

Melhor pursued an alliance with France and finally achieved this in 1667. But even before that, France sent help to Portugal in the form of a German officer named Frederick, Duke of Schomberg, who reformed the Portuguese Army and trained the Portuguese soldiers. Under his command, Portugal achieved a series of victories in the period between 1663 and 1665. Philip IV of Spain (Philip III of Portugal) lost hope he would ever regain control of Portugal during his life, which proved to be a correct assumption. After Philip's death in 1665, Melhor felt that the major obstacle to achieving peace was removed. With England and France on Portugal's side, Spain had no choice but to agree to negotiations, and the peace treaty was signed in January 1668 in Madrid. Spain finally recognized Portugal's independence, and the hostilities that tore the Iberian Peninsula asunder were mended.

Melhor's government had to deal with internal problems too, which came in the form of a conflict between conservatives and reformists. There were specific groups of people, mostly nobles and clergy with certain political influence, that wanted a more centralized administration of Portugal and the return to the old kingdom. Their opponents, although full-heartedly supporting Portugal's independence, wanted to continue the reforms started by Habsburg official Olivares. They believed that the central government was becoming too authoritative and even autocratic. They criticized Afonso's rule and the fact that, during his reign, the *cortes* was never summoned, not even for the official acclamation of Afonso as the king. They blamed Melhor for this, as he was the most influential figure in the court.

A group of prominent nobles who were traditionalists and opposed Melhor started planning a coup in 1667. Their leaders were the duke of Cadaval and the marquis of Marialva, and they managed to secure the support of Prince Peter (Pedro), the younger brother of King Afonso VI. But to be able to overthrow Afonso, they first had to deal with Melhor, so they obtained his dismissal. Then they openly sought the replacement of King Afonso with Peter. They also had the support of Luisa de Guzmán, as well as Queen Maria Francisca of Savoy, Afonso's wife, whom he had married just a year before. The royal couple never consummated their marriage, probably because Afonso was not able to perform due to his condition. Maria had their marriage annulled, and once Afonso handed the power to his younger brother, she married Peter.

At first, Peter II ruled Portugal not as a sole ruler but in Afonso's name. This arrangement lasted from 1667 until 1683. Once Peter started his sole rule, he remained in power until he died in 1706. He summoned the *cortes* in 1668 to confirm the legitimacy of his regency and started working on consolidating the Braganza regime. His supporters urged him to take the title of king immediately, but Peter II refused the crown because he was a stout follower of legal procedures. It is possible he also didn't want to simply push his brother aside. He was satisfied with the title of prince regent, which he held until Afonso VI died.

The marriage between Peter and Maria Francisca resulted in the birth of a daughter, Isabel Luísa. This princess was the only child the royal couple had, and in 1674, she was sworn in as the heir presumptive. However, this was done because the previous year, there was a plot to dispose of Peter and Maria and reinstall Afonso VI as the king of Portugal. Peter had to secure the Braganza succession, and he had the *cortes* admit his daughter as his successor. After these events, Peter's position on the throne became secure. He then started concentrating on finding a prosperous suitor for his daughter. His favorite choice was the French prince, as the marriage would secure the alliance with France. However, these negotiations were unsuccessful.

After the death of his wife Maria in 1683, Peter's behavior was worrisome. He wanted to abdicate the throne and retire to Brazil, but the Jesuit courtiers in Portugal managed to dissuade him. After grieving for Maria for the next four years, Peter decided it was time to marry again. He chose a minor princess, Maria Sophia, daughter of the elector of the Palatine. Peter's second marriage was fruitful, as Maria Sophia gave birth to five sons and two daughters. This turn of events brought even greater stability to the House of Braganza since its continuity was secured. Peter's first daughter, Isabel, died in 1690, but her death had no political consequences since the *cortes* favored Peter's newborn sons as the successors of the Portuguese throne. The last two decades of Peter's reign were uneventful. He secured the stability of his dynasty and pursued a policy of neutrality in foreign affairs.

Chapter 11 – Portugal in the 18ᵗʰ Century

Marquis of Pombal, reviewing plans for the reconstruction of Portugal after the earthquake
of 1755
*https://commons.wikimedia.org/wiki/File:O_Marqu%C3%AAs_de_Pombal_Examinando
_os_Planos_da_Reconstru%C3%A7%C3%A3o_de_Lisboa_(1883)_-
Miguel%C3%82ngelo_Lupi_(Museu_de_Lisboa,_MC.PIN.0702).png*

The Second Golden Age in Portugal

The first half of the 18th century in Portugal started with general peace and political stability. The kingdom's economy also improved, and the people were satisfied. Due to this peace, the artistic expression known as Baroque developed. This wasn't a phenomenon that occurred solely in Portugal; in fact, it didn't even start there. The origins of Baroque can be found at the start of the 17th century in Rome, Italy. But the artistic movement spread throughout Europe. Its main characteristics were pretentious and impressive architecture, elaborate interior decorations usually covered in gold, imposing yet personal writings, and ceremonial and theatrical music.

In most of western Europe, the start of the 18th century was the era of the Enlightenment. In Portugal, this movement came late, as the kingdom was busy with its revival. Even when it came, the Enlightenment only influenced certain aspects of political life. In Portugal, this intellectual movement was never all-consuming like in the rest of the western European kingdoms, such as France and Germany. Within Portugal, the main pattern of thought was strictly traditional, and there were few who promoted the ideas of the Enlightenment. They were even called out and branded *estrangeirados* ("foreignized"), as they often traveled or had contact with intellectuals outside of the kingdom and were heavily influenced by them.

The first half of the 18th century was dominated by the reign of King John V (r. 1706–1750). He was only seventeen years old when he came to the throne, but he was already determined which direction his rule would take. He was an absolutist monarch, and he modeled his rule on those of French, Spanish, and Austrian kings. He believed that secular power should always be subjected to the king, who was the absolute authority. He also believed that the future well-being of Portugal heavily depended on its overseas possessions, especially Brazil. He wanted absolute control over all the Portuguese colonies, and he was personally engaged in their government, economy, and communications.

Two years after his coronation, John married Princess Maria Anna, the daughter of Holy Roman Emperor Leopold I, thus binding the Braganza dynasty to the Habsburgs of Austria. They had six children, securing the continuation of the royal dynasty. But John V was an avid pleasure seeker, and he is known for having various mistresses from all the social layers of Portugal. He particularly enjoyed having affairs with the ladies of the church. His favorite was Paula Teresa de Silva, a Cistercian nun and the abbess of the Saint-Denis of Odivelas Monastery. Besides his adventures with women, John loved luxury and extravagance. He was a generous patron of the Baroque arts, and he especially enjoyed literature, architecture, and music. He personally oversaw many public building projects, founded libraries all over the country, and donated generously to education centers. However, he was always suspicious of the new political thought brought about by the Enlightenment.

For most of his reign, John was an exemplary monarch. He was dedicated to the government and the well-being of his country. Although he was a little restless in his youth and complained about how his royal duties prevented him from traveling the world, he quickly settled in the role of a dedicated king. In 1742, John suffered a stroke, which left him half-paralyzed. It also seriously influenced his ability to make decisions. Although he recovered physically, as much as could be expected in the 18th century, he remained weak mentally. Although his condition didn't influence Portugal's political direction much, it became obvious in 1747 when he refused to replace the aging ministers who could no longer perform their duties. Although the king lived for three more years, the leadership of the government fell on the shoulders of the royal secretary, Brazilian Alexandre de Gusmão.

When John V died in 1750, he was succeeded by his eldest son, King Joseph (José) I (r. 1750-1777). As the third child, Joseph was always excluded from Portuguese politics, but his elder brother died early, and it remains unknown why John refused to prepare his second son for the rule, even when he became the heir apparent in 1714. Nevertheless, once a king, Joseph I immediately took up the task of reforming the government. He replaced all of his father's ministers with young and able noblemen, among which Sebastião José de Carvalho e Melo, 1ˢᵗ Marquis of Pombal, stood out. He was a minor noble who previously served as a diplomat. Joseph I appointed him secretary of state of foreign affairs, a position in which Sebastião shined. This formidable minister would later be known simply as Pombal, and under his guidance, Portugal would finally give in to the reforms of the Enlightenment.

John V: Gold and Diamonds

Portugal started its colonization program with the idea of getting immense riches from its overseas possessions. But that didn't happen until the 18th century. Through the 15th and 16th centuries, Portugal received gold from São Jorge da Mina in today's Ghana. But even then, the influx of gold didn't amount to much, and the colony prospered due to the slave trade, not mining. However, the fate of Portugal was about to change when, in the late 17th century, gold was discovered in Brazil. The first shipment from Brazil to Lisbon in 1697 contained around 115 kilograms of the precious metal. However, by 1711, this number increased to fifteen thousand kilograms annually. This meant that Portugal started receiving far more gold from its colonies than any other European kingdom. In 1720, the gold import in Portugal peaked at 30,112 kilograms. For the next three decades, the amount of gold decreased, but it never went under eighteen thousand kilograms.

Brazilian gold boosted the royal treasury because the crown was entitled to 20 percent of all precious metal production. The amount of gold Portugal imported changed the pattern of international trade. The value of Portuguese products that were exported increased fivefold, and that happened in the era when European trade grew immensely due to Britain's industrial dominance. The main reason for the Portuguese export success was the Anglo-Portuguese trade treaties. In addition, Britain maintained an exchange rate that favored gold, which the Portuguese took advantage of. The Portuguese exchange rate favored silver due to the country's constant lack of it. The direct export of gold was banned in Portugal, but the precious metal still poured out due to trade and smuggling. Due to trade agreements, British ships were exempt from customs inspections when they sailed from Lisbon to Falmouth, and this proved to be the main route of smuggling gold. Brazilian gold enabled Portugal to pay for its increasing imports of wheat, textiles, cod, and other consumer goods they weren't able to produce themselves.

Just when the production of gold in Brazil reached its peak in the late 1620s, the news of the discovery of diamond deposits reached Lisbon. At this time, the main source of diamonds in the world was in British-controlled Madras (southern India), where a group of gem merchants had a monopoly on excavation and production of the precious stones. But the news of the discovery of diamonds in Brazil finally broke that monopoly, especially because the quantity in Brazil was far greater than in Madras. In 1732 and 1733, Portugal imported 300,000 carats of diamonds from Brazil, which was five times more than Madras could produce. But during the 18th century, gold was more valuable to the Portuguese crown, and its revenue from diamonds amounted to only 10 percent of the revenues gained from gold production.

The sudden influx of diamonds was welcomed by the government of John V, but it created some problems too. The new source of diamonds flooded the market, and the prices suddenly dropped. This is why, in 1734, Portugal imposed a ban on diamond excavations in Brazil and constricted it to a designated "diamond district," which was later put into the hands of monopolist contractors. These government measures stabilized the world's diamond market, and prices started increasing again. Luckily, the 18th century saw the rise of the bourgeoisie, which meant that, in Europe, the people capable of purchasing diamonds expanded. Previously, it had consisted only of European royal families and the rich nobility.

The first monopoly contractor who was given the right to deal with the Brazilian diamonds was a British company, Bristow Ward, in 1753. But such a monopoly only encouraged smugglers, and although the authorities tried to eradicate smuggling, many Brazilian diamonds reached the European market through these illegal means. Most of the illicit gems went first to London, from where they were shipped to their final buyers in various corners of Europe.

The gold and diamonds excavated in Brazil only contributed to King John V's reputation as the richest monarch of the Christian world. He was often portrayed as wasteful and prone to scandalous extravagance. But this is not the complete truth. John didn't mindlessly spend the crown's riches. Instead, he preferred to commit the wealth to a good cause, and he built many Portuguese churches and religious monuments. This might not have been the wisest investment, as these constructions couldn't return the revenue spent on the cost. However, John proved himself capable in other spheres of the economy. He used the gold and diamond revenues to reduce the overall state debt. He and his government weren't brilliant economic magnates, but 18th-century Portugal was an economically stable kingdom.

The Enlightenment and the Portuguese Public

Literacy in Portugal spread during the 18th century, especially in the urban areas. The rise of the upper bourgeoisie meant that the ability to read and write was no longer reserved for the clergy and nobility. However, it is considered that, aside from the clergy, people didn't use writing skills much, and they preferred reading.

Most printed material (around 60 percent) was religious. During the first half of the 18th century, Portugal had only one periodical, *Gazeta de Lisboa*, and it came out twice a week. Science material was the least published, and it amounted to only 4 percent of all yearly printed material. The disinterest in printed material is possibly best seen in the fact that less than one hundred books were printed per year compared to contemporary England, which published two thousand titles a year. However, many books in Portugal were imported from abroad, mainly Spain, France, and the Netherlands, but they catered only to the intellectuals who were able to read other languages.

Nevertheless, the consumption of reading material started increasing in the 18th century. Besides religious content, the population of Portugal was also interested in reading poetry, history, philosophy, and ethics. The Portuguese were not very interested in the curiosities of modern science, but some individuals strived to spread interest in scientific knowledge, such as Teodoro de Almeida. He was a Catholic priest and philosopher, as well as a leading figure of the Portuguese Enlightenment.

The Portuguese women were not yet emancipated, but literacy spread among them too. Some men considered the education of women as scandalous, even those who were usually progressive. One such man was Francisco Xavier de Oliveira (Portuguese writer), who spent many years in England. There, he received a humanist education, and he was interested in the power of reason. He claimed that educated women were no more entertaining than circuit horses. Some people promoted the education of women and claimed they were not intellectually inferior to men. Luís António Verney, a Portuguese 18th-century theologian and philosopher, claimed that educating women would benefit society, especially children that were in their care. Many nuns knew how to read, and some of them even wrote and published their own religious works.

Published material in Portugal had to undergo triple censorship. Everything planned for publishing had to be examined by the local bishop, the Inquisition, and the crown's censor. However, it is impossible to know if these legal censorship laws were practiced and to what extent. Imported books had to be submitted to the Inquisition for approval, and only then could the books be imported. Although the Holy Office kept the records of all banned heretical books, it seems it hadn't been updated since 1624. Nevertheless, it seems that the censorship worked, and it slowed down the import of progressive ideas to Portugal. Of course, an illegal network of book smuggling certainly existed, but it wasn't very widespread, and it catered only to the intellectuals.

This negative situation was also influenced by Portugal's outdated education system. The church had a monopoly on formal schooling, and the Jesuits dominated the system. Portugal had only two universities by the 18th century; there was one in Coimbra and one in Évora, and they both belonged to the Jesuits. Even in the 18th century, they were profoundly influenced by the ideas of the Counter-Reformation of the 16th and 17th centuries. The Jesuits controlled education, and they refused to change it, preferring the conservative doctrines. The main textbooks used during the reign of John V were *Doutrina Christian*, which was published in 1561, and Latin grammar, which was created in 1572. Other educational institutions broke the monopoly held by the Jesuits, but they were always short-lived and didn't offer a broad curriculum. They were known as Academia, and they were designed to educate the aristocratic youth, mainly in poetry and other forms of literature. The most prominent among them was Academia Real de Historia, but this was under the crown's control and had no relevance to the broader public.

Serious educational reforms occurred during King Joseph I's reign, led by the marquis of Pombal. Pombal started his career as a diplomat and had spent some time in England and Austria. On these travels, he realized how much Portugal's educational system lagged behind. He also developed a moderate interest in the Enlightenment, which focused on empiricism and experimental science. But after Pombal came to power, it took him almost a decade to start working on the educational reforms. In 1759, he took the first step by founding the School of Commerce, which taught young entrepreneurs such things as cost analysis, bookkeeping, different weights and their management, currencies and measurements of other countries, and other practical trade skills. Sons and grandsons of successful businessmen received priority admission to this school.

Establishing the School of Commerce was only the first step in setting the foundation for educational reform. But before more reforms could be made, Pombal first had to expel the Jesuits and break their monopoly on general education. He did this in 1759, but the consequences were painful. Most Portuguese students attended the two Jesuit colleges, and suddenly, they were deprived of their schooling. Pombal understood the seriousness of the situation, and he moved quickly. The same year, he established the Department of Education, which had the task of organizing a secular, state-controlled education system. They were to choose the curriculum, hire new teachers, and select and print the new textbooks. This new education system relied heavily on the teachings of Italian and Portuguese Enlightenment intellectuals, such as Antonio Genovesi and Luís António Verney.

More radical reforms came in 1771. A new literary tax was introduced, with the money being collected to support further reforms. The responsibility for the new education system was transferred from the directorate to the crown censorship board. This made it possible to hire new teachers, first for secondary education and later for primary. The first minister of education in Portugal was Friar Manuel do Cenáculo, who later became the bishop of Beja. He shared Pombal's interest in moderate

Enlightenment ideas and strived to eradicate the Jesuits' concept of education.

A new school was opened in 1766, which offered secondary education to the elite (meaning they were all sons of the great noble families). This royal college prepared these young minds for serving the crown. They were to be the next generation of diplomats, military engineers, or colonial and court administrators. Such schools already existed in western European countries and were already creating enlightened and intellectual men. Portugal lagged behind, but Pombal was determined to catch up. He employed teachers from abroad to teach rhetoric, mathematics, engineering, and science. In addition, the young nobles were given classes in riding, fencing, and dancing, as they had to keep up with the royal etiquettes of various European kingdoms. However, the noble Portuguese families displayed very little interest in such education, and the school survived in its original form for only six years. Because there were never enough students to justify its existence, the school was closed in 1772, but some of the professors and school equipment were transferred to the University of Coimbra, the only surviving university in Portugal (the one in Évora closed when the Jesuits were expelled).

Pombalism and the Earthquake of 1755

Sebastião José de Carvalho e Melo, later known only as Pombal, although he didn't become the marquis until later in his career, started as a diplomat to England (1739-1743) and an ambassador to Vienna (1745-1749). His travels and service abroad equipped him with the knowledge of world politics and the modern way of thinking. He learned how to maneuver governments and manage the national economy. But his experience abroad also made him aware of how backward Portugal was, as it was set in its conservative ways of the old royalty. He was determined to reform the country. He didn't have to wait long to get the opportunity to implement reforms. In 1750, King Joseph I appointed him secretary of state of foreign affairs and war. For the next twenty-five years, Pombal would come to dominate Portuguese politics and the economy. He left such a deep impression on his contemporaries and later historians that the whole period was named after him: Pombalism.

But Pombalism wasn't only a historical period; it was also the Portuguese reform movement that eventually modernized Portugal and brought the Enlightenment to the kingdom. The reforms had to be radical and swift so their opponents couldn't act against them. Pombalism also demanded that certain authorities of the elite, the church, and the crown had to be transferred to the government. In the sphere of the economy, Pombalism sought to increase the economic development of the colonies and to curb British dominance of overseas trade. Pombal didn't back down when he faced social, religious, or cultural resistance to his reforms. He simply neutralized them or completely removed them (e.g., the expulsion of the Jesuits).

Pombal wasn't alone in implementing the series of reforms. He had the help of many like-minded individuals, some of them members of his family, such as his brothers and his eldest son. He had the help of lawyers, among which José de Seabra da Silva stands out; churchmen, such as Cardinal João Cosme da Cunha; and many businessmen who saw the benefits in the Portuguese reforms. Pombalism, therefore, wasn't the effort of just one man, as it is often described in the history books, but rather an endeavor of a group of people and a collective phenomenon.

Pombal's administration displayed its efficiency and power immediately after the great earthquake of 1775, which destroyed Lisbon and was responsible for the death of thirty thousand to forty thousand people. The epicenter of the earthquake was in the Atlantic Ocean, some 290 kilometers southwest of Lisbon. If it was measured on the Richter scale, it would reach an 8.5 or even a 9. The earthquake was followed by two strong aftershocks and three tsunami waves, which reached the shores of Ireland and even the

West Indies. The waves caused the most destruction to the port of Lisbon, with 85 percent of the city being lost. Whatever buildings weren't destroyed by the earthquake and the aftershocks were taken away by the water. The parts of the city that were farther away from the shore burned in the fires that lasted for almost a week. This was caused by the many candles lit the previous day to celebrate All Saints' Day. Lisbon wasn't the only city that suffered destruction because of the earthquake. Many were affected, as the earthquake was also felt in Spain and Morocco.

King Joseph I and the royal family were not in the palace when the earthquake happened. They were in Belém, the western part of Lisbon, which was the city's outskirts. The impact there was less severe, and they all survived. The monarch was badly shaken by the events, and he quickly gathered the ministers to come up with a plan that would relieve the city from the disaster. Supposedly, Pombal advised the king to bury the dead and care for the living, but the same words were ascribed to the marquis of Alorna too. Pombal took command of the crisis, and he immediately started working on establishing order, disposing of the bodies so they wouldn't cause an outbreak of disease, and providing shelter and food for the survivors. To tackle the ensuing economic crisis that the earthquake caused, Pombal froze food prices at the pre-earthquake level, preventing famine.

Pombal saw the opportunity that the earthquake brought, and he started planning the rebuilding of Lisbon as a modern center of commerce. He employed military engineers to come up with safety and sanitary solutions for possible future natural disasters. Earthquake-resistant frames were at the core of each new house, and they were all provided with emergency cisterns. As for the city's design, Pombal chose to keep the old city center as the main square, but he renamed it the Square of Commerce. He also built four parallel streets, which extended from the main square at right angles away from the coast. These streets ended in two lesser squares, the *Rossio* and *Figueira*. The lesser streets crossed the four main ones, creating a grid. Along the sides of the main squares, Pombal built the residences for government departments and the commercial exchange. As you can probably tell, this was an exceptionally planned urban design.

The royal palace was not rebuilt during King Joseph I's life, as he didn't wish for it. After the earthquake, the king developed a fear of living within the walls, and the court was then placed on the hills of Ajuda. It consisted of a complex of canvas tents and wooden pavilions. After the death of Joseph, his daughter, Maria I of Portugal, ordered the rebuilding of the royal palace. This new palace still stands in the hills, where the old tent court used to be.

Chapter 12 – The Decline of the Empire

Maria I of Portugal
https://commons.wikimedia.org/wiki/File:Maria_I,_Queen_of_Portugal_-_Giuseppe_Troni,_atribu%C3%ADdo_(Turim,_1739-Lisboa,_1810)_-_Google_Cultural_Institute.jpg

Joseph I didn't have a son but four daughters. Because the king was very pious, all of his daughters were named Maria after the mother of Jesus. The succession was uncertain as a result. Pombal was especially good at eliminating his political enemies, and he needed a successor to the Portuguese throne who would accept him and his reforms. However, the new king would be whoever married Joseph's eldest daughter, Maria Francisca Isabel. When she turned sixteen, the court planned to marry her to her uncle, Prince Peter (Pedro). Pombal was against this idea because he was afraid Peter would create an alternative court where he would gather all of Pombal's enemies. Another proposal came from the king of Spain, Charles III, who wanted his son, Prince Charles, to marry Maria of Portugal. This was unacceptable to Pombal, who feared another unification of the Iberian Peninsula under one crown. He also realized that neither Maria nor Prince Peter was capable of leading the country, and he was sure they needed his expertise. In 1760, the couple was married with Pombal's acceptance.

The royal marriage between Princess Maria and Prince Peter proved to be fruitful, as they had six children. Their oldest son, Prince Joseph (José), displayed a high intelligence, and Pombal was determined to make a good ruler out of him. He placed him under the care and education of his friend, Friar Cenaculo Vilas Boas. When the prince turned sixteen, Pombal arranged his marriage to his aunt, Princess Maria Francisca Benedita, the youngest sister of his mother. Benedita was also very intelligent, and she was Pombal's favorite since she supported all of his policies. Pombal hoped that the young couple could somehow bypass the rule of succession and rule instead of Maria and Prince Peter. But Pombal failed to arrange this, and Maria Francisca Isabel was proclaimed Queen Maria I of Portugal in 1777 after her father's death. She was the first queen to rule Portugal, and although her uncle-husband was given the title Peter III, he couldn't rule in his own name.

The regime change meant the end of Pombal's government. Pombal's enemies, who had lain low up until that point, pressed the new queen for *Viradeira* (the turn of Pombal's policies). Pombal was replaced, as were all the ministers and royal officials loyal to him. But there was no reprisal for the atrocities his administration had committed. Pombal was allowed to quietly retire to his estate in the town of Pombal in northern Estremadura. Around eight hundred prisoners were released from their cells, among them Pombal's political enemies and the Jesuits. Those who were driven into exile by Pombal's government were allowed to come back, and noblewomen who had been forced into confinement in the nunneries because of their husband's political incorrectness were allowed freedom.

Pombal was put on trial in 1779 when he was over eighty years old. The goal of the trial was to investigate his conduct during the years of his service and to appease his enemies who demanded justice. Pombal personally defended himself, and the judges couldn't agree on how to sentence him. Queen Maria stepped in, and she declared Pombal deserved punishment, but she pardoned him due to his fragile age. Maria hoped that by recognizing Pombal's injustices, his many victims and enemies would be satisfied. Not long after, on May 8th, 1782, Pombal died of old age. The Jesuits hoped that their expulsion from Portugal would be revoked with the fall of Pombal's government, but even though Maria was willing, she could not grant them to return. The political tides had changed in Europe; even Rome suppressed the Jesuits in 1773. She couldn't allow herself to take in the religious order that was despised by everyone else.

The Enlightenment of Maria I

The most important concern of the new Marian government was the ideological subversion from outside influences and the deteriorating international military situation. In Europe, tensions were straining while the revolution raged in France. Portugal was a small power, and it had to navigate the broader political waters of the continent very carefully. Anglo-French hostilities grew during the late 18ᵗʰ century, and all of the European countries were forced to choose a side. Portugal tried to maintain its neutrality for as long as possible, but it needed to find a way to stay neutral and maintain its alliance with Britain, as the Portuguese seaborne trade and communications depended on it.

The reason for Portugal's need for neutrality was that in the early years of Maria's rule, the country repaired its relations with Spain and France. In 1785, permanent peace of the Iberian Peninsula was proclaimed after several treaties were signed that resolved the issue of some disputed territories. The peace with Spain was celebrated with the marriage of Prince John, who would later become King John VI of Portugal, to Carlota Joaquina of Spain. Maria's daughter Mariana was married to Spanish Prince Gabriel of Spain. Although Maria wished to remain neutral, she decided to recognize the independence of the British North American colonies six months before Britain did. This had a lasting influence on Brazil, which looked up to the United States and started acting against Lisbon's rule in 1789.

Portuguese society was always predominantly conservative, and the Enlightenment never spread outside of the small circle of intellectuals. Even the nobles of Portugal refused to be influenced by the new ideas, although there certainly were some exceptions. The exaggerated display of religiosity was common in late 18ᵗʰ-century Portugal, even though it was the clergy who tried to spread the enlightened ideas. The cults of various saints, pilgrimages, and religious processions were a part of daily life in Portugal. The queen was extremely pious, and she was the one setting the example for the whole society of her kingdom. Churches and religious monuments were always given priority, and the most famous construction in the Marian period was the Estrela Basilica, which was built between 1779 and 1790.

Many of the intellectuals and nobles who were forced to leave Portugal during Pombal's government now returned and brought Enlightenment ideas with them. One such individual was João Carlos de Braganza (1719-1806), a grandson of Peter II and a duke of Lafoes. He spent twenty years abroad, and he lived in England, where he joined the Royal Society. He also traveled to many countries, such as Sweden, Austria, the Middle East, France, Prussia, Switzerland, Greece, Egypt, Turkey, and Italy. He was an astound follower of the Enlightenment and critical thinking. When he returned to Portugal, he became a great patron of the arts and sciences, and he urged the government to establish a national institution that would promote scientific knowledge. Because of João's persistence, Queen Maria I finally opened the Royal Academy for Sciences in 1779. This academy remains active today, but it has a different name: the Lisbon Academy of Sciences.

The Enlightenment in Portugal always remained moderate, and the ruling class thought it was useful only to spread awareness of modern technologies. For this purpose, in 1779, the *Journal Eciclopedico* was founded, a periodical that published articles on technical innovations, economic issues, and world politics. Notions of the radical Enlightenment, such as human rights, liberty, and equality, never managed to spread in Portugal, though a small minority that dared to play with such ideas existed. However, they were strongly ostracized by the wider society, which regarded these ideas as scandalous.

Prince Regent John

Maria I is celebrated as one of the strongest female figures in Portugal's history, and rightly so. Even though she was not prepared for the rule, she proved very capable, maintaining a stable government throughout her reign. She was intelligent and clever, although she was a very anxious woman. In 1786, her husband, Peter III, died, and the queen entered a state of depression. She started displaying the first signs of madness, and on a few occasions, she had to be confined in her apartments due to a state of delirium. Her mental health only worsened, and three years later, her eldest son and heir apparent, Prince Joseph, died of smallpox. Queen Maria suffered a complete mental breakdown, and eventually, she was proclaimed unfit to rule by the royal doctors. Her second son, Prince John, had to assume the role of prince regent and rule in his mother's name.

For the next seven years, the prince maintained the political scene of Portugal. He assumed all the powers of a king, but he had to wait until his mother's death to actually assume the title. John's main preoccupation as prince regent was the international situation, especially in France, where, in 1792, the monarchy was formally abolished. A republic was put in its place. The news of the execution of King Louis XVI of France reached Lisbon in 1793 and greatly shook the aristocracy. But John knew he had to maintain good relations with France, despite the ideological differences between the two countries. He had to accept the new ambassador of the republic. However, pressed by the nobility, which supported the French monarchy, the Portuguese government made the first hostile move and denied the new ambassador access to the office. Matters escalated further when Portugal agreed to participate in the invasion of France and joined the alliance with Britain and Spain.

Portugal took up arms against France because it was pressured by Britain and Spain. The circumstances were such that almost all the European monarchs had to stand together and defend their right to lead their government. Otherwise, they might face a similar fate as Louis XVI. The Portuguese Army joined the Spanish forces, and together, they invaded France from the south, taking over the historic province of Roussillon. The army of the French Republic wasn't tested yet, and the Luso-Spanish alliance was initially successful in taking over the territory. But once they faced the fully organized and prepared French Army, they realized they were no match for it. The French defeated the Luso-Spanish army and proceeded to negotiate peace with Spain so they could detach it from Britain. This would leave France with only one enemy to deal with. The peace was signed in June of 1795, but Portugal wasn't part of it. In fact, this was a political disaster for Portugal, as it suddenly had to deal with its two allies that were now on different sides of the conflict. The next year, Spain entered the war against Britain, leaving Portugal isolated and exposed to its enemies.

Portugal had to prepare for the defense. The country was commercially and strategically important to the British, but the French and the Spanish also had political interests in it. France and Portugal entered peace negotiations, and the Lisbon government hoped it could maintain its neutrality until the conflict between France and Britain ended. Spain acted as a liaison during these negotiations, but in reality, it worked to help France reach its goal. The French demands proved too harsh for Portugal. Prince John couldn't agree with breaking the commercial ties with Britain. He needed to keep Portugal's old ally close, so cutting Britain's access to Portugal's ports was not an option. In 1799, France lost patience and started pressing Spain to allow the passage of French troops so they could invade Portugal. French leader Napoleon Bonaparte took the initiative in 1801 and sent an ultimatum to Lisbon, demanding that Portugal cut off all its ties with Britain, close its ports to British ships, and allow the Spanish Army to occupy a quarter of its territory. He gave the Lisbon government two weeks to comply.

When Portugal failed to fulfill the French demands, a short war ensued between the Portuguese and Spanish armies known as the War of the Oranges (May 20th-June 9th, 1801). Several Portuguese border towns ended up being occupied by Spain. The peace treaty, which was signed on September 29th, 1801, pressed Prince John to proclaim France as a most favored nation, to close the ports to British ships, pay a war indemnity to France, and cede some territory in Guiana to the French. In return, Portugal's neutral status was recognized, and the occupied border towns were released. Since the British failed to help Portugal in its struggle against Spain, Prince John had no choice but to accept these terms, especially because he was aware that his army was no match for the French. Early in 1802, the Anglo-French peace was signed, and Portugal didn't have to proceed with closing its ports to the British ships.

In 1802, the British and French in Lisbon challenged each other, and the animosity between the two countries continued to grow. Back in 1797, the British had brought several thousand royalist emigrants to Portugal and formed a military force there. The French found this very upsetting. The French demanded Prince John to dismiss his pro-British ministers, and when he refused to do so, Bonaparte demanded another treaty between Lisbon and Paris. He only did this, though, because the war between France and Britain was about to resume. The terms of this new treaty were the same as the one from 1801, but France also demanded Portugal pay subsidies of sixteen million francs. Britain warned that any such payment would be seen as aiding the enemy. Once again, Portugal found itself sandwiched between two of the greatest European powers.

Pressured by French diplomatic efforts, John finally dismissed his pro-British ministers and decided to alienate London rather than Paris. In their place, he employed all pro-French ministers, and with their approval, he ratified the new Franco-Portuguese treaty in 1804. But the prince had to placate the British, as he feared their response. To do so, the French ambassador Jean Lannes was dismissed. The new treaty resulted in an immediate surge of trade between Portugal and France. By the end of the year, the French imports of Brazilian cotton proved larger than the British ever were. The balance of trade with France favored Portugal, and the economic benefits were almost immediately felt. However, Portugal had to manage its now very difficult relations with Britain because Britain remained the dominant power on the seas.

The Invasion of Portugal and the Peninsular War

Prince John fulfilled all of the French demands, and he effectively closed the Portuguese ports to British ships. But he refused to arrest the British citizens living in Lisbon. This alone wasn't the only reason Napoleon decided to invade Portugal. He had planned it for a long time, as he wanted to dethrone the Braganza dynasty and form a puppet government that would answer directly to him. However, Napoleon needed a pretext for the invasion, so he sent another ultimatum to Portugal, giving Prince John's government a month to declare war on Britain, arrest all the British citizens in Portugal, and confiscate their possessions. It took John several months to make his decision, and he finally started arresting British citizens on November 5th, 1807. Great Britain responded by sending its navy, which was under the command of Admiral Sir William Sidney Smith, to block the Tagus River.

But even though Prince John agreed to all of the French terms, in October of 1807, Spain and France signed a secret treaty by which they were to occupy Portugal and split it into three administrative principalities. The central province would be under permanent military occupation until the conclusion of the European war. The southern province would become the personal fiefdom of Manuel Godoy, the Spanish secretary of state. The northern province would be given to the Spanish rulers of Etruria (Italy) as compensation for Napoleon's annexation of Etruria. The plans about Portugal's division are a clear sign that Napoleon didn't decide to invade the kingdom just because John didn't respond to his ultimatum immediately.

However, the Portuguese Braganza dynasty wouldn't give up so easily. Much earlier, in around 1801, they had planned to move the government to Brazil and defend mainland Portugal from there. Brazil was a far larger territory and much richer with resources than Portugal was. Prince John even played with the idea of permanently moving the government to Brazil. This would have made him the first emperor in the New World of equal status and power as other European rulers. The British agreed with the Portuguese plan and even urged it as early as 1803, offering their naval escort. But moving the government would be an immense upheaval, as not only the royal family but also all the ministers, their families and possessions, the whole court, and a large portion of the nobility would have to be transferred overseas. Another reason John didn't proceed with this idea was that the Brazilian trade magnates resisted the transatlantic shift of power since it would compromise their business.

The reality of the French invasion finally put the government's move into motion, and the planning began. On November 23rd, 1807, Napoleon proclaimed the Braganzas dethroned, and the Spanish Army moved into Portugal. Unfortunately, the Portuguese military leaders considered that an attack from the British was more likely than an invasion from France, so they had concentrated their army along the Portuguese coast, leaving the continental path into the kingdom open. On November 24th, Prince John ordered the transport of the whole court and government to Brazil. Thirty-six ships of the Portuguese naval force were loaded with personal possessions of ministers, their families, and the royal treasury. More than 115,000 individuals, including the royal family and the mad queen Maria I, started evacuating. They sailed on November 27th, 1807.

To this day, scholars can't agree if the evacuation of the Portuguese government was a brilliant plan to resolve the issue between Portugal and France or if it was an act of abandoning the Portuguese people who were left behind. But in reality, even if Prince John had stayed, he had no chance of fighting the French. He would likely end up executed. The flight to Rio de Janeiro (the capital of Brazil) bought him time and gave him space to coordinate the resistance to French dominance from afar. If nothing else, by sailing away, John disrupted Napoleon's efforts to effectively dethrone the Braganzas, as they remained the de facto rulers of Portugal. Nevertheless, their departure left Lisbon and all of Portugal undefended. It was left to be overtaken and partitioned by the French and the Spanish. It seemed as if Napoleon had scored a victory.

Britain observed these events as a success in its favor because the fleeing court of Prince John and the future of the Portuguese colonies now depended on British ships. The regent prince signed yet another trade agreement by which he opened the Brazilian trade fully to the British. In return, Britain promised it would never try to annex Brazil. Meanwhile, Napoleon reorganized the government of Portugal. Because the British continued to block the Tagus, he decided not to partition it with Spain. Instead, he gave the rule of Portugal to his military commander, Jean-Andoche Junot, who had served as an ambassador to Portugal back in 1805. Under his government, Portugal was put under martial law, despite the obvious support the people gave to the French. Junot also considered himself to be quite safe in Lisbon until a small group of Portuguese insurgents, aided by a British expeditionary force, stationed themselves just north of Lisbon.

Three years of constant warfare between the British and the French troops followed. Their main prize was the control over the port of Lisbon, which was strategically the best port in the world, as it was capable of receiving a significant number of ships sailing from the Americas. But on a larger scale, the war took place on the whole of the Iberian Peninsula; thus, it is known as the Peninsular War (1807–1814). In Portugal, the British took control of Lisbon in 1808 and expelled Junot and his government. Instead of waiting for the French to respond, the British proceeded into Spain but were halted there due to the heavy snow. In 1809, the British drove the French out of Porto (Portugal's second-largest city), but the French quickly reorganized and took over all of northern Portugal along with Porto. The next year, they were able to push the British farther south and march on Lisbon, but they were not able to take it.

During the next several years, there were many smaller battles across Portugal, with Britain usually taking the victory. The French never concentrated their main military power in the Iberian Peninsula because Napoleon was busy fighting on the Russian front. Nevertheless, the French put up a good fight and gave the British a hard time. In 1813, French military control of Europe came to an end, and Napoleon had to abandon some of his plans for the Iberian Peninsula. As the French retreated from Spain, the British advanced and took over Madrid in 1814. They even invaded the south of France, winning some major victories there.

In the meantime, it became obvious that Prince Regent John had no intention of returning to Portugal. Indeed, he issued a decree by which Brazil became a kingdom in its own right, one that was largely independent of Portugal. While in Brazil, John realized that the kingdom's wealth lay there and not in Portugal. He was also afraid that if he left, Brazil would somehow be lost to the Braganza dynasty and gain independence just as the United States and the Spanish American colonies had. On December 16th, 1815, he proclaimed the United Kingdom of Portugal, Brazil, and the Algarves, a crown institution that was recognized by the other European powers. The next year, Queen Maria I died, and Prince John finally became a king, ruling as John VI.

The End of the Empire

John VI was pressured to return to Lisbon by the people who stayed behind. After the end of the Peninsular War, they called for his return. He left Brazil on April 25th, 1821, leaving his son Peter as its regent. But by the time he arrived in Lisbon, the political events had led to the drawing of the first Portuguese constitution, to which the king had to swear loyalty. The constitution restricted the crown in many ways, and when John's wife, Dona Carlota, refused to follow her husband's example and agree to the constitution, she was deposed. In 1822, John VI lost control of Brazil. His son Peter led a revolt there and fought for independence from Portugal. Peter proclaimed himself emperor of Brazil. Although the revolt occurred, Portugal refused to recognize Brazil's independence for a long time. Evidence suggests that these events were staged and that Peter and his father worked together so that both Portugal and Brazil would remain in the hands of the Braganzas.

The early 19ᵗʰ century was when the revolts around Europe ended, but for Portugal, they were just beginning. The society of Portugal was divided, and two main groups formed: those who supported the constitution and liberalism and those who wanted the old monarchic regime back. The leaders of the second group were the deposed Queen Carlota and her family. They used Dom Miguel, the second son of King John VI, as an alternative to his father. They started a revolt in May 1823 in Vila Franca de Xira. They intended to restore the absolute powers of the crown. This revolt is known as the Vilafrancada, and John fully supported it. The success of this revolt was quick, and the first Portuguese constitution was abolished after only several months of its existence.

Another revolt led by Prince Miguel started on April 29ᵗʰ, 1824. The alleged reason for this revolt was the death threats the Freemasons made against the king. However, there were no death threats, and Miguel used this excuse to overthrow his father from the throne. He secured King John behind the walls of the Bemposta Palace and tried to persuade him to abdicate. The king refused and sought refuge with the British navy stationed in the port of Lisbon. The ship *Windsor Castle* acted as neutral ground. From there, John ordered his son to abandon his command of the Portuguese Army. He exiled Miguel, and the people of Lisbon celebrated the victory of the legitimate government. On June 5ᵗʰ, John returned the constitution. He also recognized Brazil's independence, mainly because the Portuguese economy was suffering due to the loss of this overseas territory. By recognizing Brazil, the two states could develop trading deals, and Peter I of Brazil continued to be the heir presumptive of Portugal and Algarve.

On March 10th, 1826, King John VI died. He was succeeded by his son, who became Peter IV. However, the same year, Peter abdicated, and his daughter, Maria II, who was only seven years old, became the queen of Portugal but under the condition that she married her uncle Miguel, who would have to accept the liberal constitution. In Brazil, he had problems with the liberals and the very conservative nobility. Although Peter was liberal himself (he abolished slavery and formed the government based on a constitutional parliament), it seemed he could never do enough to satisfy both the liberals and conservatives. He often played with the idea of abdicating. In 1831, another conflict exploded between the liberals and conservatives, and Peter acted by firing the liberal cabinet and formally abdicating on April 7th. He returned to Europe and assumed the title of duke of Braganza.

Miguel accepted Peter's proposal to marry Maria II, or so he pretended. When he came to Lisbon from his exile on June 23rd, 1828, he overthrew Maria II and usurped the throne. He didn't want to accept the Portuguese constitution. He didn't abolish it, but he avoided recognizing it. But such a violent change of the regime wasn't accepted by the liberals in Portugal, and they rebelled. This rebellion soon exploded into a civil war known as the Liberal Wars (1828-1834). Maria's father, the former King Peter IV, managed to persuade the United Kingdom and France to help his daughter retrieve the throne. Although they were reluctant at first, once their trade deals with Portugal were challenged by Miguel's reign, they joined Peter's efforts. The decisive battle occurred on May 16th, 1834, and Miguel was defeated. He was pressured to renounce all his claims to the Portuguese throne, and he was exiled to Germany. Maria II of Portugal became queen again.

Maria died in 1853 while giving birth to her eleventh child. She was only thirty-four years old. She was succeeded by her eldest son,

Peter (Pedro) V (r. 1853-1861). He is known for modernizing Portugal. Under his rule, many railroads, telecommunication lines, and roads were built. Unfortunately, Peter died young, doing so in 1861. He succumbed to typhoid fever. His younger brother, Luís I, became the next Portuguese king, but he was unprepared to rule. He proved to be an indecisive king. Two more kings ruled Portugal. During the reign of Manuel II (r. 1908-1910), a revolution happened. This time, the monarchy was finally abolished. The Portuguese Republican Party, which organized the coup, accused the regime of being incapable of adapting to modern times. The revolution was swift; it lasted for only two days (October 3rd and 4th). A republic was proclaimed, with a provisional government deciding the future of Portugal.

Chapter 13 – Portugal in the Modern World

The modern flag of Portugal dates to the period of the First Republic (1910–1926)
https://commons.wikimedia.org/wiki/File:Flag_of_Portugal.svg

During the early 20th century, the rest of Europe thought of Portugal as an incompetent and backward country. One of the reasons for this was the propaganda instigated by the British and Germans who wanted to take over Portuguese colonies. But the truth is that, at the time, Portugal was a very unstable country, with around 70 percent of its population being illiterate. The majority of the Portuguese were agricultural workers, yet the country constantly failed to feed its people. The Republicans, who overthrew the monarchy in 1910, wanted to build the country by educating its people. But although they influenced the urban centers, they were ineffective in asserting themselves in the countryside. They wanted a secular republic, but the majority of Portugal's population were villagers. They were sentimental to Catholicism and the monarchy. Because of this divide between the countryside and the cities, the First Portuguese Republic often changed its government, with none of them lasting more than several months.

The Republican leaders thought they would create a sense of national unity and patriotic enthusiasm in Portugal by entering the First World War on the side of the Allies, but Britain straightforwardly rejected an alliance with Portugal. Nevertheless, Portugal entered the war. However, fighting against Germany in France and Africa cost it enormous amounts of money. The First World War ended in 1918, with Portugal's army humiliated and the republic in great debt. The domestic economy further deteriorated when the overly centralized government decided to grant its colonies a degree of autonomy. Angola was the first to drag Portugal down. Other colonies soon followed. The economic failure of the republic and the increasing corruption among its politicians led to a military coup in 1926 and the start of a military dictatorship.

The military government, headed by General Óscar Carmona (1869-1951), started a series of policies, mainly regarding the colonies, in an attempt to revitalize the national economy. But the social unrest continued, as the people of Portugal remained divided between the liberals and those who wished for the monarchy to return. The economic situation proved to be so bad that, eventually, the military government admitted they could not repair it. They surrendered their power to the minister of finance, António de Oliveira Salazar. In 1932, Salazar became the prime minister, and he held this position until 1968 when he suffered a stroke.

Salazarism

When Salazar came to power, he proved to be a conservative and nationalist ruler, but unlike other European conservatives of the period, he detested Nazism and fascism. Salazar also hated Mussolini's and Hitler's populistic rhetoric, and he rarely showed himself in public. He also rarely spoke on the radio. Some suggested Salazar didn't like publicity because of the fear of lurking enemies, although he once explained he preferred solidarity so he could devote himself to thinking. He did create a cult of personality, but unlike others, he didn't pursue the creation of national unity by persecuting Portugal's minorities. The Catholic majority of the population saw a mix of an intellectual, high church dignitary, and an ascetic in Salazar, and they worshiped him. As such, Salazar was the founder of the Estado Novo ("New State"), his unique authoritarian regime that was headed by the intellectuals. All of his close associates were university professors.

Salazar's rule was marked by economic nationalism, but he and his propaganda continuously refused to admit the shortcomings of the government. However, he excelled in reconciling the monarchists and the Catholics with the Republicans, army, and corporations. Once united, all of these groups acted as Salazar's supporters. Since he was an economist, Salazar was the most worried about the economy of Portugal, and he was very much conscious of Portugal's reputation in the world as a weak country, one completely dependent on foreign capitalism. Salazar's main goal was to make Portugal less dependent on foreign economies and diplomacy, and he claimed he could do so only by concentrating the power in the hands of just one man. Thus, in 1939, he assumed the offices of foreign affairs, the army, and finance while continuing to be the prime minister. He became a dictator. He held the ultimate power, as he controlled all the ministries.

Salazar intended to return the Portuguese colonies to a centralized government, which would then help make Portugal economically self-sufficient. Portugal and its overseas possessions would be less dependent on imports and would turn to exports, which would bring them enough money to start developing the economy. But to achieve this, Salazar had to put restrictions on foreign investments and bring the colonies under the direct control of Lisbon. Although new foreign investments were heavily restricted, Portugal continued to safeguard the interest of its major colonial partners. Because the foreign companies were removed from the colonies, the government started importing all its overseas production to Portugal and guaranteed stable prices for it. Products, such as sugar, tobacco, cotton, maize, rice, tea, and coffee, were exported directly from Portugal's mainland.

During the Spanish Civil War and World War II, Salazar was very careful in the realm of foreign policy and opted for complete neutrality. Nevertheless, Portugal's neutrality was conceived as a means of aiding the winning side at the end of the war, whichever it may have been, so they could collect gratitude and praise later. At the end of the Second World War, the Portuguese allowed the Americans and British to use their overseas territories as bases against the Germans. When Portugal adopted the pretense of democracy in 1949, it was allowed to join NATO (the North Atlantic Treaty Organization) and collect the benefits this world organization offered. Salazar's neutrality toward foreign affairs, his policies, and his dictatorship never really clashed with Europe's major powers, so he was left in peace. But in 1958, things changed when the Cold War demanded everyone to choose a side. Portugal was to be no exception, and soon, it would hit the headlines of major European periodicals.

The first signs of trouble for Salazar's government appeared during the early 1950s when Portuguese territories in India were swarmed by insurgents who demanded independence. Some Portuguese military leaders showed sympathy for the indigenous people of their colonies and denounced the colonial regime. But the population generally didn't care, and all the defectors were either arrested or forced into exile. The faux democracy of Portugal meant that the regime groomed not only their presidential candidate but also the opposition. It was a custom that the opposing candidate would resign a day before the polls, allegedly in protest, and that Salazar's candidate would win practically unchallenged. But in 1958, a charismatic opponent appeared, one who was independent of Salazarism: General Humberto Delgado. Although he didn't have a political plan for Portugal, Delgado managed to persuade the public that Salazar's regime was to be detested. Delgado failed to win the election, and he was exiled and eventually killed by the Portuguese secret police. But it didn't matter; he had sown the seeds of discontent, and the rest would be done in time.

Portugal joined the United Nations in 1955, and when the UN mounted a Special Committee on Decolonization in 1960, Salazar opposed it. Although other countries, such as Britain, France, and Belgium, agreed to abandon their colonies, Portugal refused to do so. Because of this, the world started paying attention to Portugal even more. The decolonization idealists started accusing Portugal of various atrocities committed against the indigenous people of their overseas possessions but also the Protestant missionaries in Africa. Everyone became aware of Portugal's exploitation of the people in their colonies, as well as their brutal treatment. In 1961, Portugal lost its Indian possessions. Goa, Diu, and Daman surrendered without a struggle, and Portugal found itself without the support of foreign forces. Nobody would come and help the Portuguese retrieve their overseas colonies. This was another blow to Salazar's government, especially because other colonies started mounting guerilla wars against Portuguese rule. These wars would continue until 1972.

The Portuguese Revolution

Salazar died in 1969, one year after suffering the stroke that left him incapacitated. He was replaced by Marcello Caetano, a lawyer who started his political and academic career under Salazar's regime. Caetano lacked Salazar's authority, and his government balanced the politics of Portugal for the next five years but made no significant changes. In 1973, a group of young army officers created a secret organization, *Movimento das Forças Armadas* (MFA; the "Armed Forces Movement"), and intended to organize a coup. It was already clear that the regime had lost the people's support, especially the army, and Caetano demanded the officers swear an oath of loyalty. Several of the high-ranking officers refused to do so, and they resigned.

The coup was organized on April 25th, 1974, and the military entered Lisbon without any resistance. When they approached Caetano and the Portuguese president at the time, Américo Tomás, the two resigned. A transitional government was quickly formed under the leadership of António de Spínola, one of the military officers who refused to swear the loyalty oath. The coup was peaceful and produced no casualties. Since it had been carefully planned, the coup took the world by surprise. Many foreign ambassadors ignored the first warning signs, and even when the ministers received the warning, they ignored them. Only one press photographer happened to be present in Lisbon during the coup, and he took photographs of the key moments, which he later distributed to various world press agencies.

The people of Portugal supported the revolution but not because the opposition had a clear plan for the future. Rather, they wished for the downfall of Caetano and the Salazar regime. The people who supported the coup were diverse, ranging from Catholic traditionalists to Social Democrats to even communists and anarchists. All these factions were united by their hatred of the regime; thus, they didn't have a common goal for Portugal's future. Even the MFA manifesto that started the coup only mentioned that changes needed to be done but offered no solution to Portugal's political and economic problems. However, the new government did issue an order to cease the fighting in Portugal's African colonies, and all their soldiers retreated to their barracks, waiting to be repatriated. But nobody knew how to solve the issue of the colonies, as Portugal proved it was not ready to simply let them go.

Aside from the problem with the colonies, the MFA government had to resolve the issue of creating a new stable order for mainland Portugal. But these two issues soon proved to be inseparable. The only man with any sense of direction in which Portugal should be pushed was the acting president, General Spínola. He came up with a two-year interim period program in which a democratic institution would be built. Then he would organize a referendum that would decide the type of Portugal's future constitution. However, for this plan to work, General Spínola needed political stability in the country, which Portugal simply didn't have at the time. The left-wing politicians distrusted Spínola, and they believed he tried to deprive the colonies of their chance to gain independence. They undermined everything Spínola tried to achieve. This led the nationalist leaders in the colonies to refuse the peace offered by the Portuguese government and instead demand immediate independence.

The leftist politicians formed a coalition that forced General Spínola to resign in September 1974. General Francisco da Costa Gomes was elected as the new president, and Vasco Gonçalves became his prime minister. The government and the MFA didn't change, but they were now under the control of the leftist coalition. The leftists were afraid of a right-wing organized coup, so they rushed the negotiations with the colonies. The deal was finally reached in January 1975, and all African possessions finally became independent. With the issue of the colonies resolved, Portugal could finally turn to its internal problems.

Conclusion

After the events of 1974 and the Portuguese retreat from Africa, the Portuguese government wanted its country to assume the role of a small, not overly ambitious state. By the 1980s, the Portuguese people came to terms with their imperial past, and they started celebrating their history and the overseas discoveries their ancestors had made. In 1996, Portugal and Brazil worked together to create an international cultural and linguistic organization that promoted their countries. In 1998, they celebrated the five-hundredth anniversary of the famous voyage of Vasco de Gama and the discovery of India. With the acceptance of its past and the clear sight of the future, Portugal became a well-respected state.

But all this happened because the constitution of 1976 finally brought Portugal its first truly democratic government, which, in turn, brought stability. However, the constitution also had a clause that enabled a military council that would secure democracy. This clause was finally removed in 1980. By that time, democracy was viewed as the proper direction, and the political parties regularly rotated in power. In 1986, Portugal became a full member of the European Community (EC), which was transformed into the

European Union in 1993. Portugal became a European country with a European destiny, and it was the people who chose this path for their country.

By joining the EC, Portugal started benefiting from additional funding, which was used to finance infrastructure projects. New jobs were opened, and the economy of Portugal started growing. The nation grew, especially because many people who had resided in one of the Portuguese colonies returned home. Even some Africans chose Portugal as their home after their countries gained independence. They quickly integrated into society, making up at least 10 percent of the country. The modernization of Portugal and its growing economy started attracting immigrants, particularly from eastern Europe. Portugal was no longer a state from which people wanted to escape and seek their fortune elsewhere. It became a state that welcomed people from around the world, people who needed political, economic, and social stability.

Part 2: The Portuguese Empire

A Captivating Guide to the History of Portugal as a Colonial Power and Its Colonies in Asia, North and South America, and Oceania

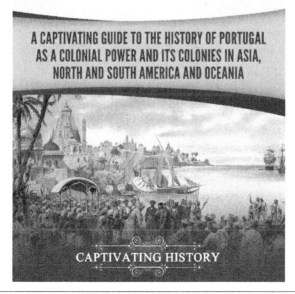

Introduction: Pre-Imperial Portugal in Brief

The Portuguese are known for their feats of exploration during the so-called "Age of Discovery." The Iberian Peninsula, which is divided between Spain and Portugal, became the launching pad for European exploration.

But before we make any attempt to understand the nature of the Portuguese Empire, it would be wise to become a little better acquainted with Portugal itself. It's important to understand the founding of the Portuguese nation and what led to its sudden rise as a maritime empire. It is also important to note that, as is the case with many other regions around the world, the Portuguese people long predate the actual Portuguese state.

The first people groups of Portugal settled the land thousands of years ago. These proto-Portuguese farmed, raised animals, and left behind elaborate burial sites for their dead. When the Romans came on the scene, they called the place "Portus Cale." The land of modern-day Portugal, along with the rest of the Iberian Peninsula, was made part of the Roman Republic and, ultimately, the Roman

Empire.

As a result, the local residents of what was then Portugal became thoroughly Romanized themselves. They adopted the Latin script for their language and Roman customs for their daily routines. They also developed Roman legal systems and forms of governance that would last, in some sense, long after the Roman Empire itself was torn down. During the Roman period, Portugal also developed many of its natural resources. Marble was regularly excavated, and gold, copper, and iron were in high demand.

The Roman period in Portugal came to an end roughly around the same time that the rest of the Western Roman Empire steadily fell apart at the seams, from 395 to 476 CE. It was during this span of time that Germanic tribes began to descend upon the western Romans.

The Germans came, and they conquered. But in many ways, they adopted the same Roman systems of those they had conquered. The Germanic interlopers even tried to imitate the Roman forms of monetary exchange, minting coins just like the Romans did. But perhaps most important for the future of Portugal, the Germans adopted Roman Christianity, and they enforced it during their rule.

These Christian foundations proved to be rather sturdy, and they were tested when the Iberian Peninsula was overrun by Islamic forces around 700 CE. Islamic powers would control Portugal and much of Spain for the next few centuries, but nevertheless, Christianity would remain strong even under Muslim rule. The Muslim armies first began clashing with the Germanic rulers of the Iberian Peninsula—the Visigoths—in 710.

These Muslim armies, which were based out of North Africa, were able to easily cross the narrow channel that separates the tip of Spain from the African continent. Once the armies arrived, the Germanic defenders, which at that time consisted primarily of

Visigoths, found themselves hopelessly outnumbered and outmatched. And in 711, the last Germanic ruler of Iberia—King Roderic—was defeated and killed.

Although they arrived as conquerors, the subsequent Islamic governance of Spain and Portugal is said to have been generally tolerant. The Muslim overlords of Spain proved to be fairly benevolent and accepting of those under their dominion. They did indeed build mosques and encouraged conversion to Islam, but they did not interfere with the Christianity that was already in place. They were also tolerant of Jewish residents, allowing them to practice and live life as they pleased.

The Islamic governance of Portugal also brought an advanced culture and technological innovations—some of it borrowed from the Greeks—that western Europe was still not aware of. Their expertise in shipbuilding, compasses, and astrolabes, in particular, would become of immense importance during the later rise of the Portuguese Empire. The Portuguese borrowed these ideas from the Muslims, and it would eventually make them the masters of the high seas.

Nevertheless, the Muslims who had brought such knowledge were themselves driven out at the start of the so-called "Reconquista" of the Iberian Peninsula. Just like the Crusades, which sought to bring the conquered Holy Land back into Christian hands, the Christians of Europe sought to recapture or re-conquer the Iberian Peninsula as well. Although the crusading Christians would have a toehold in the Holy Land for a while (from 1098 to 1291), their efforts would ultimately prove much more successful and longer lasting in Portugal and Spain.

After all, in the centuries since the Reconquista, Portugal and Spain (at least as of this writing) have not been retaken as part of an Islamic caliphate. And Portugal was ripped from Muslim hands as early as 868 when a large portion of the region that today constitutes modern-day Portugal was taken by the Christians. It was named simply the "County of Portugal."

The commander who led the successful taking of this land was Vimara Peres, who would subsequently be handed leadership of the territory. The County of Portugal continued to gain strength, and by the late 900s, the leadership was in the habit of referring to themselves as the "Grand Duke of Portugal." However, the County of Portugal faced an unforeseen threat when Vikings from the far north dropped down on the unsuspecting Portuguese in 968.

After surviving this assault, the County of Portugal became more closely connected with the Kingdom of León. The Kingdom of León had been founded as an autonomous Christian kingdom carved out of a northwestern chunk of the Iberian Peninsula in 910. In time, the County of Portugal would eventually become entirely independent, transforming into the Kingdom of Portugal in 1139.

This independence was confirmed by none other than the pope. In 1179, Pope Alexander III issued an official papal bull called *Manifestis Probatum*, in which Portugal's autonomous nature was officially recognized. The pope established that Afonso Henriques (r. 1139–1185) was the first official king of Portugal. The Portuguese Empire would ultimately be built upon the foundations of this kingdom.

An overall look at how large the Portuguese Empire was. The lines in the ocean show the Portuguese spice trade routes to Asia. The larger squares show their major factories.

Chapter 1 – Portugal Discovers the World

"I am not the man I once was. I do not want to go back in time; to be the second son—the second man."

-Vasco da Gama

If you have ever heard it said that a particular nation has discovered something, such phrases are usually a bit of a misnomer. Most of the time, those discoveries had already been discovered by someone else. For example, for a long time, people said that Christopher Columbus "discovered" America. The Americas, however, had already been discovered by the Vikings, and they had long been inhabited by various Native tribes.

In consideration of such things, it makes the claim of this discovery seem rather narrow-minded. Christopher Columbus and his men may have discovered something they themselves (as well as most of the known world) did not know existed, but that does not mean that others were not already well aware of it. In much the same way, the so-called "Age of Discovery," of which Portugal was a part, must be looked at with this same lens.

The Portuguese, who had long been locked in dynastic struggles, finally stabilized their society enough to leave their home base and discover the world. Not so much for others but for themselves. The earliest of these Portuguese expeditions seems to have kicked off around 1415 CE. During this fateful year, the Portuguese executed their conquest of Ceuta.

Ceuta was an important city and an outpost situated in an Islamic caliphate located in modern-day Morocco. Ceuta was actually the launching-off point for much of the original Islamic conquest of the Iberian Peninsula back in the 700s. Just a short distance from Spain, the city of Ceuta had long been an Islamic stronghold. The fact that the Portuguese were able to go on the offensive against the very city that had staged the conquest of the Iberian Peninsula centuries before was of symbolic as well as strategic importance.

Ceuta was strategically important because it resided on the other side of the famed Straits of Gibraltar, allowing better control over the commerce that traversed through this narrow channel of water. The conquest of Ceuta was led by none other than King John of Portugal (r. 1385–1433). King John led a strike force, which landed off the coast of Playa San Amara and managed to catch Ceuta's defenders completely off-guard. King John's invasion force consisted of some forty-five thousand troops, and they were backed up by some two hundred naval craft, which parked just offshore. This was a bit overkill, but it is a clear indication that King John was not willing to take any chances.

At any rate, the town was quickly subdued, and it fell into the hands of the Portuguese forces by the following morning. Although the taking of Ceuta may seem minor at first glance, it marks the beginning of Portuguese imperial expansion. The Christian kingdoms of Portugal and Spain had been on the defensive against Muslim encroachment for centuries. But now, with the Reconquista of the Iberian Peninsula just about complete, the Portuguese were actually going on the offensive by directly taking over territory in

North Africa, which had long been dominated by Muslim powers.

Building on these gains, in 1419, the Portuguese made their first inroads in Macaronesia—an island chain located just to the northwest of the African continent. Around the year 1419, they had subdued Madeira, an island that they would eventually make rich in sugarcane. The Portuguese then reached into the Azores by 1427, thereby ensuring their foothold in Macaronesia. Initially, the main thrust of this Portuguese expansion was to dominate the sea routes and enhance trade, although colonization for the sake of settlements would come in time.

The real goal of the Portuguese during this period was the circumnavigation of the African continent. Such a feat would allow them to bypass the traditional land routes to East Asia. After the fall of the Byzantine Empire in 1453 to the Ottoman Empire and the subsequent Muslim domination of the former land routes that ran through it, the search for a sea route to the east became all the more imperative. So, the Portuguese continued to advance down the coasts of Africa. In 1456, Portugal obtained yet another coastal acquisition when they seized Cape Verde.

They continued to progress southwest down the African coastline. By the 1460s, the Portuguese had moved into the Gulf of Guinea, which is located right along the equator, roughly at the mid-section of the African continent. The Portuguese set up shop on islands in the gulf, such as São Tomé and Príncipe. Here, they found traces of gold and other minerals.

However, the Portuguese were not the only ones vying for a spot in the Gulf of Guinea. The Kingdom of Castile had sent explorers to the region as well. The Portuguese and the Castilians would continue to butt heads, leading to the breakout of the Battle of Guinea in 1478. In a similar way to the taking of Ceuta decades prior, the Portuguese launched an overwhelming surprise naval attack on the Castilians. The Castilians were caught completely unaware, and their ships were literally blown to pieces in some cases. The ships that were not destroyed ended up in Portuguese hands, along with a considerable amount of gold, which was handed over when the Castilians were forced to give up the fight.

The Portuguese would ultimately prevail in this struggle, securing their complete domination of the Gulf of Guinea. Ensuring their monopoly, the Portuguese built the outpost of São Jorge da Mina, situated on what today comprises the coast of Ghana. The Portuguese had continued their expansive exploration in the meantime, having ventured south of the equator for the first time in 1473 and then making inroads into the Congo River by 1482.

In the following year, 1483, the Portuguese explorers would push even farther south, reaching what we now call Angola. Once ashore, in dramatic fashion, the Portuguese explorers laid claim to the land by placing a large stone monument the Portuguese called a *padrão* on the shore. The monument had an inscription that read, "In the era of 6681 years from the creation of the world, 1482 years since the birth of Our Lord Jesus, the Most High and Excellent and Mighty Prince, King D. Joao [sometimes rendered John] II of Portugal, sent Diogo Cao squire of his House to discover this land and plant these pillars."

These supposed discoveries and claims were made no matter what the previous inhabitants of the newly "discovered" lands might have thought about it. In fact, this was quite common throughout the whole Age of Discovery. But this monument was more than an attempt to stake out future territory. It was meant to serve as a marker of just how far the Portuguese had traveled up to that point in their quest to circumnavigate Africa.

A drawing by Alfredo Roque Gameiro of the erection of a padrão at the mouth of the Zaire River.

As evidence of how meticulously planned each leg of these exploratory missions was, this particular plaque had been carved several months prior to the launching of the mission. Thus, even though the actual placement of the monument was in 1483, it was inscribed with 1482—the date it was first carved back in Portugal.

In consideration of what was at stake and the resources expended, these expeditions by the Portuguese have been likened to the Apollo moon missions during the 1960s. And such comparisons would not be too far off the mark. For just like the Apollo missions to land on the moon, these efforts by Portugal took considerable sums of money, both in regards to their organization and their execution. Like the moon missions, they also took Portuguese explorers into what was then entirely unknown territory.

No outsiders had been this far down the African coast. Even Arab explorers who had long been a presence in North Africa had not sailed down the coast of West Africa like this. Much like the fears expressed by European sailors about crossing the Atlantic, Arab sailors often spoke of terrible consequences that were in store for anyone who sailed through the uncharted waters down the west coast of Africa and around the continent's southern tip.

Yet, despite such fears, the Portuguese pushed on. And they made an important discovery during these voyages. They found that although the howling winds near the shores of the African coast were often treacherous and deadly, if they just sailed a little farther west into the equatorial Atlantic, they could rely upon strong westerly winds to launch them back on course to Portugal.

This slingshot effect proved to be so helpful that it soon became a major part of their journey around Africa's southern tip. They would hug the African coast all the way to the equator, and once they reached that area, they would sail off to the west and use the strong winds to launch themselves rapidly southeast. Eventually, they made it around the southern tip of Africa. It was a moment of pure genius, and it would change the world.

Chapter 2 – The Search for India

"Each ship had three sets of sails and anchors and three or four times as much other tackle and rigging as was usual. The cooperage of the casks, pipes and barrels for wine, water vinegar and oil was strengthened with many hoops of iron. The provisions of bread, wine, flour, meat vegetables, medicines, and likewise of arms and ammunition, were also in excess of what was needed for such a voyage. The best and most skillful pilots and mariners in Portugal were sent on this voyage, and they received, besides other favors, salaries higher than those of any seamen of other countries. The money spent on the few ships of this expedition was so great that I will not go into detail for fear of not being believed."

-Duarte Pacheco Pereira

In the spring of 1488, the Portuguese first managed to sail right past the tip of southern Africa. This event dispelled the long-held belief that the Indian Ocean was "land-locked." It would be realized that by rounding the tip of Africa, one could very well make their way to the Indian Ocean and ultimately to India itself.

This expedition was led by the daring Portuguese explorer Bartolomeu Dias, who had first left on this epic voyage the previous year, sailing out of Lisbon, Portugal, in 1487. Bartolomeu Dias and his crew then reached the tip of Africa in 1488, and despite any misgivings they may have had, they successfully navigated their way around it.

However, at the time, they were unsure of exactly where they were and of how far they could go in these uncharted waters. After rounding the tip of Africa, the Portuguese sailed north along the eastern shores of the African continent. They stopped at a few places on the coast, where they noticed some native inhabitants who stared in shock at the strange ships and visitors that confronted them.

It has been said that at one point, Dias and his crew stopped to take in some water a little inland but were ambushed by some locals. Fortunately for Dias and his companions, it seemed that all their antagonists were equipped with were rocks, as they showered them with rock-like projectiles. According to the Portuguese account of what happened next, Dias took out the powerfully built Portuguese crossbow he had with him and launched an arrow at his attackers.

As a result, one was killed, and the rest fled from the scene—no doubt telling others to be wary of these strange intruders. The Portuguese then returned to their ships and resumed their journey up Africa's eastern coast. Soon, they noticed that the waters, which had cooled considerably as they rounded the southern tip, were getting warmer, indicating a return toward the equator. The crew wanted to proceed farther, but their supplies were dangerously low.

Thus, they stopped on March 12th, took a brief rest, and took the time to plant yet another monument as a mile marker. The location they had reached was situated in the Eastern Cape province, near the town of Kwaaihoek. The marker still stands to this day, and it serves as a popular tourist attraction. After they placed this marker, the crew then went back to their ships and began their fateful journey back south, back around the African continent and—or so they hoped—home to Portugal.

It was around this time that another Portuguese explorer by the name of Pêro (Pedro) da Covhilã was making an extraordinary journey of his own. Covhilã was in search of the fabled Prester John of Africa. For centuries, it had been rumored in Christian Europe that there was a great and powerful Christian monarch located somewhere beyond the Muslim-dominated lands of North Africa and the Middle East. Some tales hinted that he was in Asia, while others hinted that he was somewhere in Africa. It was believed that this isolated but powerful Christian kingdom would be a tremendous ally in the struggle of the Christian powers against Islam.

Interestingly enough, there was indeed a powerful (although perhaps not as powerful as the rumors suggested) and thriving Christian kingdom in East Africa that the larger Christian world knew practically nothing about. We are talking about the Christian Ethiopian Empire. The Ethiopian Empire had been around since 1270, and it was one of the very first countries to officially adopt Christianity, doing so in the 4th century under the Kingdom of Aksum.

Initially, Ethiopia had solid relations with other neighboring regions that had also turned to Christianity. After Islam swept through what had previously been a Christian-based North Africa around 700 CE, Ethiopia suddenly found itself cut off from the rest of the Christian world.

So, just like the myth of Prester John suggested, there was indeed an isolated but thriving Christian kingdom cut off from the rest of Christendom, south of the Islamic bloc. Covhilã was in search of this long-sought-after realm, but he didn't take a powerful armada of ships around the tip of Africa to find it. Instead, he simply disguised himself and quietly traversed the treacherous overland routes, journeying through the Holy Land, Saudi Arabia, and into the Horn of Africa.

From here, he proceeded to the Ethiopian Empire, where he was cordially greeted by Ethiopian Emperor Eskender. But although he was treated well enough, Eskender actually forbade Covhilā from leaving his realm. He essentially kept Covhilā as a highly pampered prisoner in his kingdom. Such things seem to only add to the mystique of medieval Ethiopia since so many legends of mythical realms speak of intrepid explorers entering paradises but never returning.

In Eskender's royal court, Covhilā was treated as a guest of honor. He was given all he ever wanted, except for one thing—a way to return home. But as mysterious as such actions might seem, there are a few reasons why the Ethiopian monarch may have acted in this manner. In those days, Ethiopia was very secretive and deeply concerned about potential intrusions from outsiders. And one can hardly blame them, considering how much outside powers ended up exploiting so many African kingdoms.

In many ways, Ethiopia's best defense from outside manipulation was its sheer remoteness. Ethiopia was hard to find—and the ruling powers thought it prudent to keep it that way. Although Covhilā was not allowed to leave, he was indeed treated with great distinction. He was made a member of the king's court and eventually married an Ethiopian woman, with whom he raised a family. Covhilā would ultimately die, with his Ethiopian friends and family members at his side, in 1526.

Nevertheless, the friendship that had been forged between Portugal and Ethiopia would prove pivotal for the latter. In the following year, 1527, a Muslim power rose up in eastern Ethiopia. A military leader by the name of Ahmad ibn Ibrahim al-Ghazi cobbled together an army that threatened the entirety of the Christian Ethiopian Empire. The struggle would go on for decades. By the 1530s, Ethiopian Emperor Lebna-Dengel (also known as

Dawit II; Dengel is an Amharic variation of David, as in King David of the Bible) was throwing the full might of his army against the Islamic forces, but his enemy continued to gain the upper hand.

The emperor himself ultimately fell in battle but not before sending off an urgent request for military aid to the Portuguese. These entreaties would lead to the Portuguese intervening in the conflict in 1540. Portugal only sent four hundred troops, but they were equipped with the latest weaponry. These hardened Portuguese fighters were enough to tip the scales in favor of the Ethiopians. At the Battle of Wayna Daga in 1543, the Muslim forces of Ahmad ibn Ibrahim were finally defeated, with Ahmad being one of the casualties.

The assistance of the Portuguese no doubt helped to ensure that the only indigenous Christian nation left in Africa was allowed to remain standing. It is somewhat ironic that for centuries, the Christians of Europe whispered about a powerful Christian king of the East—Prester John—hidden somewhere behind the Muslim forces. The tales often spoke of how this great Christian king would rise up to aid the Christians of Europe during their darkest hour.

In reality, though, it was the Christians of Europe who ended up aiding Christian Ethiopia in its darkest hour. Say what you will about the Portuguese and some of their later exploitations of the natives, but if they had not ventured to Ethiopia in the 1540s, the empire might well have been conquered by Muslim forces. Although forced conversion goes against Islamic law, the Muslims still placed an exorbitant tax on those who did not convert. If one could not pay this tax, a person could be sentenced to death, exiled, or forcibly converted. (Typically, they were more lenient to those who practiced Judaism and Christianity, although the tax still applied to them.) The Portuguese arriving when they did turned out to be a miracle for the continuity of the Ethiopian civilization and the longevity of its long Christian heritage.

But we are getting ahead of ourselves in the discussion of the general chronological progression of the Portuguese Empire. Putting aside these events of the 1500s, let us transport ourselves back to the 1480s when both Pêro da Covhilã's overland journey and Bartolomeu Dias's sea journey were still under way. This decade was a pivotal one for Portugal. Columbus had yet to discover the New World for Spain, so the Portuguese were the ones making most of the major discoveries.

That fateful 1492 voyage of Columbus was, of course, mainly launched to search for a new route to India. Ever since the fall of Constantinople to the Ottoman Empire in 1453, overland routes to the Far East had been cut off. This event was what first led the heads of state in Europe to contemplate the discovery of a new route via the high seas. And as a lasting hallmark of his true intentions, Christopher Columbus was Genoese (some believe he might have been Portuguese, Spanish, or even Polish; as of this writing, genetic testing is being conducted on his remains), but he sailed for the Spanish Crown. Upon landing in the Americas (more precisely, the Bahamas) in 1492, he called the native inhabitants Indians.

This, of course, reflects what his prime directive was. The goal was not to discover the Americas but to find an alternative route to India. And Columbus sincerely believed he was in India at the time. He had sailed west across the Atlantic in the hopes of finding the backdoor to India. Little did he know that there was a whole continent in his way. The Portuguese, on the other hand, were working on a route that would take them south around the tip of Africa and up to India. And they were quite confident that they would be able to do it.

In fact, they were so confident that in 1485, some three years prior to Dias's circumnavigation of Africa, King John (João) II of Portugal was openly bragging to the pope that his explorers would soon be sailing to India. In 1488, however, Bartolomeu Dias's expedition did not make it to India. He ultimately had to turn back before reaching the Indian subcontinent. But his journey around the southern tip of Africa paved the way for future expeditions to follow in his footsteps.

The political happenings in Portugal proper would postpone these follow-up trips. On July 13th, 1491, for example, King John II's presumptive heir to the throne—Prince Afonso—abruptly perished from a horse-riding accident. This set Portugal up for a succession crisis. Figuring out who would be next in line to King John II became absolutely paramount.

It was soon determined that the crown would go to "Manuel, Duke of Beja. King John II actually had a son born out of wedlock named Dom Jorge, whom he wished to pass his throne to, but when it was clear that such a thing would never be seen as legitimate, he finally settled on his cousin, Manuel, instead. King John II ultimately perished in 1495, and the reins of power were officially handed over to Manuel.

King John II was only forty years of age when he passed. The fact that the king died so early in his reign bears testament to the importance of having a successor. Fortunately for Portugal, Manuel was ready to take on the burden of leadership as soon as King John II passed. There are those, of course, who have suggested that perhaps King John II's demise was not a natural one and that he was poisoned to hasten the succession of Manuel to the throne.

But besides whispered rumors, there is no evidence that this was the case.

King John II's death seemed to have taken most people by surprise. He was at the height of his power, and in the previous year of 1494, he had overseen the forging of the famed Treaty of Tordesillas, which basically divided all of the new territories beyond Europe's frontiers between the Portuguese and the Spanish.

Ever since Christopher Columbus led Spain into the Americas in 1492, it was clear that Spain would be Portugal's main competitor in the search for new land. The 1494 Treaty of Tordesillas, which was sanctioned by none other than the pope, sought to avoid any future friction by having these two Catholic powers agree ahead of time on who would claim what. This treaty essentially divided the spoils of newly found territories between the two, with the arbitrarily created Tordesillas line situated some 370 leagues west of the Portuguese-controlled Azores. Spain had access to the territory west of the line, and Portugal had access to the territory east of it.

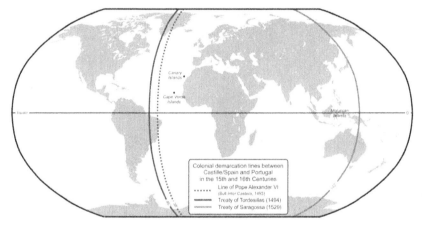

The lines of the Treaty of Tordesillas and the later Treaty of Zaragoza (Saragossa)

Lencer, CC BY-SA 3.0 <http://creativecommons.org/licenses/by-sa/3.0/>, via Wikimedia Commonshttps://commons.wikimedia.org/wiki/File:Spain_and_Portugal.png

It is amazing that Portugal and Spain could agree to such things diplomatically and without coming to blows over who controlled what piece of colonial real estate. Disputes would indeed arise many years later, but for quite some time, both parties would abide by this ruling.

It has been suggested that the final hammering out of these terms during the last days of Portugal's King John II, combined with the uncertainty of the succession of the new king, Manuel I, in 1495, were all factors that delayed the next major Portuguese expedition. It was not until two years after Manual took the throne that the famed navigator Vasco da Gama disembarked from Portugal. Vasco da Gama would not only follow in the path laid by Bartolomeu Dias in 1488 when he rounded the southern tip of Africa; Vasco da Gama would push even farther. He would end up finding the greatest prize of all—a route to India itself.

Chapter 3 – The Journey of Vasco da Gama

"I am not afraid of the darkness. Real death is preferable to a life without living."

-Vasco da Gama

The soon-to-be-famous explorer Vasco da Gama sailed out of a Portuguese port in the summer of 1497. In his possession were two letters. One was made out to Prester John, who was now believed to be the emperor of Ethiopia. And the other was meant for the Raja or ruler of the region of southern India known as Calicut. Portuguese intelligence had long found out that Calicut was a major hub in the Indian spice trade. And since this was a major industry that the Portuguese wished to become involved with, it was only natural that they would go to its source.

It has long been said that the voyages of discovery, both to the Americas and India, have revolved around the search for spices. In modern times, it might be hard for us to understand why it seemed so imperative for Europeans to find new ways to access something as seemingly trivial as pepper, nutmeg, ginger, cinnamon, cloves, and the like. But these things must be taken into perspective.

Indian spices played a major role in the economies of countries at the time. Spices were a much sought-after yet rare commodity due to the distance of Indian ports from most of their would-be customers. And ever since the fall of Constantinople in 1453, Arab armies blocked the route by land. Arab merchants had largely become the middlemen, which only served to ratchet up the price that European merchants paid to acquire these goods.

The monopoly that these traders had over spices would be akin to one group of people having an iron grip on something as crucial for modern-day life today, such as microprocessors. The world is run on computers, and computers need microprocessors. In the 1400s and 1500s, Indian spices were seen as an incredibly valuable commodity.

Let us delve deeper into our modern-day example. As of this writing, Taiwan makes more of these microprocessors than anyone else. Taiwan is currently able to trade openly with the world, and there isn't much of a problem with the status quo of this arrangement. However, China considers Taiwan a part of its territory and would like to reclaim it. If China were to suddenly seize the independent republic of Taiwan by force, China would then have a complete monopoly on microprocessors. Such a thing would be akin to the fall of Constantinople. Such a development would have a significant impact on the global economy since the world would depend on China for much-needed computer chips. If it really did come to this, then it could be argued that it would take a modern-day Vasco da Gama to break up this monopoly by somehow wresting control of this commodity back from the Chinese.

At any rate, moving on from our example, the very same sort of geopolitical stakes was at work during Vasco da Gama's voyage in 1497. The trek was not made merely because some Europeans desperately needed access to spices to liven up their food—it was to break up a monopoly that was crippling much of the European economy. And da Gama would be ultimately successful in that task.

Along with his letters of introduction, Vasco da Gama's crew was also equipped with various real-life sample products of the things he wished to gain during the trip. He had samples of gold, seed pearls, and, of course, the much-coveted spices. If Vasco da Gama and his explorers encountered a language barrier, these products would be used as visual aids to help them communicate what they wanted with the local inhabitants.

Just imagine Vasco da Gama pulling up at a port in India and showing the curious locals samples of spices. Just by sight, they would know what Vasco da Gama and his crew were after, and they would be able to lead them to the right people to begin the necessary transactions to get them.

The first leg of this epic voyage had Vasco da Gama and company heading southwest from Portugal. About a week into the trip, the explorers reached the Canary Islands. By the end of July, they had passed the Cape Verde Islands. After they were about seven hundred miles south of the Cape Verde Islands, Vasco da Gama's ships did what, at that time, was still quite unexpected. They all headed west and sailed to the mid-point of the Atlantic before utilizing the westerly winds to send them sailing right toward the tip of South Africa.

Since no one on board these vessels at the time had any assurance that this tactic would send them back on course, it was a daring move. It was just about as daring as the Apollo astronauts heading out into the unknown depths of space to land on the moon. And when taken into consideration, the Portuguese explorers were actually a lot more daring since these bold sailors had no mission control to radio back to in case there was a problem. No—these Portuguese explorers were completely on their own.

They did have the example of Bartolomeu Dias's previous trek to follow, but they sailed much farther west than Dias ever did, taking full advantage of the westerly winds. The fact that they knew how to do this has led some historians to speculate that there must have been other tentative expeditions in between Dias and da Gama, but there is no clear evidence to back such theories up.

At any rate, even with the westerly winds helping to push them toward the tip of Africa, it still took several more days to round it due to the ships being battered with stormy winds. Upon rounding the tip of Africa, the ships made a pit stop on the east side of Africa's tip. Here, they rested and made contact with some of the locals. This contact was noted by one of the expedition's crew members, who took note of how the local residents greeted them.

Our anonymous man wrote, "They brought with them about a dozen oxen and cows and flour or five sheep. As soon as we saw them we went ashore. They forthwith began to play on four or five flutes, some producing high notes and other low ones." The man then went on to state, "The captain-major then ordered the trumpets to be sounded, and we, in the boats, danced, and the captain-major did so likewise when he rejoined us."

It was not always this easygoing for these intrepid explorers, however. By mid-December, the crew had reached the point where Bartolomeu Dias had stopped his own expedition in 1488 to turn back for Portugal. Instead of turning back, Vasco da Gama and his crew braved the stormy winds that battered the coasts of southeastern Africa and pushed farther north up the African coast. In early January of 1498, ten years after Dias's fateful decision to turn back, these explorers found themselves in what to them was a brand-new land.

They immediately noticed the uniqueness of the settlements they saw along the coast. These villages were much denser, and some had impressive mosques with tall minarets. Upon making landfall, the Portuguese found that the locals were not quite as astonished as other locals had been to see them. They actually seemed to expect them, as if the arrival of faraway visitors was more or less routine.

It was soon discovered that many of the locals were part of the Bantu people. This provided a breakthrough moment for the expedition since they had interpreters on board who were familiar with the Bantu language. The crew was greeted well by the locals, and the men were able to stop, replenish their supplies, and rest a bit before moving farther north along the East African coast.

Vasco da Gama's expedition sailed north up the strait between the East African coast and the island of Madagascar in early spring, and by March, the Portuguese made their way to the famed port of Mozambique. The locals at this port spoke Arabic, and they were able to converse freely with the crew's Arabic interpreters. In this trading town, they met rich Muslim traders decked out in expensive clothing and the finest gold and jewels.

The merchants were used to receiving faraway visitors, but they were indeed curious as to where their guests were from. Initially, these Mozambique merchants assumed that the Portuguese must be Turks who had somehow discovered a new route to the east by sea. After several conversations between the locals and interpreters, the crew realized that the locals assumed they were Muslims just like them. The Portuguese quickly decided that given the hostilities between these two religions in those days that it was probably in their best interest for the merchants of Mozambique to continue operating under this assumption.

After a local sultan greeted the visitors, he asked to see examples of the Turks' famed bows and well-crafted Qurans. The crew sought to keep up the façade. Da Gama had his interpreters concoct a likely story, informing the sultan and anyone else who might happen to ask that while they were not from Turkey, they were from a country near Turkey. Perhaps by using such vague statements, these Christian explorers felt a little better about the deception.

It was certainly a gross exaggeration to suggest that Portugal was anywhere near Turkey. Portugal is thousands of miles away from Turkey. And as it pertained to their exquisite, well-crafted Qurans? These Portuguese sailors claimed that their books were far too sacred to risk damage by carrying them over the sea. As for their famous bows, the Portuguese were more than ready to brandish their best crossbows and put on a demonstration from the decks of their ships for those interested.

One of the Portuguese chroniclers wrote that their hosts were "much pleased and greatly astonished." After getting into the good graces of this local sultan, the Portuguese requested and were granted a couple of local navigators who could show them how to best traverse the Indian Ocean.

However, one of these pilots would realize what was going on with these so-called "Muslims." Just as they were preparing to make their way to India, one of the navigators realized the façade for what it was—that these Muslims were actually Christians. He made a break for it and literally jumped ship. The Portuguese tried to track the runaway pilot down, but they could not catch him.

Bad weather then arrived, and the Portuguese, along with their remaining navigator—now turned veritable hostage—were forced to remain where they were. They were in desperate need of water, and after the storm died down, they made landfall in Mozambique under cover of darkness. The next day, they ventured out to a spring to get water but found their path blocked by several local guards.

It was quite clear now that the people of Mozambique knew that the Portuguese were not who they said they were. Unable to get what they wanted from the increasingly hostile locals, the Portuguese, with their better-armed naval craft, would soon resort to an early form of gunboat diplomacy. They parked their ships near the watering hole, and if anyone came near the crew as they disembarked to get water, the ship's cannons roared to life. The

Portuguese retrieved water for the last time on March 25th before heading out of Mozambique for the last time.

The next major port these intrepid explorers reached was that of Mombasa. Today, Mombasa is the second-largest city in Kenya, but back in the 1500s, Kenya as a nation did not exist. Mombasa was a thriving port city in what was then known as the Swahili coast. Mombasa played a big role in trade across the Indian Ocean, with skilled local navigators crossing back and forth between East African port cities like Mombasa and the bustling ports of India.

The Portuguese were received well at first, but after a few weeks, relations soured. One night, some local men were caught trying to sabotage the rigging on some of the ships. They had swum up to the ships while they were parked and attempted to cut the lines. The would-be saboteurs were chased off before any major damage occurred, but it was clear to the Portuguese that it was time to move on.

It was now mid-April, and the Portuguese made their way some seventy miles north, landing at the next major hub on the Swahili coast—the port city of Malindi. Malindi had long been a trading hub in the region, trading with merchants as far away as Saudi Arabia, India, and at times even China. In 1414, the famed Chinese admiral Zheng He sailed into Malindi's ports. Vasco da Gama and company were following in the footsteps of previous navigators such as these when they landed at Malindi in the spring of 1498.

It was here that the Portuguese first came into contact with Indian merchants, whom they actually mistook for the Eastern Christians that they were so desperately looking for. Shortly after their arrival, they made contact with a group of Indian merchants who they managed to erroneously project their own beliefs upon. These men were Hindu believers, yet after they were shown a painting of Jesus and Mother Mary, their reaction convinced the Portuguese that they were Christians. The men obviously sensed the reverence of the religious icons, and they bowed down in reverence and were heard shouting what the Portuguese thought to be "Christ! Christ!" Some historians have since concluded that the Indian merchants were most likely exclaiming, "Krishna! Krishna!"

It is not too hard to imagine that the Hindu believers mixed up an image of Christ with Krishna since the depictions of the two have always had some similarities. Even some of the attributes given to Krishna could be said to be similar to Christ. Little did the Portuguese know then that they could very well have been mistaking *Krishnians* for *Christians.*

At any rate, according to journals from crew members, it seems the Portuguese had a jolly time in Malindi, and the local sultan even gave them another navigator who was more than willing to lead them to India proper. On April 24th, Vasco da Gama and his ships left Malindi and headed for the Indian port of Calicut.

Their trip from the coasts of East Africa across the Indian Ocean to India would take just a few weeks, with the crew making landfall in India in late May. In far-flung India, they would find those with whom they could converse freely. Most of the Portuguese crew knew how to speak their sister language of Spanish. This would prove important because shortly after their arrival in India, they came across a couple of merchants who originally hailed from the North African nation of Tunisia, who spoke fluent Spanish.

The merchants were apparently quite surprised to see these European explorers. They were particularly amazed that they had somehow made their way to India. It has been said that Vasco da Gama sent one of his scouts, a man by the name of João Nunes, to speak with the locals. One of the first things that these Spanish-speaking merchants asked him was, "What the devil has brought you here?" To this question, João Nunes gave the now famous reply, "We have come to seek Christians and spices."

For the Spanish conquistadors of the Americas, it has long been said that their main motivations were for "God, gold, and glory!"

For the Portuguese then, it could be said that the simplistic anthem they sang was for "Christians and spices!" After all, Vasco da Gama had two letters of introduction, one for the famed Christian king Prester John and another for the Raja.

Vasco da Gama hoped to cut a lucrative trade deal in exotic Indian spices with the Raja. Da Gama and a small company of his were scheduled to meet with the local Raja, known as the Samoothiri Raja, on May 28th. They had an anonymous chronicler with them who recorded parts of this momentous event. Before meeting with the Raja, they met with the Raja's subordinate governor, referred to as his *bale*. The *bale* led them to a welcoming committee at a local home, where they were given a fine meal of rice and fish. Although his companions dined in style, da Gama himself, always a bit paranoid in new and unfamiliar surroundings lest someone slip him some poison, refused to eat any of it.

After the meal came to a close, da Gama and company were directed to a couple of boats that had been joined together so that the group could travel by river to reach the Raja's palace. Once the river took them as far as it could, da Gama was placed in a palanquin. This was a kind of large box that was used as a carriage. It rested on long poles and was lifted up on the shoulders of others so that those inside could be literally carried to their destination.

Seated in his palanquin, da Gama was able to observe the crowds that had gathered along the way to watch this strange procession. Prior to reaching the palace, they stopped at what was most likely a Hindu temple, but da Gama and company, who were still quite confused about Hinduism, took it to be a church of some unknown Christian sect. Da Gama took the time to pray inside the temple before he was led back out and brought the rest of the way to the Raja's palace.

The chronicler who accompanied da Gama described the interior of the palace as being quite magnificent. He later wrote that it was "a great hall, surrounded with seats of timber raised in rows above one another like our theaters, the floor being covered by a carpet of green velvet, and the walls hung with silk of various colors." Within this grand palace, da Gama would first gain an audience to the Raja.

After the introductory greetings had been conducted, da Gama requested and was granted the opportunity to speak with the Raja in private. It was not completely done in private, of course, since interpreters were required. But the meeting was shielded from the vast majority of curious onlookers, so it was about as private of an audience as Vasco da Gama would be able to get. Da Gama proceeded to inform the Raja of the great mission he had been charged with by Manuel, King of Portugal.

He spoke at length of how his countrymen had been seeking a new route to India for some sixty years—ever since the fall of Constantinople. Along with seeking to reopen trade with India, da Gama also spoke of how he was seeking out Christian kings. It remains unclear what the Raja thought of the notion of the Portuguese seeking out "Christian kings." Much of what da Gama was saying was probably lost in translation, and the context may have been completely misunderstood.

But the Raja did understand the basics of da Gama's intention to reopen trade with India. After laying down the basics of why he had come to India, da Gama and company bid the Raja farewell and retired for the evening. As was customary, the next day, da Gama had goods unloaded from his ships to give to the Raja as presents. These goods were intercepted by the Raja's governor, who immediately considered them not to be adequate as royal presents.

The governor is said to have remarked that any gift given to the great Raja "should be in gold," not the measly brass bracelets, beads, and other cheap trinkets that the Portuguese apparently had on board. Da Gama was deeply frustrated at this turn of events, and he is said to have protested that he was "no merchant but an ambassador." He also insisted that if he were able to make a return trip, he would be sure to have "far richer presents" the second time around.

Da Gama was on a voyage of discovery; thus, he was not quite prepared to shower a local potentate with gifts. His men were lucky to have just reached India alive and with their ships in one piece. It was for this reason that da Gama promised that their gifts would be much better on a return visit since the major hurdle of simply navigating to India had been achieved.

Da Gama told the governor that he wished to have another audience with the Raja so that he could better describe the plight he was in. He was granted this audience, but he was told that he was only allowed to have two of his men accompany him. Da Gama was deeply suspicious of these developments and feared for their safety, lest they suddenly be seized and held hostage. Nevertheless, he didn't see any other option but to take the Raja up on his invitation.

The Raja was greatly confused as to why they would come to a place renowned for exotic trade goods with only mere beads and other trinkets. Da Gama once again tried to explain himself, stating that this expedition was one of "discovery." He had to explain the risk of traveling into unknown waters and how the king of Portugal was not willing to load up ships with silver and gold only for them to possibly fall off the edge of the earth (some did indeed still speculate that such a thing might happen).

In the end, it is thought that da Gama's efforts to explain the nature of his expedition managed to partially appease the great Raja. He was then given permission to have his ships unload goods at the docks and sell and trade whatever they were able to.

But this was most certainly not the end of Vasco da Gama's problems in India. After leaving the palace, he asked for small boats he could use to transfer himself to his ships, which were cautiously waiting a short distance away. The governor then made what he no doubt thought was a reasonable request, as he asked da Gama to have his ships pull in closer to shore. Da Gama, however, was intensely suspicious of his hosts. He feared that if the ships actually pulled into port, they might somehow be trapped and blocked from leaving. Da Gama's Indian hosts, on the other hand, feared that if they granted da Gama's request and paddled him all the way out to his ships that da Gama and company might simply take off without paying the customary service charge, which all visiting craft were obligated to pay.

This disagreement of how to get da Gama back onto his ships led to an incredibly uneasy situation. Da Gama became increasingly incensed at the hold-up. He told the governor that he would like to speak with the Raja once again. This was agreed to, but as would be expected in a busy kingdom such as the Raja's, it would take some time for another meeting to be arranged.

In the meantime, da Gama was kept in a local house, surrounded by armed guards. He was increasingly feeling more like a hostage than an esteemed guest. The chronicler who was still in da Gama's company at this time recorded just how incredibly dire the ordeal had become.

The chronicler wrote, "We passed all that day most anxiously. At night more people surrounded us than ever before, and we were no longer allowed to walk in the compound, within which we were, but confined within a small tiled court, with a multitude of people around us. We quite expected that on the following day we should be separated, or that some harm would befall us, for we noticed that our jailers were much annoyed with us. This, however, did not prevent our making a good supper off the things found in the village. Throughout that night we were guarded by over a hundred men, all armed with swords, two-edged battle axes, shields and bows and arrows. While some of these slept, others kept guard, each taking his turn of duty throughout the night."

One with a more positive outlook could perhaps convince themselves that the armed guards were there to protect da Gama and his companions. But as the situation seemed to be deteriorating, it is quite understandable why da Gama and his crew might have come to fear the worst. The next day, however, it seems that the misunderstandings were eased over, and it was made clear to da Gama that it was simply "the customs of the country" that certain protocols needed to be followed.

There was no mysterious plot afoot; the Indian Raja was just trying to make sure that his visitors followed typical procedure. The Raja was willing to make an exception, though, and agreed that if the Portuguese crew went ahead and brought their goods to the docks, the ships could remain at sea. Da Gama and his companions could be brought to them in the manner in which they requested. Upon returning to the craft waiting for their return, the chronicler captured the relief felt by all, writing, "At this we rejoiced greatly."

After a lack of interest was displayed in the landed goods, da Gama requested the Raja to send some of his men to deliver the trade goods to the city of Calicut, where other commerce was being conducted. This way, they would have a better chance of gaining the interest of passing merchants. The Raja graciously obliged this request.

The proceeds that the Portuguese gleaned were disappointing, but they did manage to raise enough money to buy some spices, gold-worked objects, and other valuable commodities. This small sampling of Indian goods would at least serve as proof of the potential wealth that could be gained by free and open trade with India.

At this point, da Gama was ready to leave, but he still had one more card he wished to play. He wanted to request for the Raja to allow him to leave behind some of his crew so that they could establish a permanent trading post. Da Gama sent a crew member by the name of Diogo Dias back ashore so that he could deliver this request to the Raja. Diogo was subsequently informed that to do such a thing, a "trading tax" would be required.

Diogo intended to return to the waiting ships to deliver this information to da Gama, but he ended up being held hostage in a nearby house. Diogo was apparently being held as an attempt to force the Portuguese to pay all of the fees that were due. Da Gama was quietly informed of what was happening, and he decided to play it off as if he was not in the least bit concerned. On August 15th, some of the Raja's entourage rowed up to da Gama's ships and offered to trade some goods. He had everyone pretend that everything was normal.

It is believed that these men were sent to da Gama in order to gauge the temperament of the visitors, and da Gama's cool composure managed to lull them into complacency. On August 19th, after twenty Indian traders and dignitaries boarded one of da Gama's ships, he suddenly turned on them and had his guests held hostage. Da Gama, of course, was operating on the cold calculus that he could use these hostages to get Diogo back. The gambit worked, and Diogo was successfully exchanged for some of the hostages that da Gama held.

But the key phrase here is "some of the hostages." Da Gama, proving just how ruthless he could be, made sure to keep a few on board as future bargaining chips and insisted that the rest of the hostages would be released after his remaining merchandise was restored to him. So, until all of his unsold goods were transported back to his ships, at the Raja's own expense at that, he was not going to release the rest of the hostages.

Da Gama was certainly playing hardball. For a guy who tried his best to impress the Raja upon his first meeting with him, da Gama's tactics had changed considerably. The actions that da Gama took next, however, are rather puzzling. Once the goods were rowed back up to the ships, Vasco da Gama suddenly decided to have his ships turn speed in the other direction, leaving the goods behind and keeping the terrified hostages on board.

This seems incredibly cruel and duplicitous on da Gama's part unless there was some other reason lost as to why he might have done this. Was the increasingly edgy and paranoid da Gama afraid he was about to fall into a trap? It remains a bit unclear. At any rate, this first seaborne voyage to India by Portugal achieved a major milestone, although it left much scandal and outrage in its wake.

Chapter 4 – Tragedy and Triumph

"And it all goes to pay the carriers, the ships and the dues of the sultan. So going the other way it's possible to strip out all these costs and middlemen. Which is why I hold the sultan; these kings and the Muslims will do all they can to rebuff the Portuguese king in this business. If the king continues it will be possible to sell spices at the port of Pisa many times more cheaply than at Cairo, because it's possible to get them there at a much lower cost."

-Girolamo Sernigi

Vasco da Gama and his crew returned to Portugal in the summer of 1499. This successful voyage was followed by yet another in 1500–this time led by a Portuguese nobleman, Pedro Álvares Cabral. This mission sought to fulfill the one objective that Vasco da Gama's mission had been unable to. Cabral and his associates would attempt to install a permanent Portuguese trading post.

The Portuguese had a good handle on how to circumnavigate the tip of Africa so that they could reach India by this time. It is interesting to note that the exact methodology was considered a state secret. The Portuguese knew how to make this treacherous voyage, but they did not want any other nation to know what they knew. All sailing charts and related information about how these expeditions were made were ordered to be kept secret under the pain of death.

For the Portuguese, their secret route to India was something akin to the Manhattan Project. And it was not entirely unlike the development of the nuclear bomb, for it, too, would come to change the world. Pedro Álvares Cabral did indeed follow the path laid out by Vasco da Gama, but the westward winds proved a little stronger than anticipated. His ships were actually pushed far enough west to reach the eastern coasts of Brazil.

This would prove to be a pivotal discovery, though, at the time, the crew had no idea where they had ended up. Here, the explorers would find a large amount of a form of red dyewood. The Portuguese already referred to this commodity as brazilwood or, as it was said in the Portuguese dialect of the time, *pau-brasil.* The whole territory came to be named after this red-hued brazilwood. But there was more to this land than redwood.

Brazil, of course, was already inhabited by various native groups. This Portuguese expedition would encounter some of them, and the crew was found to generally admire the society of the natives. Though the natives were far different from their own people, they were seen as a peaceful and even noble group of people. They were seen freely roaming the forests of Brazil without much worry or concern of anything.

As the expedition's chronicler, Pêro Vaz de Caminha, documented of the encounter, "They seem to me to be people of such innocence that, if we could understand them and they us, they would soon become Christians, because they do not seem to have or to understand any form of religion. For it is certain that this people is [sic] good and of pure simplicity, and there can easily be stamped upon them whatever belief we wish to give them."

Although Pêro no doubt thought he was being charitable at the time, his words today would be roundly condemned. While praising the locals for their "simplicity" and "innocence," he desired to "stamp upon them" the Portuguese belief systems. Of course, one must consider the context of the times in which these Portuguese explorers lived.

Christians in general and the Portuguese and Spanish in particular were locked in what they viewed as a life and death struggle with Islam. And as both Islam and Christianity continued to compete for dominance in this zero-sum game of religious outreach, these new unknown people with no apparent religious affiliation, such as those encountered by the Portuguese, were essentially seen as a group of religiously neutral individuals who needed to be coerced into the Christian fold.

At any rate, this accidental landing in Brazil would encourage another expedition in 1501 and yet another in 1503, leading to eventual settlements being established. But as it pertains to this particular voyage with Cabral at the helm, India was still the prime objective. And in early May, they left this strange new land to once again head southwest toward the southern tip of Africa.

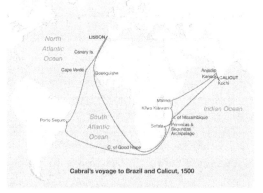

Cabral's route in 1500.
Cabral_voyage.png: Lecen (based on work created by Castoro. See File:MONDO3.GIF)derivative work: Odysseus1479, CC BY-SA 3.0 <https://creativecommons.org/licenses/by-sa/3.0>, via Wikimedia Commons https://commons.wikimedia.org/wiki/File:Cabral_voyage_1500.svg

Several weeks later, they reached and then circumnavigated around the tip. By mid-June, the Portuguese had managed to make landfall on the other side in Mozambique. Here, the local sultan was hospitable enough, allowing them to replenish their stores of water and even giving them a local man to help lead them to the nearby trading port of Kilwa. After a brief pitstop in Kilwa, they then moved up the coast to the port of Malindi, where they obtained another local navigator to help ensure the smooth crossing of the Indian Ocean.

It seems that even though the Portuguese were doing their best to follow the instructions of their predecessors, they still depended upon some local help to make sure they stayed on track. Shortly after Cabral and his company arrived, they learned that the Indian Raja—the Samoothiri Raja—who had previously hosted Vasco da Gama had passed and that he had been replaced by his nephew.

One might think this was good news for Cabral and his crew since the relations between da Gama and the old Raja had become so antagonistic. But despite the new leadership, it was not long before tensions between Cabral and the new Raja began to become frayed as well. In the Portuguese proto-gunboat diplomacy style, Cabral met the new Raja with a more aggressive attitude. On behalf of the king of Portugal, Cabral demanded "preferential tax tariffs" as well as "low prices for spices," with the promise of a permanent Portuguese trading post to boot. But probably the most galling was Cabral's request to have the Muslim merchants banned from conducting trade since, as Pedro Cabral insisted, this "would comply with his duty as a Christian king."

The Portuguese, you see, were still locked into their misunderstanding that Hindus were some sort of strange Christian sect. They still believed that the Raja and his court were Christians. As such, they made demands of this supposed Christian Indian king, just as they would their Christian counterparts in Europe. By the time the Raja's interpreters translated half of the things that

Cabral was saying, he was no doubt appalled. Who were these aggressive strangers? And who gave them the right to make such outrageous demands?

One could only imagine the Raja asking himself such questions. But the Raja realized that he was dealing with a foreign power that could bring considerable damage to his kingdom, so he settled upon a cautious form of appeasement, at least to buy himself some time. The Raja did not outright deny many of the demands, but he was not exactly clear on whether all of them would be granted. At any rate, after weeks of negotiations, Cabral's ships were loaded up with plenty of spices and other precious goods.

But there was a problem—the local Arab merchants, rightly realizing that the Portuguese were threatening to push them out of this lucrative trade, began to run interference and slow the loading of Cabral's ships. They also noticed that some of these same merchants had their own ships rapidly loaded up, stealthily sailing out of the harbor with a full load.

Cabral lodged an official complaint with the Raja about this, and the Raja, feeling the full pressure of his demanding guests, consented to allow the Portuguese to pursue any merchant craft seen to be engaging in this sort of unlawful behavior. It was not long before Cabral seized one of the crafts. This action, however, lit the fuse of long-simmering hostilities between the Portuguese and Arab merchants. Soon, a huge group of angry merchants stormed the recently established Portuguese trading post. They were hellbent upon taking their vengeance out on the hapless Portuguese stationed there.

The Portuguese traders were forced inside a nearby building, locking themselves behind a large gate. The Portuguese then clambered up onto the wall and began firing on the crowd with their crossbows, killing and injuring several. Cabral, in the meantime, received word about what was happening on the ground and sent some smaller boats equipped with swivel guns and had them fire into the crowd.

The guns could not effectively reach the rioters, so they did not deter them from continuing their siege of the compound. The attackers then set fire to the wall and actually managed to burn it to the ground. The wild crowd then charged up toward the building the Portuguese were now hiding in. It was at this point that the Portuguese inside decided to make a run for it, hoping to outrun their attackers and reach the gunboats that were nearby.

Running at full speed, they managed to get to the beach but were frustrated to find that the gunboats were still a distance away. They were forced to get into the water and swim for it. The mob managed to catch up to them at this point, and before they could swim toward safety, many were hacked to pieces with scimitars or even torn limb from limb with the bare hands of the angry rioters.

In the end, it has been estimated that some fifty Portuguese were killed in this massacre, while a mere twenty managed to make it to the safety of the boats. Cabral, of course, was quite infuriated, and he soon demanded the Raja to take action against these aggressors. But the Raja essentially kept quiet. It is likely he was unsure what to do, so he simply refused to respond. This led Cabral to seek vengeance on his own. He arbitrarily hunted down ten different craft belonging to the Arab merchants. He brought them to port and then had all on board the ship killed right then and there for all to see.

It was a truly dreadful scene. As one chronicler put it, "And thus we slew to the number of five hundred or six hundred men, and captured twenty or thirty who were hiding in the holds of the ships and also the merchandise; and thus we robbed the ships and took what they had within them. One had in it three elephants which we killed and ate, and we burned all nine of the unloaded ships."

The brutality of these actions would shock just about anyone. Even the elephants were not spared; they, too, were consumed, as well as the empty ships. It was overkill for a previous wrong that these particular men may not have had anything to do with.

As brutal as all of this is, one must keep in mind the background of Portugal and the Iberian Peninsula to understand their mindset at the time. The Portuguese truly felt that they were on the front lines of a holy war, and more often than not, they gave no quarter to their perceived enemies, either at home or abroad. Cabral, however, had a thirst for vengeance that seemed to go above and beyond even what was typical for the time. And after this particular display, he actually fired upon the city of Calicut itself, demolishing many buildings near the coast.

He then washed his hands of the Raja altogether and sailed north to the city of Cochin (Kochi), where the local potentate was a known rival of the Raja of Calicut. This was apparently planned all along; Cochin had been reserved as an alternative in case things did not work out in Calicut. Here at Cochin, the Portuguese would begin a classic divide and conquer strategy in regard to India. They would align themselves with one of the Raja's rivals so as to better insert themselves into India's geopolitical and global affairs.

Forgetting all about their failed attempt to install a trading post in Calicut, the Portuguese now put all of their focus on Cochin. And soon, friendly relations were established. The Portuguese were able to create a permanent trading post in Cochin, and they had their ships loaded up with precious goods without any delay. At Cochin, they were also first introduced to a few actual Indian Christians.

It was from this rare segment of Indian society that the Portuguese learned the truth. They discovered that while there was a very small population of Christians in India, they were an extreme minority. They soon began to understand more about the main religion of India—Hinduism—from these local Christians.

In the meantime, Cabral received a warning from the locals that the Raja of Calicut was planning to strike out against him and his crew. It was learned that a fleet of some eighty ships was on its way to launch an assault against them. Pedro Cabral did not want to stick around for an all-out naval battle, so he loaded his ships and quietly slipped away to avoid conflict.

Cabral made one more pitstop in nearby Cannanore (Kannur) to get some more goods before disembarking from India altogether. Cabral and company ended up returning to Portugal in the summer of 1501. It had been a hard journey, and of the thirteen ships that had left the previous year, only seven returned. The rest had been either lost or abandoned, with the survivors piling into the seven operable vessels to make their way back home.

Pedro Cabral's expedition was viewed as both a triumph and a tragedy. Many were aghast at the reports of what had happened to the Portuguese trading post in Calicut, but others still saw the potential for great wealth—including, of course, King Manuel of Portugal. The Portuguese were determined to press on. Cabral apparently had had enough, though. None other than Vasco da Gama would be tapped for the next major expedition to India.

Chapter 5 – Establishing Permanent Outposts

"My son is dead, as God willed and my sins deserve. The Venetians and the Sultan's Muslims killed him. As a result of this, the Muslims in these parts are hopeful of great help. It seems to me that this year we cannot avoid a trial of strength with them, which is the thing I most desire, because it seems to me that with God's help we have to remove them totally from the sea, so that they do not return to this land. And if our Lord is served by my ending my days in this way, I will have obtained the rest I seek."

-Francisco de Almeida

The already legendary Vasco da Gama disembarked for his second grand expedition to India in early 1502. As usual, the crew sailed around North Africa, swung west at the equator, then used the westerly winds to launch themselves southeast toward the tip of South Africa. After rounding the cape, Vasco da Gama went to the now familiar stomping grounds of Mozambique and took some time to reestablish relations with the local leaders.

From here, he went on to the port of Kilwa, where he sought the audience of the local sultan. Vasco da Gama was able to intimidate the sultan enough to convince him to cooperate, and a lasting trade relationship was established. The Portuguese ships then sailed up to the port of Malindi, where they were given a more or less friendly welcome. By September, they had reached Mt. Deli, where they rested for a bit and restocked their dwindling supplies.

In the vicinity of Mt. Deli, the crew spotted a large Arab ship sailing nearby. The ship was called the *Miri*, and it was full of religious pilgrims who were traversing across the Indian Ocean from Calicut. They were on their way to Mecca. Da Gama, displaying his full ruthlessness and utter contempt for Muslims, ordered his ships to attack this unarmed vessel.

After looting the now disabled ship, Vasco da Gama ordered it to be set ablaze and proceeded to watch as everyone on board suffered a terrible death. Many brutal incidents often occurred between Muslims and Christians in those days, but this incident was viewed to be outrageous, even in that day and age. Many among Vasco da Gama's own crew began to wonder just how cruel and cold-hearted their captain really was. One remarked over the senseless violence that some of the wealthier crew probably would have been more than willing to pay a big ransom if the ship were spared. The chronicler thought it was big enough "to ransom all of the Christians held in Fez."

The writer was referring to Fez, Morocco, where many kidnapped Christians had been taken by Muslim forces and held for ransom. As cruel as kidnapping someone for profit might be, at least there was some hope that the victims might be returned to their family members. Vasco da Gama was taking things much further by refusing to even consider a ransom. He was engaging in a shade of brutality that was darker than usual.

The sad fate of the *Miri* was sealed on October 3rd when it was set ablaze and turned into nothing more than flaming ash and cinders floating on the waters. Vasco da Gama's own chronicler lamented the monstrous callousness displayed, acknowledging, "That with great cruelty and without any pity the admiral burned the ship and all who were in it." After this outright atrocity was committed, Vasco da Gama crossed the Indian Ocean and landed in the Port of Cannanore to restock. He was soon on his way to Calicut.

It seems that Vasco da Gama was eager to get vengeance for past slights, as he really laid down the hammer on the Raja once he reached Calicut. By now, the residents of Calicut had received word of what had happened to the *Miri* and were practically frightened into submission. The Raja sent a letter to da Gama in which he declared his desire for peaceful relations. In his overtures, he even offered to reimburse da Gama for the goods that had been abandoned on his previous expedition.

As for the lives that were lost on both sides, the Raja was more realistic in his acknowledgment that this could not be rightfully reimbursed. But the Raja was magnanimous enough to offer an olive branch and suggest that they should both essentially forgive and forget. Even though the Raja was not actually the Christian king that da Gama had once taken him for, these were most certainly Christian values on display. After all, the greatest attribute of Christianity is forgiveness.

But Vasco da Gama ultimately proved how unchristian he could be, as he let his bitter and vengeful nature get the better of him. And his mind for vengeance was ultimately made up when his Indian ally in Cochin sent word to Vasco da Gama that the Raja of Calicut had sent a secret letter to him around the same time, suggesting that the rivals forget their differences and join forces against the Portuguese. Having heard about this, Vasco da Gama was not in any mood for mercy.

Messengers from the Raja appeared at the port to record Vasco da Gama's demands. They found that these demands were not going to be easy ones. Vasco da Gama demanded something to which the Raja could never agree. He not only demanded financial compensation for the attack on the previous Portuguese outpost, but he also demanded that all Muslim merchants be barred from further trade. In the draconian statement he handed off to the Raja's emissaries, Vasco da Gama declared that "otherwise he did not wish to make peace or any agreement with him, because Muslims were enemies of Christians and vice versa since the world began."

The Raja obviously could not take such absurd and belligerent demands seriously. But at the same time, he did not have any more bargaining chips left against the gunboat diplomacy of the Portuguese. He sent back an apologetic response, but he insisted that he could not expel the Muslim merchants. Upon receiving this refusal to his unreasonable demands, Vasco da Gama promptly seized the dignitaries of the Raja and set in motion his own personal war against the Indian potentate.

He had the ship's guns lowered and began blasting everything in reach into smithereens. There was eventually a lull in the fighting, and the Raja sent word that there would be a peaceful resolution. But the Raja, desperate to get rid of the Portuguese, had something else in mind. In the dead of night, he had a squadron of some eighty ships sneak up on the Portuguese craft.

The ships opened fire at close range and threatened to sink the Portuguese ships. The only thing that saved the surrounded Portuguese craft was the sudden arrival of ships under the command of Vicente Sodré, who had stayed behind in Cannanore. Vicente arrived just in time to engage the Raja's craft, allowing Vasco da Gama's ships to break free and then turn around and attack the Raja's ships. The Raja's ships were no match and were forced to flee.

The infuriated Vasco da Gama fired off another message for the Raja in the meantime, stating, "Oh miserable man, you had me called and I came at your request. You have done all that you could, and you would have done more if you could. You have had the punishment that you deserve: when I return here I will pay your due—and it won't be in money." Da Gama ultimately left India behind in the spring of 1503; behind him, he left a trading post in Cochin and Cannanore, while Calicut was practically buried in rubble.

After da Gama's departure, the fragile Portuguese outpost at the allied Indian port of Cochin was vulnerable to reprisal. And soon after, the Raja struck, launching a massive assault on Cochin. The Portuguese and their Indian allies were forced to flee to the island of Vypin that summer, where they remained under constant siege. In September of 1503, their lives were secured when Francisco de Albuquerque, along with two other ships, arrived fresh from Portugal.

These ships were then followed by four other Portuguese ships, which were led by Francisco's cousin, Afonso de Albuquerque. This relief force allowed the beleaguered defenders to return to Cochin, but the extra manpower would not be able to stay. By the spring of 1504, the ships once again loaded up with spices and readied themselves to head back to Portugal.

It is a bit mind-boggling that after such ferocious attacks, the Portuguese were still doing business with the Raja of Calicut, but this was precisely the case. Even after all of this fighting, the Raja and the Portuguese craft had entered into what historian and writer Roger Crowley has referred to as a "cynical truce." It was quite cynical on the part of the Portuguese traders since the Portuguese knew that as soon as they got their spices and left, the Raja would wage war on their Portuguese countrymen who remained at Cochin. And it was cynical on the part of the Raja as well since he was trading goods with men whose countrymen he was still plotting to slaughter.

But this was indeed the state of affairs at the time. And sure enough, as soon as spring arrived, the Portuguese ships laden with spices left for Lisbon, Portugal, once again. Around one hundred Portuguese were left to defend Cochin, along with a few small craft. All of them were directed by Duarte Pacheo Pereira. It has been said that the cynical Portuguese who sailed their ships back to Portugal were almost certain that the men left behind would all be dead by the time they returned.

But the cunning and strategic Duarte Pacheo Pereira would prove them wrong. The Raja did indeed launch his forces against Cochin shortly after the spice ships left, striking out against the absurdly small garrison on Cochin that March. Considering the fact that the Raja was sending tens of thousands of troops against a pitiful band of Portuguese defenders, the Indian ruler of Cochin actually recommended that they all abandon the post and leave him to beg the Raja for forgiveness.

This was ostensibly an act of mercy on this potentate's part since he figured that the Portuguese would meet certain death—or perhaps even worse—should they stay to face the Raja of Calicut's wrath. However, Duarte was not one to back down, and he pledged his allegiance to the leader of Cochin, declaring, "We will die serving you if necessary." Duarte worked like a madman and began to set about erecting defenses all over Cochin, placing makeshift stockades of stakes wrapped in steel chains at every strategic point. He then positioned all of the artillery in narrow fords and waited for the enemy forces to arrive.

The Raja of Calicut's army was massive. But other than just marching headlong toward Cochin, their strategy was lacking. And despite their best attempts to rush through the defenses Duarte had laid, they were consistently mowed down by heavy Portuguese artillery at every turn.

Incredibly enough, this small group of Portuguese defenders managed to successfully repulse the Raja's troops on seven different occasions. By July of 1504, the humiliated Raja had had enough, and he called off the attack. He was so thoroughly disgraced that he actually resigned from office, handed power over to his nephew, and became a Hindu monk.

Shortly after the Raja's defeat, a relief force from Portugal arrived with huge ships and massive artillery bristling from their decks. These reinforcements probably expected to find Duarte and the rest of the defenders dead, but they instead found them victorious.

The Portuguese now had a frightening mystique of being unstoppable, and many more local Indian rulers began to openly embrace the Portuguese out of fear for their cities and people. In the meantime, the Muslim merchants from Mecca were being systematically shut out, and many were forced to leave their old outposts behind, as the ban on Muslim merchants that Vasco da Gama had called for essentially came into being.

Several more Portuguese settlements in India were established. These settlements were put under the administration of Francisco de Almeida, the first viceroy or governor of what would become Portuguese India. King Manuel of Portugal himself delegated this authority, fully knowing that due to the distance and impossibility of back-and-forth communication, a permanent Portuguese presence with local Portuguese leadership must be established.

Almeida left for the Indian outposts in March of 1505. Before landing in India, however, he had some business to take care of on the East African coast. Almeida visited the port of Kilwa. Vasco da Gama had established relations with Kilwa in previous years, and the sultan there had promised trade as well as an annual tribute to the Portuguese. This sultan had since put an end to these friendly relations.

Almeida sought to pick up where Vasco da Gama had left off, landing his ships in full force and demanding tribute. The situation quickly broke down from here, and Almeida ended up attacking the port. Almeida himself led the charge, and he personally planted a Portuguese flag on Kilwa soil. The sultan and many of the residents fled before them, allowing the Portuguese to seize the deserted settlement.

The Portuguese hastily constructed a fort and made loyal subjects of those who remained. They also installed a local merchant as their new point man in Kilwa. Almeida himself was ecstatic over these results. This can be seen in the letter he fired off to the king of Portugal shortly after, stating, "Sire, Kilwa has the best port of any place I know of in the world, and the fairest land."

From here, Almeida approached the port of Mombasa. Here, however, he met fierce resistance from the local sultan, who tried to throw everything he could at Almeida. The Portuguese were once again able to use their shipboard cannons, as well as muskets on the ground, to blast the inhabitants into submission. On the heels of this seizure, Almeida and company would cross the Indian Ocean and then make landfall in India proper later that summer. It could be said that this was the moment that the Portuguese overseas empire began in earnest.

Chapter 6 – Conflicts of Interest

"I am a man who, if you entrusted me with a dozen kingdoms, would know how to govern them with great prudence, discretion and knowledge. This is not because of any special merits of my own but because I am very experienced in such matters and of an age to tell good from bad."

-Afonso de Albuquerque

Francisco de Almeida left his post as governor in 1509, and he was replaced by Afonso de Albuquerque. Just prior to leaving his post, Almeida struck a stunning blow to the local Islamic powers by using his naval forces to sink a joint Egyptian/Gujrati (Indian) fleet in February of 1509. This fleet was essentially the only real naval opposition left in the region that could have stood up against the powerful Portuguese galleons.

Only one of the Gujarati carracks proved to be formidable. This was a twin-decked behemoth that held some four hundred fighting men. The ship was said to have held out against the Portuguese until the very end of the battle. The ship itself was too close to shore for the Portuguese to safely board and attempt to take over. In the end, they were forced to simply continue taking potshots at the craft from a distance.

It took a whole lot of effort, but the ship finally began to sink. It never capsized; it just slowly began its descent under the waves. This allowed those on board to escape the doomed ship by simply hopping off and swimming to shore. These were the lucky ones, as it is estimated that some 1,300 Gujaratis perished during the course of the fighting. And as for the Portuguese? It is estimated that around one hundred Portuguese lost their lives, with maybe around three hundred being severely injured. This was indeed a clear and indisputable victory for the Portuguese fleet.

On the heels of this victory, Almeida's term as governor ended, and it was time for his successor, Albuquerque, to succeed him. However, Almeida was not quite ready to hand over power, and he bluntly informed the would-be governor that he would have to wait to assume office until the weather was favorable enough for him to set sail back to Lisbon.

This meant that Almeida would remain the acting governor until the end of the monsoon season. This dicey situation of having two governors in the Portuguese Indies would not be resolved until November of that year when a man by the name of Fernandes Coutinho, the so-called Marshal of Portugal, arrived on the scene. Fernandes had been given full royal authority to ensure that the peaceful transition between Almeida and Albuquerque took place.

The day after Albuquerque took official control as governor, Almeida hopped onto a ship and sailed away from India. Interestingly enough, it has been said that a fortune teller of some sort had actually warned Almeida against the trip, predicting that he would perish before reaching Portugal. It is a bit odd that such supposedly fervent Christians would resort to fortune tellers, but in the long lonely nights at their posts, it seems that such things often became hard to resist.

At any rate, the prediction was seemingly fulfilled, and Almeida would indeed perish on the trip. The incident occurred in March of 1510, shortly after rounding Africa's Cape of Good Hope. The crew landed to gather wood, water, and other resources when they were ambushed by some locals. They were taken by complete surprise, and in the vicious attack, it is said that some fifty crew members—including Almeida—were killed.

It is rather ironic that so many men died doing such a simple task. During the massive naval battle in which Almeida put down the Egyptian/Gujarati fleet, around one hundred Portuguese perished, but that was facing large ships and cannons. Here, about half that number were killed just getting a drink of water. At any rate, Almeida would not see Portugal again; he was buried not far from where he was slain on the African coast.

Although Albuquerque was in charge as governor, the marshal brought instructions directly from the king of Portugal that Albuquerque was supposed to follow. It had been determined that Calicut should be seized. The Raja of Calicut had long resisted the Portuguese, but now these newcomers to the Indies were determined to quite literally force the doors of Calicut wide open.

The plan was to land a joint armada, with part of the fleet led by Albuquerque and the other part led by Marshal Coutinho. Upon landing, both groups were to storm Calicut together, taking the fight all the way to the Cerame—the Raja's own personal pavilion where he held audiences. It is incredible to think of how rapidly the situation had changed since Vasco da Gama first met with the Raja on bended knee in humble humility.

The Portuguese were confident in their force of arms. It seems they were done with any and all efforts of diplomacy and were ready to storm the pavilion outright. On January 2nd, 1510, under cover of darkness, Albuquerque's squadron made landfall off the shores of Calicut just south of the Cerame. Marshal Coutinho was then supposed to land his contingent to the north of the Cerame so that it would be attacked from both sides at the same time.

Such a feat would have no doubt been absolutely devastating, but Governor Albuquerque's men had other plans. These rough and tumble warriors were just itching for a fight, and despite their rules to stand down and wait for the Coutinho's forces to arrive, they began to make inroads toward the pavilion of their own accord. Coutinho was delayed, though, because his ship accidentally overshot its landing, ending up too far north.

In the meantime, Albuquerque was beginning to lose control of his rowdy troops, who were more than ready to sack Calicut. Realizing that any attempt to stop them might backfire with an all-out mutiny, he decided to go ahead and order them to attack. The energized Portuguese assailants then rushed forward with pikes, swords, and firearms, ready to mow down anyone that stood in their way.

The Raja had placed several barricades and heavily armed guards in the path of the Portuguese, but they proved ineffective at holding their ground against this tidal wave of aggression. Many were killed in the attempt. While Coutinho's troops were still floundering in the waters, Albuquerque's men reached the pavilion and actually ripped the ornate doors from their hinges with their axes. These were then hurriedly sent back to the ships, both as loot and as a souvenir of their conquest.

Albuquerque did not want his troops to proceed any farther without the reinforcements of Coutinho, and he put a contingent of troops at the gates to keep them from moving forward. Marshal Coutinho, in the meantime, had finally arrived, but by now, he could hear the sounds of a battle already underway. Coutinho became infuriated, thinking that Albuquerque was attempting to somehow outdo him.

Albuquerque anticipated as much, and he had a message sent to Coutinho that sought to give him credit for the events, stating, "You are the first captain to have landed men and entered the city of Calicut, and you have gained what you sought—the doors of the Cerame are now on board." But this attempt to share credit with Marshal Coutinho only infuriated him further. Taking it as an insult, Coutinho is said to have muttered in disgust, "What is this Afonso de Albuquerque? Your words are nothing but a puff of air."

At any rate, Albuquerque did not have the intended effect of making the late-coming marshal feel as if he were part of the team. Instead, Coutinho shot back, "This honor is yours. I don't want any of it." The fact that such a petty grievance would jeopardize the mission seems absolutely absurd, but for these men, who lived and breathed their own unique sense of honor when it came to warfare, such matters were indeed important. And the fact that Marshal Coutinho was left out during the initial siege rendered him absolutely uncooperative with Albuquerque. He had other plans.

In a bid to gain glory for himself and his contingent, he ordered the four hundred men under his command to march all the way to the Raja's palace, which was situated some three miles farther inland. This was a dangerous proposition since it meant the troops would have to pour through the narrow streets and alleys of Calicut to get there. Put in such a position, they could be ambushed rather easily. The rapid march of Coutinho was fairly successful, and despite some loss of life, he was indeed able to get to the courtyard of the palace with most of his troops intact.

It was here, however, that all hell broke loose, as the Raja's royal guard surged out to greet them. They set off a blistering barrage of arrows, and many of the Portuguese fighters soon took on the appearance of porcupines with shafts sticking out of their armor and, for the less fortunate, out of their bare flesh. The Portuguese were finally able to push the defenders back, forcing the guards to turn their attention to evacuating the Raja rather than defending the palace.

With its defenders gone, the Portuguese burst into the palace and, in a complete frenzy, began grabbing up all of the treasure that they could find. The Raja, who had been safely evacuated from the premises, began to redirect his royal guard. He sent a large force of them (about four hundred in total) back to the palace to take on the distracted Portuguese, who were busy sifting through the palace treasures. Ironically enough, the besiegers would soon be under siege themselves.

Coutinho's luck had not completely run out yet, as Albuquerque and a contingent of his own troops had just arrived on the scene. Albuquerque realized how dire the situation was, and he quickly set up a perimeter. He and his men were able to temporarily hold the Raja's forces back. Albuquerque knew that this perimeter would not last long, so he sent word to Coutinho that his time was up and that they all needed to evacuate Calicut immediately.

Since he was still looting the palace, Marshal Coutinho refused to heed the warning. This led an entirely frustrated and flabbergasted Albuquerque to head into the palace himself and directly order the marshal to make a tactical withdrawal. Albuquerque pleaded with Coutinho, saying, "In the name of the king, we ask you to leave. We mustn't stay here a moment longer. If we don't, we're all dead. The route by which you came is all on fire, and we're going to have great trouble getting away."

To these desperate words, Coutinho is said to have laughed. In full bravado, he declared that he would make sure that he was the "last to leave" and that after looting all the treasures from the palace, he would set the whole place ablaze. Bewildered, Albuquerque ordered his men to begin the evacuation, leading in the front, with the marshal's men following from behind. True to his word, Marshal Coutinho remained in the rear, flanked by just a small contingent of troops.

Some of these Portuguese fighters wielded a heavy piece of artillery called a *berço*, which proved quite effective in knocking back the surge of attackers that swarmed on all sides as the Portuguese passed through the narrow streets and alleys of Calicut. However, as the winding path narrowed, the heavy artillery did not have enough room for the men to operate them, and they had to be left behind. Without this firepower to back them up, the Raja's forces were able to swoop down on them with increasing aggression.

At one point, a group of them managed to outflank Marshal Coutinho and his entourage. Marshal Coutinho is said to have swung around to face his attacker, only to have the back of his foot chopped right off by one of the many sword-wielding hands that thrust at him. This caused the marshal, who was a large, heavy man, to fall right to the ground. His defenders tried to help their fallen leader, but the big man proved to be too difficult to pick up.

Nevertheless, his guards felt compelled to stand and fight around their injured liege. They fought until they, too, were cut down. Soon, all of these slain Portuguese would have their decapitated heads hauled off by their jubilant opponents. Albuquerque, who was at the front of the retreating Portuguese column, soon learned of what was happening and attempted to lead troops to the rear to see if they could be of assistance.

They could not make much headway, and Albuquerque himself was soon subject to a grievous injury. An arrow sank through his left arm, and a dart hit him in the neck. Just as he was coming to grips with these injuries, a bullet managed to strike him right in the chest. As Albuquerque fell to the ground, it was believed that the governor was dead. The sight of the slain commander caused the Raja's troops to be energized.

They surged forward in a frenzy to seek more vengeance against their enemies. Before they could seize the fallen Albuquerque, four of his loyal guards put him up on a large shield. They ran through the whirlwind of arrows, darts, and bullets, rushing Governor Albuquerque toward the ships waiting on the coast. The closer they got to the beach, the safer they were. The longboats were situated with *berço* artillery, which were ready to provide cover for the retreating Portuguese.

Soon, the large cannons from the waiting galleys began to erupt, annihilating any of the pursuing Indian warriors who dared to get too close. Upon returning to the safety of the waiting ships, in what was perceived to be a miracle to all involved, it was discovered that Albuquerque was not mortally wounded after all. Governor Albuquerque would, in fact, recover. His left arm would never be the same, but he would go on to live and rule Portuguese India.

Chapter 7 – Making Major Inroads

"It seems to me that if you make yourself powerful in the Red Sea, you will have all the riches of the world in your hands, because all the gold of Prester John will be available to you—such a huge sum that I don't dare speak of it—traded for spices and the merchandise of India. I take the liberty of writing like this to you your Highness, because I have seen India on both sides of the Ganges and I observe how our Lord is helping you and placing it in your grasp. Great tranquility and stability have come over India since your Highness gained Goa and Malacca and ordered us to ender the Red Sea, seek out the Sultan's fleet and cut the shipping lanes to Jeddah and Mecca. It is no small service that you will perform for our Lord in destroying the seat of perdition and all their depravity."

-Afonso de Albuquerque

India's most powerful self-ruling polity at the time of Portuguese imperial expansion under Governor Afonso de Albuquerque was that of the Hindu-based Vijayanagara Empire. As mighty as this polity was, it was landlocked at the time, and it was mostly concentrated on the eastern side of India. A rival of Vijayanagara, the Bijapur Sultanate, which was situated just to the west of Vijayanagara, had a powerful seaport on the southwestern side of India called Goa. This city was situated between the settlements of Kerala and Gujarat.

Goa was indeed a strategic outpost, and the fact that it sat on an island in the middle of two formidable rivers made it a fortress that could be easily defended. If the Portuguese had such a piece of real estate under their control, they would be much better positioned to get a handle on the Indian spice trade. The Portuguese established friendly relations with Vijayanagara, and it was not long before they began to plot with their new ally for the seizure of Goa.

Goa itself had been fought over between the Vijayanagara Empire and the Bijapur Sultanate many times. It just so happened to be under the control of the Bijapur Sultanate when the Portuguese began plotting to take it. Governor Albuquerque would end up waging open warfare against the Bijapur Sultanate, and he would manage to successfully seize the port from its grasp.

Besides aligning himself with the Hindu rulers of the Vijayanagara Empire, Governor Albuquerque had a surprising ally in the form of an Indian pirate by the name of Timoji. Timoji provided his own band of two thousand fighters, who attacked Goa on the ground while Portuguese ships blasted the Bijapur defenders from the waters. It was not long before Goa's defense gave out completely, and those who remained sued for peace.

Albuquerque, unlike previous Portuguese belligerents, demonstrated a much more tolerant approach. He declared that under Portuguese rule, the residents of Goa had nothing to fear and that he would make sure that both the Hindu faith as well as the Muslim faith would be tolerated. For a group of religious zealots whose own king had commissioned them to wage a holy war against Islam in the Indian Ocean, this was a great departure from what had been the typical stance of the Portuguese against other religions in general and most certainly Islam in particular.

Along with these peaceful overtures toward the faithful, Albuquerque also pledged to help out the residents of Gao by lowering the amount of taxes levied against them. Governor Albuquerque officially took up residence as the ruler of Goa on March 1ˢᵗ, 1510.

Many of the Hindu-believing Indians were relieved to be rid of the growing Islamic incursion that had been in their midst. Although Albuquerque was working for the Catholic Portuguese king and, by extension, the pope, he quickly found it more expedient for his more temporal purposes to practice a form of religious tolerance when it came to Hindu beliefs.

However, Albuquerque's religious tolerance proved to have its limits when it came to the practice of immolation, which was sometimes carried out by Hindu widows. This involved a widow throwing herself on her husband's funeral pyre and being burned alive. Albuquerque, just like the British centuries later, made sure that this lethal ceremony was shut down.

To further endear himself to the people, Albuquerque eased taxation and created his own currency. The currency, in full recognition of the crusading spirit that drove the Portuguese, was called the *cruzado*. Interestingly enough, Albuquerque launched a festive parade of sorts to introduce the coin to the populace. He had men carry the new form of currency in silver basins, while a full band, along with circus-style performers, followed the procession. Heralds declared in both Portuguese and the local tongue that the coins were "the new currency of the king our lord, who ordered that it should run in Goa and its territories."

Governor Albuquerque's mention of "the king our lord" was, of course, his effort of giving faraway King Manuel of Portugal credit for the seizure of Goa. Governor Albuquerque would come to rule Gao as if he were the king himself, though.

In the meantime, the man that Albuquerque had deposed—Yusuf Adil Shah—was already planning his return. And by April 1510, he had assembled a large force, with freshly recruited troops from Persia and remote regions of Central Asia. Incredibly enough, the force he cobbled together was said to be forty thousand strong. To say that this massive recruitment was slightly overkill on Adil Shah's part is an understatement, but he obviously did not intend to lose—the huge army he brought bore testament to this. This army was led by Adil Shah's loyal general, Palud Khan. This massive army, which came on a huge armada, first cut through the Hindu pirate Timoji's fleet as if it were nothing.

The force then managed to reach the outskirts of Gao proper. General Khan showed some surprising restrain, offering Governor Albuquerque the opportunity to not only retreat but also save considerable face. Khan knew that his forces would not be able to lose, but he most likely figured that he could probably take Gao without having to fire a shot if he could just convince the Portuguese that they were beaten.

General Khan even sweetened the deal by offering to find the Portuguese somewhere else farther down the coast where they could build a fortress. Now, it is unclear whether the general would actually make good on this deal; he very well could have changed his mind later and simply blow the Portuguese out of the water upon their retreat. Governor Albuquerque, for one, was not about to put his trust in General Khan's offer.

So, despite the incredible odds against them, Albuquerque obstinately refused to come to terms with his opponents. It has been said that General Khan was amazed at the audacity and boldness the Portuguese displayed in the face of certain defeat, but nevertheless, he ordered his troops forward so that the invasion of Gao could commence. In early May, with the monsoon rains pouring from the skies, the massive horde attacked Goa.

The pitiful group of defenders situated on the outer perimeter of the outpost was quickly overrun and decimated. It was not long before what remained of the Portuguese fighters found themselves seeking refuge in Gao's citadel. They held their ground here for several days, but they eventually came to terms with the fact that the walls around them were about to come crumbling down. Governor Albuquerque finally accepted reality and organized a plan to evacuate Gao.

The Portuguese fought a desperate rear-guard action all the way, but the Portuguese fleet was able to successfully sail to safer harbors on May 31ᵗ. Prior to leaving, some of Albuquerque's subordinates had actually suggested firing on Gao, but Albuquerque stayed their hand, insisting that they did not want to destroy structures that they would soon be coming back to reclaim.

Yes, Albuquerque, even while in full retreat, was determined to take back Gao at all costs. After deserting Gao, Albuquerque ended up docking at the island of Anjediva. Shortly after their arrival, they were met by a small fleet of Portuguese ships captained by Diogo Mendes de Vasconcelos. Diogo and company had just returned from even farther east, specifically from Malacca, a trading hub situated on the Malay Peninsula.

Diogo had been on a separate mission authorized by the king of Portugal to set up shop in Malacca, but he had been driven out. Hearing of this defeat while also still reflecting on his own expulsion from Gao, Albuquerque was immediately interested in backing a second attempt on Malacca. But before such a thing could be carried out, the governor's main focus was retaking Gao.

After Albuquerque's trusted informant Timoji brought him word that hostilities had erupted between Adil Shah and the Vijayanagara Empire, he knew that the moment to reclaim Gao was already at hand. Even so, it took a couple more months for Albuquerque to get his forces prepared for this latest attempt at seizing Gao. Back at his temporary headquarters in Cochin, Albuquerque assembled a war council on October 10th, where he cobbled together a group of captains loyal to him who were willing to take part in the fight. The governor then fired off a letter to King Manuel back in Lisbon to document his reasoning.

This missive read, in part, "You will see how good it is, your highness, that if you are lord of Goa, you throw the whole realm of India into confusion. There is nowhere on the coasts as good or secure as Goa, because it's an island. If you lost the whole of India, you could reconquer it from there."

Soon after setting down his rationale, Albuquerque led his forces back to Gao, approaching this fortified island on November 24th, 1510. The Portuguese fleet, along with auxiliary forces of local allies, then launched a two-pronged attack on Gao on November 25th. Adil Shah had directed his men to erect defensive barricades, but once the Portuguese made landfall, the rapid rush of energized Portuguese fighters was able to easily knock them down.

They surged onward to the city gates of Gao. Here, one daring Portuguese fighter seemed to use his javelin as a long jumper would in the Olympics. He thrust the javelin into the city walls and actually managed to propel himself up into the air over it. This daring soul then clambered up onto a parapet, and with a Portuguese flag in hand, he began shouting, "Portugal! Portugal! Victory!"

It has been said that the city defenders were so stunned that many of them turned away from their posts defending the gates to gape at this crazed Portuguese fighter suddenly towering above them, right within the city walls. It was in this moment of distraction that the Portuguese tore through the city gates and surged into Gao. The fighting that ensued was bitter, bloody, and close quarters.

The defenders fought vigorously, but soon the ferocious onslaught had them on their heels. They sought to retreat across the waterways. Once they reached dry land, many were cut down by local Portuguese allies who met them on the other side. It took several hours, but Albuquerque successfully retook Gao and decisively defeated his enemy.

It was not long after Gao was back in the Portuguese fold that Albuquerque began to once again discuss the prospect of taking Malacca with Diogo Mendes de Vasconcelos. There were already sixty Portuguese hostages being held by the sultan of Malacca, Mahmud, from the previous failed attempt. Albuquerque sailed off to Malaysia in April of 1511 to repatriate his countrymen and make Malacca his own. With him were eighteen ships filled with some seven hundred Portuguese soldiers, along with three hundred auxiliary fighters picked up from the Malabar coast.

Here, they were met with a new fighting element: the high-walled, huge junks (a type of ship) of East Asia. These ships proved much more resistant to artillery. As one of the Portuguese put it at the time, they were "no less strong than a castle, because it is of three or four decks one on top of another so that artillery does not harm it." At any rate, the fleet successfully made their way to Malacca on July 1st, and the mission to seize this valuable outpost commenced shortly thereafter.

However, the group briefly paused their advance after the sultan reached out for a peaceful solution. The sultan was no doubt intimidated by the huge fleet, and he now sought to use his Portuguese prisoners from the previous failed expedition as a bargaining chip. Sultan Mahmud wanted to cut a deal with the Portuguese in which the safe passage of ships would be allowed in exchange for the peaceful repatriation of the Portuguese prisoners of war.

Albuquerque insisted that the Portuguese prisoners must be given to him safe and sound before he entered into any further agreements. The sultan was not about to agree to such terms, yet he delayed and dragged on the discussions as much as possible in the hopes that the bad monsoon weather would arrive, thereby forcing the Portuguese to call the whole thing off. Albuquerque was well aware of this delaying tactic, and after a couple of weeks of stalled negotiations, he decided to commence with the bombardment of the city.

Once Sultan Mahmud's city was wrecked, he began to sing a different tune. He actually dressed up the prisoners of war in fine clothes and sent them off to Albuquerque. However, just as the sultan must have feared, this was not enough for Albuquerque. Now, Albuquerque was demanding that the sultan not only establish a Portuguese trading post but also sponsor the building of a Portuguese fortress, as well as give them money to cover all of the damages that they had suffered.

The bitter irony was not lost on Sultan Mahmud since it was obviously the Portuguese who had caused most of the damage. These were obviously terms that the sultan could not accept. As such, he immediately began fortifying Malacca with trenches and defensive barriers. He also laid out elaborate traps for the Portuguese on the shores by installing iron spikes covered in hay and other rubbish, as well as sacks of gunpowder to work as makeshift landmines.

The strategic thrust in the seizure of Malacca was the taking of the grand bridge that ran toward the center of the settlement. This bridge crossed over the river that divided the city. It was realized that by taking this bridge, the Portuguese would essentially divide Malacca in half. It was in pursuit of this purpose that Albuquerque split his troops into two groups. One would make landfall on the western side of the river, while the other would make landfall on the right.

Upon hitting the beaches, the Portuguese and their allies were bombarded with cannon blasts, arrows, and poisonous darts shot from blowguns when they got too close. The cannons were largely inefficient in causing much damage. The Portuguese were used to facing off against arrows; during most battles in this period, arrows were the main offensive weapon of their opponents.

However, the poisonous darts caused great fear among the Portuguese. The weapons could only be used in fairly close range, but they were quick and stealthy. The dart itself did not inflict much pain, but those injected with its venom would soon start feeling the effects. And as their condition worsened, most would drop dead in a matter of days. This slow, painful, and seemingly irreversible death sentence terrified these hardened fighters the most.

Nevertheless, they pushed on. Upon reaching the bridge, the most fantastic battle scene took shape when the Portuguese forces were confronted by Sultan Mahmud's war elephants. These huge elephants had been outfitted to serve as living tanks and literally ran over anyone who approached. Many of the Portuguese fighters fled before these awesome beasts, but a few of them were bold. Instead of fleeing, they took their long lance and shoved it right into the lead elephant's eyes and stomach.

This caused the animal to become enraged and bewildered from the terrible blows it had sustained. It then turned on its own rider, knocking him off. Without the rider, the elephant became uncontrollable. Like a contagion, the madness spread. Soon the defenders were in a full-on panic, running from their own elephants. The Portuguese took control of the bridge soon after.

But even though the Portuguese had their opponents on the run, it was the very elements of Malacca that were taking a heavy toll. By this point, it was the middle of the day, and the sun was bearing down on the fighters. Already worn out from their fighting and standing there on that bridge with their previous adrenaline draining away, the awful heat began to sink into their systems. Feeling like they were being baked alive in their armor, the Portuguese realized that they were unable to progress any further.

Albuquerque realized this much as well, and as much as it grieved him to do so, he was forced to call off the attack. As the Portuguese withdrew, the sultan was able to rebuild his defenses once again while he awaited the next round of the siege. That next round came on August 10th, 1511. This time, the Portuguese were able to break through Sultan Mahmud's barricades and charge right into the city. After several hard-fought battles at close range, Malacca was in Portuguese hands.

The Portuguese were greatly assisted by local Hindu merchants in the establishment of this outpost. They helped the Portuguese become the new middlemen in regional trade goods. While they consolidated their position in the region, the Portuguese constructed a sturdy fortress, which they named the A Famosa.

In good time, Malacca would be used as a springboard to explore nearby Indonesia, especially the Maluku Islands (Moluccas). They had to put down local resistance first, though, which was done in stunning fashion in January of 1513 when Portuguese ships managed to wipe out an entire fleet of Javanese ships. That same year, on the other side of the Indian Ocean, a Portuguese expedition was launched to storm into the Red Sea and seize the port of Aden, which is situated on the Arabian Peninsula.

Despite all of the previous Portuguese victories in the open waters of the ocean, they were soundly repulsed by the galleys of Aden's defenders in the shallow waters of the Red Sea. The galleys of Saudi Arabia proved very effective in these low-lying waters. Even without any wind to blow their sails, their rowers were able to maneuver them rapidly around the Portuguese craft.

Shifting gears away from the Red Sea, the Portuguese would eventually manage to secure Hormuz on the Persian Gulf in 1515. This conquest would make the Persian Gulf a part of the Portuguese domain, with the local shah becoming an official vassal of Portugal. However, despite this success in the Persian Gulf, all repeated attempts to seize Aden would be easily swatted back by the mighty defenders of the Red Sea.

In 1514, the Portuguese sent an expedition under Jorge Álvares even farther abroad. Jorge and his compatriots ended up all the way in China, becoming the first travelers from Europe to make such a trek. The Portuguese would learn that one of the complications that they had inherited with their seizure of Malacca was the fact that the local sultan actually paid an annual tribute to the Chinese emperor.

These were matters that the Portuguese would soon have to sort out with their new Chinese neighbors in their Malaysian neighborhood. Nevertheless, the Portuguese Empire was indeed on the rise, and it would remain so for quite some time.

Chapter 8 – Toward a More Perfect Union

"When I arrive with a fleet the first thing they try to find out is how many men and what armaments we have. When they judge us invincible, they give us a good reception and trade with us in good faith. When they find us weak, they procrastinate and prepare unpredictable responses. No alliance can be established with any king or lord without military support."

-Afonso de Albuquerque

Not long after the Portuguese deposed him from Malacca, the former potentate of the region—Sultan Mahmud—appealed to the Chinese to whom he had formerly been paying an annual tribute. The response of the Chinese was lackluster at best since they felt that the loss of one measly vassal in Southeast Asia was the least of their concerns.

For centuries, China had placed its primary focus in regards to security on its northern grasslands. Ever since Genghis Khan and his Mongol horde had swooped down on China in the 13th century, the northern frontier was always of the gravest concern. Soon enough, the Portuguese would make their presence known even to the Middle Kingdom of China.

The preeminent Portuguese enforcer, Governor Afonso de Albuquerque, passed away on December 15th, 1515. He was succeeded by a man by the name of Lopo Soares de Albergaria. Albergaria was handpicked by the king of Portugal as a successor primarily because of his noble roots and his perceived loyalty. Albergaria was actually chosen to succeed Albuquerque before the prior governor had died, and he left in the spring of 1515 to replace him.

King Manuel would only learn much later of how Albuquerque had passed before Albegaria's arrival. Albergaria was indeed loyal to the Crown, but he was not quite the rugged warrior and fearless sea captain that Albuquerque had been. Even Manuel realized this. Prior to receiving word that Albuquerque was dead, he actually had second thoughts about his selection.

After Albergaria had already set sail, Manuel received word that the Mamluks were saber-rattling against Portuguese interests. Fearing that Albergaria would not be able to mount a stand against them as effectively as Albuquerque, he began to reconsider Albuquerque's removal. It was only later on that Manuel learned that Albuquerque was already dead.

Nevertheless, despite these misgivings and the big shoes he had to fill, the new governor, Albergaria, would break a lot of new ground on his own. Shortly after leaving Lisbon, Albergaria sent a delegation to Ethiopia to seek an audience with the Ethiopian emperor, who was still often perceived by the Portuguese as the legendary Christian king, Prester John.

This delegation was led by Portuguese ambassador Duarte Galvão. These forged relations would bear fruit decades later in the 1540s when a joint Portuguese/Ethiopian force successfully repulsed Islamic forces hellbent on extinguishing the Christian

Ethiopian Empire from the Horn of Africa.

In the meantime, the Portuguese would lose their window of opportunity as it pertained to their crusading dream of storming the Red Sea, taking Saudi Arabia, and then marching all the way to Jerusalem. Their old foes, the Mamluks, who had ruled from Cairo, Egypt, had been deposed by the Islamic Ottoman Empire. With its head in Istanbul (Constantinople), Turkey, the Ottomans of the 1500s were still quite a force to be reckoned with. And from 1517 onward, it would be primarily the Ottomans that the Portuguese would have to deal with as their main adversaries on the high seas.

But they certainly were not the only ones. As mentioned, the eastward expansion of the Portuguese had already reached China. It was actually that same fateful year of 1517 that a Portuguese delegation first attempted to set up official trade relations at the port of Canton, China. Initially, the Chinese were fairly friendly—if not ambivalent—when it came to the Portuguese presence.

But it would not take long for relations to break down. Exacerbating the situation was a Portuguese explorer-turned-pirate by the name of Simão de Andrade, who began to openly raid Chinese settlements on the coast. Such actions obviously would not be too endearing to the Chinese. And in 1521, the situation would erupt into a fully-fledged battle between a Portuguese fleet and Ming China.

The Portuguese were parked in China's Guangzhou harbor, attempting a rather heavy-handed approach with the Chinese to open up trade. The Chinese had had enough and sent out their most powerful ships to send the Portuguese packing. The Portuguese initially attempted to fight back, but after the Chinese unleashed a fireship, they were forced to flee.

After this exchange, the Chinese government, by imperial decree, put an official ban on all trade with the Portuguese. The ban would not be lifted until 1554. It was only a few years after this ban was lifted that the Portuguese were allowed to establish a trading post in nearby Macau. The word "allowed" is a bit of a loaded term since the Portuguese had already established an outpost on their own accord.

Even though initially, the Chinese had the Portuguese paying them "rent" (otherwise known as "custom duties") for this piece of real estate, the Portuguese would soon have complete control over all of Macau, culminating in a 1783 declaration of Macau being an official Portuguese territory. In a bizarre sense, the Portuguese could be viewed almost as squatters on Chinese territory, who, after many years, declared themselves the rightful owners! But this is basically what happened, and Macau ultimately would not be returned to China until 1999.

Taking our chronicle of Portuguese history back to the 1500s for a moment, the year 1521 was indeed a momentous one for the whole Portuguese Empire. Not only was it the year that the Portuguese were checked by China, but it also marked the passing of King Manuel. His successor to the Portuguese throne and ultimate inheritor of the Portuguese Empire was King John (João) III.

Although Manuel oversaw the greatest and most rapid expansion of Portuguese power, it literally came at a cost. And as much revenue as the spice trade brought in, Portugal was encumbered by many debts to keep its overseas empire up and running. It was this debt that King John III would have to come to grips with and carefully manage.

The population of little Portugal had grown in the meantime, and for many, the prospects of living in one of the overseas Portuguese colonies was finally starting to seem more appealing than remaining in crowded and stifling Lisbon. For most, the surest path to success was either through the clergy, the king's court, or by trying one's luck overseas. As a popular saying of the times described the state of affairs, "Those wishing to stay afloat, must choose Church, Court, or Boat."

And one of the places that the Portuguese were now frequently hopping on a boat to immigrate to was the new colony of Brazil. By 1534, Brazil had been divided into many regions, which were being settled under the leadership of the donatários, which means "endowed one." These were often noblemen who had been given a piece of territory called a donataria. Donatários were put in place to lead each of the colonial settlements in a region of Brazil that was being settled. The donatários were responsible for the well-being and security of the settlers.

To provide further security to the people in this faraway land, the position of governor-general of Brazil was established in 1549, with the role going to Tomé de Sousa. Under de Sousa, Brazil would become prosperous, and it would also become deeply involved in the slave trade.

The Portuguese had dabbled with slavery to some extent from the very beginning of their forays into West Africa. And now, there was a steady stream of African slaves (primarily from the Portuguese outpost in Angola) being brought to Brazil, in particular, to tend to sugarcane and other cash crops that were grown in the colony.

The proceeds of Brazilian sugarcane would come to be a dominant feature of the Portuguese Empire by the year 1575. Incidentally enough, all of this coincides with the establishment of the Portuguese capital of Luanda in Angola. This city was linked directly to the sugarcane market in Brazil, and it became a hub for slave trading. While all of this was going on, the nobles of Portugal began to contemplate a possible merger with Spain.

Portugal and Spain share the Iberian Peninsula, and they had long divided the spoils of extraterritorial possessions with each other. Many of the elites in both Portugal and Spain began to consider how a union of the two crowns—and the peninsula itself—might work to their benefit. This discussion then came to a head in dramatic fashion in 1578 when the king of Portugal—Sebastian I—presumedly perished during an expedition in Morocco.

Sebastian was only twenty-four years old at the time, and he had no heir. Along with forcing a desperate search for the next ruler, Sebastian had also racked up terrible debt fighting in Morocco. Whoever succeeded him would have to deal with paying for the expenses. In the immediate aftermath of his demise, the throne ultimately went to Sebastian's grand-uncle, Cardinal Henry. Yes, Henry was a Catholic priest, which perhaps makes an unusual choice for a king. But at this point, he was simply the closest in the dynastic line.

Priests, of course, are not known for marrying or having children (at least legitimate ones), so when Cardinal Harry perished just a couple of years later in January 1580, there was still no heir apparent. Instead, immediately after his passing, a board of five governors was established as an interim government to run the Portuguese Empire.

In the meantime, the grandchildren of former King Manuel I rose up as claimants. Philip II of Spain was himself a strong contender. But so was António, Prior of Crato. António was popular with many Portuguese, and although an official successor had not yet been declared, he attempted to ride his popularity all the way to the throne of Portugal. However, the five governors did not recognize him, and they held further debates on just who would ascend the throne.

Philip II initially sat on the sidelines to see if he might be selected by the panel. He was a powerful contender since, as mentioned, there was a strong faction who wished for the Iberian Union that Philip II would bring. Philip II was also already an experienced monarch in his own right.

But as the days wore on, it was clear that he was not going to easily take the throne through this board. And soon enough, Philip

II grew tired of waiting for the verdict. In the end, a military force decided who the crown would go to, as Philip made the bold move to send his armies to Portugal to seize the throne by force. This led to the Battle of Alcântara on August 25th, 1580—a horrible struggle that left thousands of Portuguese dead, wounded, or captured. The casualties were not nearly as bad for the Spanish forces, who only lost around five hundred troops.

Philip II would then go on to officially assume the kingship of Portugal in 1581, establishing the long-sought-after Iberian Union. In order to smooth over the tragic bloodshed that had transpired to make this union happen, Philip granted a general amnesty to those who had challenged his quest for the Portuguese throne. It was not all bad news for the Portuguese either since Spain's massive wealth of silver (mostly mined from the Americas) was a welcome relief to Portugal's treasury, which was practically empty. Spain also sent extra military forces to Portuguese acquisitions.

Philip II was the head of a huge empire even before the union, with holdings in the Americas and the far-flung Philippines (named after Philip no less), and he was not able to remain in Portugal for long. By 1583, he had left for Madrid, where he created what was known as the council of Portugal so that he could be better kept abreast of Portuguese affairs.

In the meantime, he placed a nephew of his, Albert of Austria, in charge as a viceroy in Lisbon, Portugal. Albert turned out to be a schemer. He secretly opened up a dialogue with Queen Elizabeth I of England, a country that was at odds with Spain at the time due to the fate of the Protestant Netherlands, which Spain was desperate to bring back into the Catholic fold. The Netherlands had been fighting for its independence since 1568, and the Iberian Union had only made their struggle more frantic.

In desperate need of an ally, the Dutch had won a major coup by getting Britain on their side. Protestant England and Catholic Spain then came to blows with each other in 1588. Philip II actually attempted to invade England, but it did not turn out well for him at all. Spain ended up losing an entire armada of ships after their abortive attempt was beaten back by the English.

The emboldened English went from the defensive to the offensive, and they decided to meddle with local affairs in the Iberian Peninsula by landing in Portugal in 1589 and attempting to restore local Portuguese power. This bid failed spectacularly, but the English were much more successful in keeping the Dutch Netherlands free of Spanish interference. And ironically enough, it would be the resurgent and free Dutch who would come to haunt both the Spanish and Portuguese empires more than anything else.

Chapter 9 – Portuguese Empire under Siege

"So long as they are upheld by justice and without oppression, they are more than sufficient. But if good faith and humanity cease to be observed in these lands, then pride will overthrow the strongest walls we have. Portugal is very poor and when the poor are covetous they become oppressors. The fumes of India are powerful—I fear the time will come when instead of our present fame as warriors we may only be known as grasping tyrants."

-Afonso de Albuquerque

It has long been one of the ironies of history that although the Iberian Union was forged in the name of empowering both the Spanish and Portuguese empires, it would significantly weaken both. And it was shortly after this development that the Netherlands won its struggle against Spain, gained independence, and then went on to wallop Portuguese territories.

The Iberian Union did not bring more security to the Portuguese; rather, it helped turn them into targets of Dutch aggression. An increasingly aggressive Dutch naval power attacked the Portuguese more than the Spanish. The Dutch thought they could gain ground by stabbing the soft underbelly of imperial Portuguese holdings.

The Portuguese were spread thin, and they held their territories with a small number of troops. The Dutch would very much come to mimic the Portuguese in these tactics, but they posed a greater threat to the Portuguese than anyone else at the time since their ships and armaments were roughly on par with them. Unlike the Egyptians and Indians, whom the Portuguese larger depended on due to their faster ships and more powerful guns, the Dutch were able to match or even exceed the Portuguese in just about every fashion.

Helping to fuel the aggression and animosity between the two was the fact that the Dutch were just as fervent Protestants as the Portuguese were Catholics. The ensuing struggle between the Dutch and the Portuguese, therefore, was one of both material and religious conquest. The Portuguese came to view their Dutch adversaries with absolute contempt. As one Portuguese historian put it in 1624, "The Hollanders are merely good gunners and are otherwise fit for nothing save to be burned as desperate heretics."

The Portuguese viewed the Dutch as demented Protestants who believed in doctrinal errors, whereas the Dutch viewed the Portuguese as religious tyrants in league with a pope whom they frequently referred to as nothing short of the "antichrist." But as much as they expressed their mutual distaste over their respective belief systems, there were moments early on when the Portuguese and Dutch actually found some common ground and cooperated with each other.

When the Dutch showed up in Indonesia in 1596, for example, after a perilous voyage that killed most of their crew, the Portuguese were the ones who gave them assistance. The Portuguese already had outposts in Indonesia, and they directed the Dutch to the local ruler who would give them trading rights. But this cooperation certainly would not last long. And the first major strike by the Dutch against Portuguese possessions occurred during the years 1598 and 1599, with attacks launched on both Príncipe and São Tomé.

The Dutch tended to raid Portuguese islands and coastal enclaves that were fairly isolated and quite easy to launch hit-and-run attacks against. It would have been a much different story if the Dutch had attacked, for example, Spanish holdings in Mexico. Against a well-consolidated colony on land such as this, they would not have fared as well. But the string of settlements the Portuguese had established on isolated island chains and remote coastlines proved to be much easier targets. The Dutch would slowly graduate to taking on larger Portuguese holdings, most notably Brazil, in 1624.

In between these major strikes, the Dutch were not above engaging in piracy. Ever since the audacious seizure of the Portuguese flagship *Santa Catarina* in 1603, just about any Portuguese craft found isolated on the open waters was fair game in the minds of the Dutch. Ironically enough, the Dutch essentially began treating the Portuguese in a strikingly similar, ruthless manner as the Portuguese had treated most Muslim-based ships in the previous century.

Just as the Portuguese typically considered it fair game to seize the ships of Muslim merchants in the Indian Ocean for no other reason than disdain of their religious faith, the Protestant Dutch were now essentially doing the same thing to the Portuguese due to their disdain of Catholicism.

Just a couple of years after the seizure of *Santa Catarina*, two integral Spice Islands—Tidore and Ambon—were taken by the Dutch in 1605. The Portuguese, of course, were not completely defenseless against this onslaught, and they fought back as vigorously as they could. At times, they were quite successful in repulsing the Dutch advances. This was the case in 1622 when they easily pushed back the Dutch who were attempting to invade

Macau.

After they were beaten back by the Portuguese, the Dutch then had the audacity to raid the Chinese coastal city of Fujian before issuing demands to the Chinese to cease trading with the Iberian Peninsula. China was slow to answer, but a couple of years later, it did—and in a big way. The Chinese sent out a large army of tens of thousands of men, which successfully expelled the Dutch from their holdings in nearby Taiwan.

That same year, the Portuguese lost their outpost on the Persian Gulf. This was not due to Dutch interference but rather the English. The English had also begun operating in the region, and due to their technical assistance with artillery, the Persian forces were able to finally expel the Portuguese from their midst.

Soon, though, the English became increasingly alarmed at the progress of the Dutch, and they soon began to change course. They went from an ambivalent to somewhat hostile tact toward the Portuguese to engaging in diplomatic relations. The two forged a basic alliance, which led to the Anglo-Portuguese Truce of 1635.

As much trouble as the Dutch were causing the Portuguese in Asia, their efforts to hamper Portugal's African settlements were much less successful. Several efforts—including two swipes at Mozambique—were repulsed until the Dutch finally decided to simply establish a settlement of their own, which they did in 1652 at the Cape of Good Hope.

The Dutch would be pigeonholed in this meager outpost for quite some time, almost like they were in some sort of colonial quarantine, while the Portuguese continued to expand their landholdings in Africa during this period. The Dutch were a little more successful in their efforts to pressure Portuguese holdings in Angola. In August of 1648, they managed to establish alliances with both the king of Kongo and the queen of neighboring Jagas. With this coalition, the Dutch drove the Portuguese into toeholds in the

Kwanza Valley.

However, they were able to regroup, and with the help of auxiliary forces shipped in from Brazil, they were quickly able to retake the Angolan capital of Luanda, followed by the rest of Angola itself. The end of hostilities between the Dutch and the Portuguese was then in sight, and an official peace treaty was signed between the two parties in 1663. That very same year, the Iberian Union, which for nearly one hundred years had bound the fate of Spain and Portugal together, finally came undone.

Upon Portugal's renewed independence, her empire—particularly Portuguese holdings in Asia—had shrunk considerably. Portuguese India was down to the merest of toeholds. This fact was duly noted by a Jesuit priest by the name of Padre Manuel Godinho that same fateful year of 1663.

Padre Manuel had traveled from India to the Persian Gulf and then back to Portugal, reporting, "The Lusitanian Indian Empire or State, which formerly dominated the whole of the East, and comprised eight thousand leagues of sovereignty, including twenty-nine provincial capital cities as well as many others of lesser note, and which gave the law to thirty-three tributary kingdoms, amazing the whole world with its vast extent, stupendous victories, thriving trade and immense riches, is now either through its own sins or else through the inevitable decay of great empires, reduced to so few lands and cities that one may well doubt whether that state was smaller in its very beginning than it is now at its end."

Yes, by the time Portugal had regained mastery of its own destiny, the Portuguese Empire had indeed contracted considerably. From here on out, despite a few toeholds in Asia, the heart and soul of the Portuguese Empire would be primarily in South America and Africa.

What the Portuguese (green) and Dutch (blue) holdings looked like after the Dutch-Portuguese War.
https://commons.wikimedia.org/wiki/File:DutchPortugueseWar1661.png

Initially, the major export from Portugal's Brazilian holdings in South America was its namesake, brazilwood. But the land would prove to be much more profitable than that. In 1693, both gold and diamonds were located in the region of Minas Gerais. This Brazilian gold rush brought in a large number of immigrants, and this part of Brazil became alive with activity. Due to these developments, and combined with losses in Asia, Brazil became the main hub of imperial Portugal.

Around that very same time, the Portuguese were also looking for gold and other precious resources in their holdings in southeastern Africa. These efforts led them to expand their territory farther west, with the ultimate dream of linking their colony in Mozambique on Africa's eastern coast all the way to Angola on Africa's western coast.

Their efforts, however, were hampered by a local Bantu chief called Changamire, who rose up to lead a resistance against Portuguese expansion. Changamire would continue to stand up to the Portuguese until his death in 1695. After this powerful chief's death, the Bantu once again became too divided among themselves to pose much of a threat to the Portuguese.

During this time of resurgence, there were many notable Portuguese who would attempt to distinguish themselves. Among them was a member of the famous da Gama family—João da Maia da Gama. João da Maia da Gama was born in 1673, so he was separated from his famous relative and Portuguese pioneer, Vasco da Gama, by a couple of centuries. In 1692, as a young man, he headed for what remained of the Portuguese outposts in India. By 1693, he was in Goa, and he was soon taking part in naval battles against English ships, which had aligned themselves with forces from Omani Sultanate.

João ended up fighting off and on in the Persian Gulf over the next few years before heading back to Portugal, arriving back home in 1699. After returning to Portugal, da Gama fought in the War of the Spanish Succession, which had a direct impact on the Portuguese. He also assisted in the destruction of a naval blockade of the Straits of Gibraltar, which had been carried out courtesy of the French in the year 1705.

A few years later, in 1708, da Gama arrived in Brazil, where he was made the governor of the Brazilian region of Paraíba from 1708 to 1717 and then governor of Maranhão e Grão-Pará from 1722 to 1728. Perhaps proving his relations to the great explorer Vasco da Gama, on the heels of João da Maia da Gama's governorship of Maranhão, he went on an exhausting expedition from Maranhão all the way to Pernambuco.

It was a trip that would take up most of the year 1729. In 1730, Pernambuco had been taken by the Dutch, and the Portuguese settlers there would remain under Dutch rule for decades. In the end, the settlers themselves decided to cast off the yoke of Dutch oppression, rising up against the usurpers in 1745.

It was a long and protracted struggle, but by 1754, Pernambuco was once again part of Portuguese Brazil. However, it would take nearly ten years for the Dutch to acknowledge this fact, doing so only in 1761. This would come to serve the Portuguese Empire well since Brazil would someday become a fallback position when Portugal itself came to be threatened.

Chapter 10 – The Age of Pombal and Beyond

"The cultivation of literary pursuits forms the basis of all sciences, and in their perfection consist the reputation and prosperity of kingdoms."

-Sebastião José de Carvalho e Mello (Pombal)

By the 1750s, the Portuguese Empire had entered into the so-called "Age of Pombal." It is called this because the entire age was named after one of the most powerful and influential figures in Portuguese history—Sebastião José de Carvalho e Melo, 1st Marquis of Pombal. It is from this title that we get his more widely known moniker of "Pombal."

Sebastião, better known as Pombal, began life in relative obscurity. His family did have some connections to the nobility, but it was lacking in scope. After his father abruptly perished when Pombal was twenty-one years old, the chance for his own upward mobility seemed grim. Pombal managed to marry into a more prosperous family, as he wed the niece of the count of Arcos. However, it should be noted that most of her household was against the match.

Nevertheless, this union brought much more clout to Pombal, and from here on out, he was able to slowly rise up the ranks. In 1739, he became the ambassador to Britain, and in 1745, he was made ambassador to Vienna, where he stayed until 1749. In both of these postings, Pombal became acutely aware that the Portuguese Empire was increasingly behind its European rivals in almost every sphere.

He marveled at the technological innovations taking place in Britain and the strong bureaucracy that had been established in Vienna, which was, in those days, the seat of the Holy Roman Empire. During his foray at Vienna, Pombal's wife passed. Pombal didn't hesitate to find a new bride, and once again, he chose a woman of high birth, the daughter of an Austrian count no less— Eleonora Ernestina von Daun.

Eleonora was actually the lady-in-waiting for the Holy Roman empress. This brought Pombal right to the top echelons of European nobility. Incidentally enough, the king of Portugal, John (João) V, was actually married to a Viennese noble, Maria Anna, who is sometimes dubbed the "Austrian Queen." Pombal's wife was on close terms with Maria Anna, and it was through this connection that Pombal was able to secure a transfer back to the Portuguese court in 1749.

Pombal was now a veteran politician. He was well connected to high-ranking officials both at home and abroad. Back in Portugal, his first objective was to catch the Portuguese Empire up in the areas Pombal felt were seriously lagging. At the king's court, Pombal pushed for many initiatives in an attempt to jumpstart the Portuguese Empire and make it better equipped to deal with the most pressing matters of the 18th century.

Pombal's chance to really make a difference came in 1750 when King Joseph (José; his father died in late July 1750) made him his secretary of state for foreign affairs and war. It was at this point that the Portuguese Empire entered into the so-called "Pombal Age," and it would last for several decades.

The first major incident that occurred during Pombal's tenure was the tremendous earthquake that erupted in the Portuguese capital of Lisbon on November 1ˢᵗ, 1755. To say that this earthquake was incredibly destructive would not be an understatement. The quake is believed to have clocked in at around nine on the Richter scale. Just to give some reference, the only known earthquake to have been larger was the one that hit Chile in 1960, which was recorded at a record 9.5 on the Richter scale. This earthquake affected all of Portugal, and the initial tremors were immediately followed by a couple of terribly devastating aftershocks.

Several major towns in Portugal were literally leveled to the ground. In the immediate aftermath, it was quite clear that Portugal—the seat of the Portuguese Empire—was in a state of emergency. It was something akin to what Rome must have been like after it burned, and Nero was blamed for fiddling too much. However, the devastation that was wreaked upon Portugal was far greater than what Rome experienced.

The earthquake was followed by many fires, which was largely attributed to the fact that the quake happened on All Saints' Day. All Saints' Day is a day of reverence of the saints. On this day, Catholic believers light a multitude of candles. It has been widely theorized that the earthquake knocked down many of the candlelit altars, which resulted in numerous outbreaks of fire.

It has been said that after it was all over with, about 90 percent of the residences in Lisbon alone were no longer suitable for human habitation. One can only imagine the survivors literally clawing their way out of the burned-out rubble only to find themselves homeless and left to wander the ruined landscape of the city. This terrible situation would prove to be just the kind of apocalyptic climate in which a form of martial law and a would-be dictator might emerge.

And that was basically the framework that Pombal found himself working under. However, not all was lost; the king had survived, mainly due to the sheer coincidence that he and his family were away at a country resort far from the epicenter of Lisbon. Yet, upon the king's return, Pombal was the one who took on a leading role in advising the king, famously instructing the worried monarch to "Bury the dead and care for the living."

In other words, despite the devastation, King Joseph was informed it would be best just to cut their losses as quickly as possible and simply move on. The dead were already gone; it was time to focus on the future of those who had survived. Such advice perhaps is lacking in sentimentality, but on a logical level, it is sound enough. The Portuguese Empire needed to rebuild and move on, lest one of their enemies should somehow try and use their current hardship against them.

Seeing Pombal as an indispensable executive in this crisis, he was given great authority to ensure that order was established in the chaos. Just as he had described, Pombal directed the burying of the dead and then moved on to look after the living. The death toll was so high and the burden of finding a final resting place so enormous that the vast majority of the deceased were simply given a burial at sea—a more polite way of saying that they were systematically disposed of by dropping them into the ocean.

As for the living, Pombal enacted programs that would give survivors a temporary roof over their heads. He also saw to it that anyone dastardly enough to loot through the ruined hovels would be prosecuted. He posted Portuguese troops on every corner and authorized them to put a stop to any unauthorized rummaging through the wreckage. In Pombal's mind, it would all be sorted out in due time but only in an orderly fashion under his direction. There would be no wanton looting in the streets.

In yet another parallel to when Rome burned, giving Emperor Nero the excuse to build brand new buildings, Pombal seized the same opportunity. He realized that the leveling of Lisbon allowed him to finally embark upon his great dream of modernizing the capital of the Portuguese Empire. Aiding in this was the fact that the spooked king—Joseph I—decided he did not want to rebuild his ruined palace.

This cleared the way for Pombal to erect a modernized administrative center instead. These subtle moves away from the monarchy translated into many other ruined buildings and locales being transformed as well. The Palace Square, for example, was rechristened as the Square of Commerce. In all of these renovations, it was clear that the monarchy had been diminished and that businesses had risen to prominence instead.

In the rebuilding of the capital, Pombal relied upon military engineers to construct sturdy and stable infrastructure. The care with which this was done is evident, as all of the new residences were erected upon a well-planned grid. Each building was created with an earthquake-resistant inner frame, as well as a cistern.

Pombal wanted to make sure that these many upgrades would not be forgotten. He wanted future generations to be able to continue to make these kinds of improvements. It was with this intention in mind that, in 1756, Pombal established a school of architecture.

After rebuilding Portugal's infrastructure, Pombal sought to rebuild the general economy of the Portuguese Empire. And a big part of that was done through better streamlining how Portugal conducted trade. At this point in time, the British were the most dominant in overseas commerce. However, Britain was an ally, so any competition had to be done in a manner that would not provoke the British. This prompted the so-called "Pombaline plan" of monopolies. This plan revolved around the creation of independent companies that could work as autonomous monopolies.

One of the most successful of these companies was the Grão Pará and Maranhão Company, which was given a twenty-year monopoly over all trade conducted in the Amazonian sector of Brazil. This company worked on weeding out independent Portuguese traders who were cutting deals with British merchants in favor of individual profit over the general well-being of the Portuguese Empire's economy.

The plan worked well enough, and these internal developments seemed to go under the radar as far as Britain was concerned. Further streamlining the control of economic trade was the establishment of a national treasury for all imperial revenue and expenditures, which was established in 1761. This development allowed all profits to be directed to this one official repository.

But this state of affairs came under scrutiny in 1762 after Portugal was drawn into the Seven Years' War. Portugal had initially remained neutral, but after Portugal's refusal to stop trade with Britain, Spanish soldiers declared war on the Portuguese Empire. Portugal turned to its ally, Great Britain, and the Spanish troops were ultimately repulsed. Portugal managed to come out on the winning side of the conflict.

However, the close operations between Britain and Portugal had made Britain better aware of Portugal's trade strategy with its monopolized companies. Britain did not like what it saw and ordered the Portuguese to ensure fairer trade.

Pombal, in the meantime, had begun a real reign of terror both at home and abroad. In Brazil, the Jesuits were viewed with the utmost suspicion over Pombal's accusations that they were not following protocol. He also claimed that they were hoarding money. Pombal circulated many anti-Jesuit tracts during his reign, and much of the subsequent Portuguese rancor against the Jesuit order dates back to these actions during the Pombal Age.

Pombal also persecuted any and everyone who he felt to be somehow disloyal to him or the Portuguese Empire. Many of these were locked up on obscure charges and held indefinitely. One of Pombal's biggest purges occurred back in 1758 when an assassination attempt was made on the king of Portugal. The king was actually visiting his mistress, Teresa Leonor de Távora, when his entourage was ambushed.

The king received two minor gunshot wounds but was quickly on the mend. Pombal, however, was ready to go to war. He arrested not only the king's mistress but also nearly everyone associated with her, including about a dozen Jesuits for reasons only entirely known to Pombal. Pombal stated that he thought they plotted to overthrow the monarchy.

Pombal took the plot against the king personally, and many historians believe that there is good reason for him to have done so. Just prior to this attempt on the king's life, several nobles had met with him and attempted to convince the king to get rid of Pombal. The nobles did not like Pombal's policies, and they requested that the king remove him from office. It is believed that after the king refused to listen to their pleas, the nobles entered into a conspiracy to get rid of the king instead. Getting rid of the king, after all, would get rid of Pombal.

If this were indeed the case, it is really no wonder that Pombal—a vindictive enough character as it is—would have gone to such extreme lengths to destroy those who had sought to do him harm. But his ability to pursue his opponents would only last as long as he was in power. It is said that by the time of King Joseph's death in 1777 and Pombal's oust from power, around eight hundred souls were finally set free from their bonds.

Upon taking the reins from her deceased father, Queen Dona Maria I ordered the release of all of Pombal's political prisoners. Shortly thereafter, Pombal sent the queen his official resignation. Many of those who gained their release with the ascension of

Queen Dona Maria were itching for revenge against Pombal and urged the queen to go further and hold Pombal criminally accountable for his actions.

But any such attempt to follow this course invariably led to a dead end since all of Pombal's actions had been co-signed by the deceased king. And since Queen Dona Maria was not about to convict her late father along with Pombal, she was forced to just quietly put both Pombal and the whole Pombal Age to the side.

After the end of Pombaline Portugal, the Portuguese Empire began its long march of decline. The first indication that the empire was beginning to fall apart at the seams occurred in 1789 when Minas Gerais, a profitable province of Brazil, began asserting itself as an independent state. However, this bid for independence did not last long, and its ring leaders were quickly rounded up and arrested. But this was just the first of several revolts that would rise up throughout the next few decades.

The real game-changer came after the French Revolution and the subsequent rise of Napoleonic France. Napoleon would threaten Portugal and the Iberian Peninsula as a whole, and the entire Portuguese royal court was forced to evacuate to Brazil in 1808. This led to the 1815 declaration of the United Kingdom of Portugal, Brazil and the Algarves, in which Brazil's Rio de Janeiro rather than Portugal's Lisbon became the capital of the Portuguese Empire.

The United Kingdom of Portugal, Brazil and the Algarves.
https://commons.wikimedia.org/wiki/File:Portuguese_empire_1800.png

The royal court would eventually make its way back to Portugal in 1821, but the previous shift in power had emboldened Brazil to vie for its own independence. This independence was declared on September 7th, 1822, with surprisingly little resistance from the Portuguese Crown. The remnants of the Portuguese Empire would then refocus its interests almost solely on Africa.

The two jewels left in Portugal's crown were now Angola on the west side of Africa and Mozambique on the east side. In between these two was a whole corridor of unclaimed territory. By the late 1880s, when the so-called "Scramble for Africa" was in full force, the Portuguese dreamed of finally connecting these two Portuguese colonies together.

The British, who sought to link up their holdings in Egypt to their territory in South Africa, did not approve of this venture, and they did everything they could to prevent it. This led to the British Ultimatum of 1890, in which the British issued direct demands to King Carlos I of Portugal (r. 1889–1908) to cease and desist with any further attempts to link up the two colonies. The fact that the Portuguese king was so easily cowed by the British was not forgotten by his Portuguese detractors, and it would ultimately lead to his death.

King Carlos was assassinated by his critics on February 1st, 1908. A few years later, in 1914, World War One broke out. What remained of the Portuguese Empire would face even more dire challenges with the rise of German aggression. During the war, the Germans sought to seize Angola from the Portuguese. Repeated acts of aggression led to Portugal's entry into the war against Germany in 1916.

Along with supplying troops to the Western Front, Portugal was on the frontlines of submarine warfare, along with the British, in and around their colonial possessions of Angola and Mozambique. Portugal came out on the winning side of this war and was able to keep its colonial possessions, but it was just a matter of time before these colonies would seek independence on their own.

The first big push for the Portuguese to decolonize their overseas possessions occurred in the aftermath of World War Two. In the late 1940s, Portugal was being pressured to rid itself of its last footholds in India. The Portuguese leader at the time—strongman António de Oliveira Salazar—refused, citing the holdings as being essential to the welfare of Portugal.

Nevertheless, in 1954, Portugal lost two of its outposts due to local insurrections, and in 1961, the Indian military unilaterally seized and dismantled the final Portuguese settlement in India. During that same fateful year, Angola also rose up to shake itself out of Portugal's grip. This was followed by similar uprisings in Guinea in 1963 and Mozambique in 1964.

After the Portuguese possessions in Africa freed themselves, the next to declare independence was East Timor in Southeast Asia in 1975. The last vestige of what had been the Portuguese Empire, the old trading outpost in Macau, was handed over to China on December 20th, 1999. It was this final release of overseas territory that finalized the complete and utter dissolution of what had been one of the greatest empires the world has ever known.

Conclusion: The Pride of the Portuguese

The rise of the Portuguese Empire was quite an unexpected and incredible feat. The tiny nation of Portugal was carved out of the Iberian Peninsula after Islamic armies subdued almost all of the peninsula. Once the Reconquista had run its course, Portugal proper rose to prominence as a small but determined country, perched right on the Atlantic seaboard.

It was from this little perch that the Portuguese sailed forth into the unknown to find both new routes as well as new lands. Expeditions were commissioned by the Portuguese monarch to round the tip of Africa. Bartolomeu Dias succeeded in this mission and literally charted the course for those who would follow. This paved the way for explorers and conquerors like Vasco da Gama to solidify these gains for the Portuguese Empire.

As for those who bore witness to the arrival of these foreign explorers, the initial reaction was one of astonishment. The fact that the Portuguese could travel such a great distance seemed nothing short of a miracle. And when the strangers proclaimed that it was

"Christians and spices" that they were after, it struck those who heard it as both incredible and incredulous.

But these were indeed the primary motivators of the Portuguese voyages to India. Ever since the fall of Constantinople in 1453, the overland routes had been largely blocked off, and the merchants of the Islamic world had a monopoly over the Indian spice trade, ferrying goods from India to Saudi Arabia and Egypt, then overcharging the Venetian middlemen who dealt with them at sky-rocketing rates.

The Portuguese sought to cut out these middlemen once and for all by going directly to the source of this great wealth of trade goods. This not only altered the entire state of the global economy but also opened up new lands for exploration. Soon, Portugal would have an empire that spanned the Americas, Africa, India, and Southeast Asia. Portugal was on top of the world, but from here on out, it was just a slow and steady decline.

Spain attempted to merge with the Portuguese Empire, and then the Dutch attempted to supplant them. Portugal was greatly weakened by the 18th and 19th centuries, but it continued to hang on. It was not until the aftermath of the two world wars that the local residents of Portugal's imperial holdings began to become vocal about the chances of their own independence.

Even then, however, Portuguese strongman António de Oliveira Salazar tried to hang on, but the die had already been cast. By 1999, with the handover of Macau to China, it was at its end. Nevertheless, the sheer audacity of little Portugal's endeavors is still a point of pride with many Portuguese since it reveals an ingenious and indomitable spirit that continues to live on.

Here's another book by Captivating
History that you might like

HISTORY OF
EUROPE

A CAPTIVATING GUIDE TO EUROPEAN HISTORY, CLASSICAL ANTIQUITY, THE MIDDLE AGES, THE RENAISSANCE AND EARLY MODERN EUROPE

CAPTIVATING HISTORY

Free Bonus from Captivating History (Available for a Limited time)

Hi History Lovers!

Now you have a chance to join our exclusive history list so you can get your first history ebook for free as well as discounts and a potential to get more history books for free! Simply visit the link below to join.

Captivatinghistory.com/ebook

Also, make sure to follow us on Facebook, Twitter and Youtube by searching for Captivating History.

References

Anderson, J. M. (2000). *The History of Portugal*. Westport, Conn: Greenwood Press.

Gomes, R. C. (2007). *The Making of a Court Society: Kings and Nobles in Late Medieval Portugal*. Cambridge: Cambridge University Press.

Levenson, J. A. (1993). *The Age of the Baroque in Portugal*. Washington: National Gallery of Art.

Marques, A. H. (1976). *History of Portugal*. New York: Columbia University Press.

Maxwell, K. (1995). *Pombal, Paradox of the Enlightenment*. Cambridge: Cambridge University Press.

Maxwell, K. (2003). *The Making of Portuguese Democracy*. Cambridge: Cambridge University Press.

McMurdo, E. (1888). *The History of Portugal, from the Commencement of the Monarchy to the Reign of Alfonso III*. London: S. Low, Marston, Searle, & Rivington.

P. O. M. (1969). *A History of Iberian Civilization*. New York: Cooper Square.

Savory, H. N. (1968). *Spain and Portugal: The Prehistory of the Iberian Peninsula*. London: Thames and Hudson.

Silva Tavim, José Alberto Rodrigues da. (2015). *In the Iberian Peninsula and Beyond: A History of Jews and Muslims (15th - 17th centuries)*. Newcastle upon Tyne: Cambridge Scholars Publ.

Conquerors: How Portugal Forged the First Global Empire. Roger Crowley. 2015.

A History of Portugal and the Portuguese Empire, Vol 2. A. R. Disney. 2007.

The Portuguese Seaborne Empire: 1415-1825. C. R. Boxer. 1969.

A History of Modern Ethiopia. Bahru Zewde. 2001.

Printed in Great Britain
by Amazon